Mark H

# ONE J
# AHEAD

# THE TOP NH HORSES
# TO FOLLOW FOR 2017/2018

# THE AUTHOR

Mark Howard is 42 and graduated from Manchester University with a BA Honours Degree in History. For the last 24 years, he has written the National Hunt horses to follow book *One Jump Ahead*. He also writes the Flat racing equivalent, *Ahead On The Flat*. In addition, he appears as a pundit on *Racing UK* (Sky Channel 432) and, prior to that, Attheraces. He has also written for *The Irish Field*, *Sports Advisor* and *Racing & Football Outlook* (*Borderer* & *Trainer File*).

**FRONT COVER: WAITING PATIENTLY** (Brian Hughes), who was featured in the *Top 40 Prospects* last season, wins the Grade 2 Star Sports Cheltenham Preview Evening Novices' Chase at Haydock (21/1/17).

**BACK COVER: RAVENHILL ROAD** (Kaine Wood) wins the Spire Brewing Company - Chesterfield Standard Open National Hunt Flat race by fourteen lengths on his Rules debut at Market Rasen (15/10/16).

Front cover photograph supplied by GROSSICK RACING PHOTOGRAPHY. The Steadings, Rockhallhead, Collin, Dumfries. DG1 4JW. Telephone: 01387 750 512.

Back Cover photograph supplied by MICK ATKINS Photography & Media. The Elms, Goodmanham, York. YO43 3HX. Telephone: 07764 160600. www.mickatkins.com

**Published by *Mark Howard Publications Ltd*. 69, Fairgarth Drive, Kirkby Lonsdale, Carnforth, Lancashire. LA6 2FB.**
**Telephone: 015242 71826**
**Email: mark.howard@mhpublications.co.uk**
**Website: www.mhpublications.co.uk**

(Please note: If you are currently NOT on the *Mark Howard Publications* mailing list and you would like to be, and therefore receive all information about future publications then please post / email / phone your name and address to the above).

Printed by H&H REEDS PRINTERS. Southend Road, Penrith, Cumbria. CA11 8JH. Telephone: 01768 864214. www.hhreedsprinters.co.uk

All information correct at the time of going to press. Every care is taken with compilation of *One Jump Ahead*, but no responsibility is accepted by the publishers, for error or omissions or their consequences.

**ISBN: 978-0-9929224-4-3**

# CONTENTS

# INTRODUCTION

Welcome to the 25th edition of *One Jump Ahead*, which I hope readers will find informative and value for money. As far as last winter was concerned, Richard Johnson won his second jockeys' title with a total of 188 winners. Runner-up Brian Hughes had a fantastic season, too, with 144 winners. It is the third consecutive time the Irishman has broken the hundred barrier as he continues to rule the roost in the North.

Nicky Henderson claimed his fourth trainers' championship and reclaimed the crown he lost to Paul Nicholls four years ago. It was a memorable campaign for Seven Barrows with 154 domestic winners and Buveur D'Air providing his trainer with his sixth win in the Champion Hurdle, the brilliant Altior was unbeaten in six races over fences, including in the Arkle Trophy, and another novice Might Bite atoned for a desperately unlucky defeat in the Kauto Star Novices' Chase at Kempton, by winning at Cheltenham and Aintree in the spring. Ironically, Nicholls had his best ever season, numerically, with 171 winners, which was seventeen more than Henderson, but his total prize-money of £2,528,736 was a little over £300,000 shy of his nearest rival. Henderson trained eight Grade 1 winners last season with Nicholls being responsible for two.

The trainers' title in Ireland was even closer with Gordon Elliott, who led by £400,000 going into the final week of the season, being reeled in by Willie Mullins on the final day, at the Punchestown Festival. Once again, it was the runner-up who sent out more winners with 193 (compared to 180 for Mullins) but the Closutton handler earned £200,000 more with total prize-money of £4,580,200. Mullins and Elliott trained 8 and 6 winners respectively over the five days at the Punchestown Festival. Similar to the UK, Mullins, who was winning the championship for a tenth time, trained twice as many Grade 1 winners as Elliott in 2016/2017 with a tally of 20. Ultimately, that proved the difference.

On the same theme, I am delighted to include an interview with Elliott's former assistant Olly Murphy who only took out a licence this summer. The son of Bloodstock agent Aiden Murphy, Olly has made an excellent start to his new career from his Warren Chase Stables base near Stratford Upon Avon with winners under both codes. Two other new names in the *Talking Trainers* section are Tom Lacey and Colin Tizzard. The former has handled a number of promising youngsters who started their careers in English points, while the latter needs no introduction following a stellar campaign last winter with 57 domestic successes, 9 Grade 1 winners, a Hennessy Gold Cup and Welsh National and three victories at the Punchestown Festival.

News broke in late August that one of the most influential National Hunt stallions in recent years, Presenting, had died at the age of 25. Based at Glenview Stud in Fermoy, County Cork in Ireland, he was a Group 2 winner on the Flat for George Strawbridge and John Gosden and was placed in the 1995 Epsom Derby behind Lammtara. Crowned champion sire on four occasions, he was responsible for 20 individual Grade 1 winners, including Cheltenham Gold Cup winners Denman and War of Attrition. His progeny also featured Dunguib, First Lieutenant, No More Heroes, Weapons Amnesty and Yorkhill.

Finally, thank you to all those who have helped with the production of *One Jump Ahead* – from owners, trainers, jockeys, bloodstock agents, secretaries, photographers, proof readers etc – and subscribers for your continued support, it is much appreciated. The whole purpose of the book is to try and identify future stars hence the *Top 40 Prospects* is virtually full of unexposed youngsters, with a large proportion being trained in Ireland. Enjoy the winter.

*Mark Howard*

# FOREWORD
## by Nick Luck
### Broadcaster of the Year 2007, 2008, 2009, 2011, 2013 & 2014, 2016

It must be early September. As I look out of my office window, the leaves are just starting to turn; downstairs, the heating is on. Endless pictures of children smiling weakly in their new school uniforms are appearing on Facebook. Paul Nicholls has just had his open day and said he isn't chasing the trainers' championship.

And Mark Howard has been in touch asking if I can write the Foreword to *One Jump Ahead*. Predictable, yes, but these autumn crumbs of familiarity offer significant reassurance in these uncertain times; times in which the world order is being shaken by Trump, North Korea and Olly Murphy's strike-rate.

The Flat season may have many of its biggest prizes outstanding, but I know that OJA regulars will have been feeling a quickening of the pulse this last fortnight with news of sundry stable stars having "summered well" and coming back into training "like a bull." Thistlecrack apparently looks like "a mare in foal". I'm hoping he has the foal soon, so that he's fit enough to win another King George just like last season. I admit to a little misty eyed fondness for that performance, as it was the last big race we covered on Channel 4 Racing. That aside, it was the most exciting display of power and aggression that I've seen in a steeplechaser since Denman's Gold Cup win. Truth is that neither ratings nor time matched the impression, but you can't put a number on how a sporting experience makes you feel, and that was exhilarating in its execution.

Aside from Thistlecrack's much missed Cheltenham conqueror Many Clouds, the shining light of the staying chase division was the ruthlessly efficient Sizing John, knocking out Gold Cups at Leopardstown, Cheltenham and Punchestown a bit more easily than he was credited. Trainers often moan that their horses are underrated, but Jessica Harrington's protestations were entirely valid. Top class jumpers these days tend to be heavily indicative of the sport's power bases, and Thistlecrack and Sizing John are testament to the need to take the Tizzard and Harrington teams (battling for the title of longest overnight sensation) every bit as seriously as Nicholls, Mullins and Henderson.

As such, it's no surprise that Mark has ensured some strong Tizzard copy in this year's edition, nor that he has included the aforementioned Murphy, a man whose thirst for instant success in the summer made Dan Skelton look like Captain Tim Forster. He has the hallmarks of a serious operator, and is a likeable and popular character. Rather more of the old school is the considered and unshowy Tom Lacey, but he too warrants a place in Mark's Hall of Fame this year.

It's great to have *One Jump Ahead* back. Mark is such a thorough and experienced researcher that a flick through here will not only point you towards a few decent winners, but will also tell you quite a lot you didn't already know. Something of a rarity nowadays. Here's hoping the season is much like this book: plenty of entertainment at very little cost.

# TYPE OF TRACK

| Course | Sub-course | Description |
|---|---|---|
| AINTREE | National Course | Left-Handed, Galloping |
| | Mildmay Course | Left-Handed, Tight |
| ASCOT | | Right-Handed, Galloping |
| AYR | | Left-Handed, Galloping |
| BANGOR-ON-DEE | | Left-Handed, Tight |
| CARLISLE | | Right-Handed, Stiff / Undulating |
| CARTMEL | | Left-Handed, Tight |
| CATTERICK BRIDGE | | Left-Handed, Tight / Undulating |
| CHELTENHAM | | Left-Handed, Stiff / Undulating |
| CHEPSTOW | | Left-Handed, Stiff / Undulating |
| DONCASTER | | Left-Handed, Galloping |
| EXETER | | Right-Handed, Stiff / Undulating |
| FAKENHAM | | Left-Handed, Tight / Undulating |
| FFOS LAS | | Left-Handed, Galloping |
| FONTWELL PARK | Chase Course | Figure of Eight, Tight |
| | Hurdle Course | Left-Handed, Tight |
| HAYDOCK PARK | Chase Course | Left-Handed, Galloping |
| | Hurdle Course | Left-Handed, Tight |
| HEREFORD | | Right-Handed, Tight |
| HEXHAM | | Left-Handed, Stiff / Undulating |
| HUNTINGDON | | Right-Handed, Galloping |
| KELSO | | Left-Handed, Tight / Undulating |
| KEMPTON PARK | | Right-Handed, Tight |
| LEICESTER | | Right-Handed, Stiff / Undulating |
| LINGFIELD PARK | | Left-Handed, Tight / Undulating |
| LUDLOW | | Right-Handed, Tight |
| MARKET RASEN | | Right-Handed, Tight /Undulating |
| MUSSELBURGH | | Right-Handed, Tight |
| NEWBURY | | Left-Handed, Galloping |
| NEWCASTLE | | Left-Handed, Galloping |
| NEWTON ABBOT | | Left-Handed, Tight |
| PERTH | | Right-Handed, Tight |
| PLUMPTON | | Left-Handed, Tight / Undulating |
| SANDOWN PARK | | Right-Handed, Galloping |
| SEDGEFIELD | | Left-Handed, Tight / Undulating |
| SOUTHWELL | | Left-Handed, Tight |
| STRATFORD-UPON-AVON | | Left-Handed, Tight |
| TAUNTON | | Right-Handed, Tight |
| TOWCESTER | | Right-Handed, Stiff / Undulating |
| UTTOXETER | | Left-Handed, Tight / Undulating |
| WARWICK | | Left-Handed, Tight / Undulating |
| WETHERBY | | Left-Handed, Galloping |
| WINCANTON | | Right-Handed, Galloping |
| WORCESTER | | Left-Handed, Galloping |

# IRELAND

| | |
|---|---|
| BALLINROBE | Right-Handed, Tight |
| BELLEWSTOWN | Left-Handed, Tight / Undulating |
| CLONMEL | Right-Handed, Tight / Undulating |
| CORK | Right-Handed, Galloping |
| DOWNPATRICK | Right-Handed, Tight / Undulating |
| DOWN ROYAL | Right-Handed, Tight / Undulating |
| FAIRYHOUSE | Right-Handed, Galloping |
| GALWAY | Right-Handed, Tight / Undulating |
| GOWRAN PARK | Right-Handed, Tight / Undulating |
| KILBEGGAN | Right-Handed, Tight / Undulating |
| KILLARNEY | Left-Handed, Tight |
| LEOPARDSTOWN | Left-Handed, Galloping |
| LIMERICK | Right-Handed, Galloping |
| LISTOWEL | Left-Handed, Tight |
| NAAS | Left-Handed, Galloping |
| NAVAN | Left-Handed, Galloping |
| PUNCHESTOWN | Right-Handed, Galloping |
| ROSCOMMON | Right-Handed, Tight |
| SLIGO | Right-Handed, Tight / Undulating |
| THURLES | Right-Handed, Tight / Undulating |
| TIPPERARY | Left-Handed, Tight |
| TRAMORE | Right-Handed, Tight |
| WEXFORD | Right-Handed, Tight |

# ACKNOWLEDGEMENTS

I would like to thank all the following Trainers who have given up their time, during the summer, to answer my inquiries:

*Talking Trainers*: Brian Ellison, Harry Fry, Philip Hobbs, Malcolm Jefferson, Alan King, Tom Lacey, Olly Murphy, Paul Nicholls, Ben Pauling, David Pipe & Colin Tizzard, plus Venetia Williams & Richard Woollacott. Thank you also to the following secretaries for organising the appointments/answering queries: Ruth Jefferson (Malcolm Jefferson), Hannah Roche & Sarah (Paul Nicholls), plus Lauren (Tom George), Carolyn Harty (Nicky Henderson), Hannah McVeigh (Jonjo O'Neill), Sarah (Venetia Williams).

Thank you also to Anthony Bromley, David Minton & Bernice Emanuel (Highflyer Bloodstock), Nick Luck (Foreword), Declan Phelan (Ireland), Graham Wylie, Mags O'Toole, Rich Ricci, Joe Chambers (Racing Manager for Rich & Susannah Ricci), Michael Shinners & Ruairi Stirling (Skybet), Jonathan Neesom (Racing UK), Ian Robinson (Imperial Racing), Mick Atkins, Jon Hughes (Owners For Owners) & James Couldwell (valueracingclub.co.uk).

# The TOP 40 PROSPECTS FOR 2017/2018

## AIONE (FR)

4 b g Coastal Path – La Horquela (IRE) (Acatenango (GER))
OWNER: Mrs S.RICCI
TRAINER: W.P.MULLINS. Bagenalstown, Co.Carlow.
CAREER FORM FIGURES: 1
CAREER WIN: 2017: May DROMAHANE Good 4YO Mdn PTP 3m

Willie Mullins and Gordon Elliott, who fought out such a fantastic finish to the Irish trainers' championship last season, have invested heavily in the point-to-point scene once again. I have included three in the *Top 40 Prospects* who will be trained by the former with the first being this four year old who registered a two and a half lengths victory at Dromahane in May.

Bought for €35,000 as a three year old at the Tattersalls Derby Sale, Irish point expert Declan Phelan reports: **"The vibes were positive for this tall, white faced bay gelding, prior to his late season debut at Dromahane (Left-Handed). Encountering good ground, jockey Rob James bounced him out in front at the start and he was never headed. At times, he jumped a little to his right, yet he maintained a decent gallop and, once turning downhill to the third last, he lengthened nicely and always kept a three or four lengths cushion between himself and his nearest pursuers and won snugly. The winning effort may have lacked a wow factor, nonetheless, he displayed characteristics suggesting he can keep going at a decent clip for three miles and he has loads of scope in the jumping department. I gather Mullins expressed an interest pre-race in acquiring him contingent on performance, and after the win, he sealed the deal with vendor Donnchadh Doyle. It is noteworthy that the French based stallion Coastal Path supplied two point winners in Ireland this spring from his current four year old crop, and Willie Mullins snapped up both: clearly the exploits of Bacardys (another Coastal Path) has influenced the master of Closutton. The stallion Coastal Path is himself a half-brother to another active and popular jumps stallion Martaline, and I note his stock stay very stoutly and find under pressure. Aione may have some speed injected by his damline as that bloodline is mainly ex-Flat stock. He is a surefire bumper winner this winter for new owner Rich Ricci and, with natural progression, could be capable of featuring in some of the high brow bumpers next spring."**

The Ricci's won the Cheltenham Festival bumper in 2012 courtesy of Champagne Fever but were denied the opportunity last spring when the unbeaten and ante-post favourite Getabird suffered an injury in February, which ruled him out. Granted better fortune this time around, they may have another major contender next March.

**POINTS TO NOTE:**

| | | |
|---|---|---|
| Probable Best Distance | - | 2 miles |
| Preferred Going | - | Good/Soft |

| GOING: | R | W | P | TRACK: | R | W | P |
|---|---|---|---|---|---|---|---|
| Good | 1 | 1 | 0 | Left Handed | 1 | 1 | 0 |

| TRIP: | R | W | P | JOCKEY: | R | W | P |
|---|---|---|---|---|---|---|---|
| 3m | 1 | 1 | 0 | R.James | 1 | 1 | 0 |

# AMOOLA GOLD (GER)
4 b g Mamool (IRE) – Aughamore Beauty (IRE) (Dara Monarch)
OWNER: MR & MRS GORDON PINK
TRAINER: D.SKELTON. Shelfield Green, Alcester.
CAREER FORM FIGURES: 2

Since leaving his role as assistant to Paul Nicholls and taking out a licence in 2013, Dan Skelton has accumulated seasonal tallies of 27, 73, 104, 118 and the Warwickshire based handler has already past half of last year's total this time around. Lodge Hill Stables appears to be particularly strong in the novice hurdle division with Captain Forez and Cause Toujours likely to spearhead their challenge.

Skelton sent out 10 bumpers winner during 2016/2017 and a couple of those are featured in the *Top 40 Prospects*. The once raced Amoola Gold didn't manage to get his head in front but he is a promising sort nevertheless. Bought as a yearling for €17,000, the Mamool gelding was sent off 14/1 for a sixteen runner bumper at Kempton in February, but those close to the yard were expecting a bold showing. Held up early on, he made stealthy headway inside the final half a mile only to find the Pam Sly trained Haafapiece a length and a quarter too strong. Admittedly, the winner has been beaten a couple of times since but Amoola Gold shouldn't have any trouble going one better having reportedly thrived during the summer.

Indeed, he has grown considerably since his debut run, by all accounts, and is viewed as a useful prospect in the making. While his future lies over fences, he can develop into an above average middle distance novice hurdler this winter.

**POINTS TO NOTE:**

| Probable Best Distance | - | 2m 4f |
|---|---|---|
| Preferred Going | - | Good/Soft |

| GOING: | R | W | P | TRACK: | R | W | P |
|---|---|---|---|---|---|---|---|
| Good/Soft | 1 | 0 | 1 | Right | 1 | 0 | 1 |
| | | | | Tight | 1 | 0 | 1 |

| TRIP: | R | W | P | JOCKEY: | R | W | P |
|---|---|---|---|---|---|---|---|
| 2m | 1 | 0 | 1 | H.Skelton | 1 | 0 | 1 |

# ANNAMIX (FR)
4 gr g Martaline – Tashtiyana (IRE) (Doyoun)
OWNER: Mrs R.RICCI
TRAINER: W.P.MULLINS. Bagenalstown, Co.Carlow.
CAREER FORM FIGURES: 2

Despite tasting Grade 1 success on five occasions during the last campaign, good luck was in short supply for Rich and Susannah Ricci during the winter with triple Cheltenham Festival winner Vautour suffering a fatal injury following a freak accident at home, Champion Hurdler Annie Power was retired, 2/9 favourite Douvan fractured his pelvis in the Queen Mother Champion Chase and setbacks sidelined Faugheen and Getabird, which meant the pair never left their boxes at Closutton in the middle of March.

One race, however, which has been kind to the famous pink and green silks in recent years is the Skybet Supreme Novices' Hurdle. Champagne Fever (2013), Vautour (2014) and Douvan

(2015) scored in consecutive seasons, while Min chased home Altior in 2016. The word from across the Irish Sea is that the once raced Annamix is expected to develop into Willie Mullins' number one contender for the Festival opener this time around. Ireland's champion trainer is seeking his sixth win in the two mile event. Like Vautour, the Martaline gelding was trained in France by Guillaume Macaire and was bought soon after finishing two and a half lengths runner-up behind his stablemate Mick Taros (seventh and second since) in the Prix De Saint-Voir at Vichy (2m 1f : Holding) in September. It was eight and a half lengths back to the third. Annamix's race is available to watch on *Youtube* - the grey showed a tendency to jump to his right. Therefore expect to see improvement when he races left-handed. Over the years, it has become a tradition of Mullins to leave the three year olds he has purchased in late Autumn/ early winter off until the following season, hence Annamix didn't race again.

Don't forget Vautour finished second in both his races for Macaire before developing into one of the best National Hunt horses of recent times until he met a cruel end last Autumn. Annamix's Irish debut is eagerly anticipated and it is hoped the Martaline gelding develops into a high-class novice and lines up for next March's Supreme Novices' Hurdle. If the vibes are accurate, there is a very good chance he will.

**POINTS TO NOTE:**

| | | |
|---|---|---|
| **Probable Best Distance** | - | **2 miles** |
| **Preferred Going** | - | **Good/Soft** |

| **GOING:** | **R** | **W** | **P** | **TRACK:** | **R** | **W** | **P** |
|---|---|---|---|---|---|---|---|
| Holding | 1 | 0 | 1 | Right | 1 | 0 | 1 |
| | | | | Galloping | 1 | 0 | 1 |

| **TRIP:** | **R** | **W** | **P** | **JOCKEY:** | **R** | **W** | **P** |
|---|---|---|---|---|---|---|---|
| 2m 1f | 1 | 0 | 1 | Kevin Nabet | 1 | 0 | 1 |

# APPLE'S SHAKIRA (FR)
**3 b f Saddler Maker (IRE) – Apple's For Ever (FR) (Nikos)**
**OWNER: J.P.McMANUS**
**TRAINER: N.J.HENDERSON. Lambourn, Berkshire.**
**CAREER FORM FIGURES: 1**
**CAREER WIN: 2017: May VICHY Very Soft Hdle 2m**

French trainer Emmanuel Clayeux has been responsible for the best two juvenile hurdlers in Britain and Ireland during the last couple of seasons. Apple's Jade won three of her four races, including a demolition job at Aintree, during the 2015/2016 campaign, while Defi Du Seuil cleaned up with seven consecutive wins last winter. The pair started their careers under the tutelage of Clayeux.

Apple's Shakira is a full-sister to the former and she won the same three year old fillies' event (Prix Colonel Bidault) at Vichy in May, which Gordon Elliott's five times Grade 1 winning mare landed in 2015. Partnered by Arnaud Duchene, she destroyed her twelve rivals by upwards of eight and a half lengths (runner-up and stablemate hasn't raced since). Bought by J.P.McManus (won the last two Triumph Hurdles), she was reportedly very impressive and has joined Nicky Henderson. The Seven Barrows team have already won the Triumph Hurdle on six occasions and it is possible Emmanuel Clayeux may have supplied them with a major contender for the 2018 renewal. She could be out of the top drawer.

**POINTS TO NOTE:**

| | | | | | | | |
|---|---|---|---|---|---|---|---|
| Probable Best Distance | | - | | 2 miles | | | |
| Preferred Going | | - | | Soft | | | |

| GOING: | R | W | P | TRACK: | R | W | P |
|---|---|---|---|---|---|---|---|
| Very Soft | 1 | 1 | 0 | Right | 1 | 1 | 0 |
| | | | | Galloping | 1 | 1 | 0 |

| TRIP: | R | W | P | JOCKEY: | R | W | P |
|---|---|---|---|---|---|---|---|
| 2m | 1 | 1 | 0 | A.Duchene | 1 | 1 | 0 |

# BACARDYS (FR)

6 b g Coastal Path – Oasice (FR) (Robin Des Champs (FR))
OWNER: SHANAKIEL RACING SYNDICATE
TRAINER: W.P.MULLINS. Bagenalstown, Co.Carlow.
CAREER FORM FIGURES: F1 – 1313 – F11P1
CAREER WINS: 2015: Apr QUAKERSTOWN Yielding/Soft 4YO Mdn PTP 3m; Dec
LEOPARDSTOWN Heavy NHF 2m: 2016: Apr AINTREE Soft Grade 2 NHF; Dec
LEOPARDSTOWN Yielding MH 2m: 2017: Feb LEOPARDSTOWN Soft Grade 1 NH 2m 2f;
Apr PUNCHESTOWN Good/Yielding Grade 1 NH 2m 4f

Amateur Patrick Mullins rode three Grade 1 winners last season, including two on the same day, namely Bacardys and Wicklow Brave, on the fourth day of the Punchestown Festival in late April. Indeed, the former also provided Mullins with his other win in the Deloitte Hurdle at Leopardstown in February.

The six year old, who started his career in point-to-points with Pat Doyle, looks tailormade for the RSA Chase at the Cheltenham Festival. Despite the fact he has yet to race beyond two miles five under Rules, the Coastal Path gelding appears to be crying out for further and the 16/1 currently on offer looks attractive. A smart bumper performer, who finished third in the championship event at Cheltenham in 2016, he gained compensation at Aintree next time. Switched to hurdling last winter, he won three of his five races and failed to complete on the two other occasions – fell three out on his hurdles debut at Cork and he was badly hampered by the fatal fall of Consul De Thaix when strongly fancied in the Neptune Investments Novices' Hurdle at Cheltenham before being pulled up. Bacardys provided Mullins with his sixth win in the Deloitte Hurdle at Leopardstown staying on strongly to lead close home. **"He could easily go up to two and a half and three miles might end up his best trip,"** remarked Patrick Mullins afterwards. However, his best performance to date came in the Grade 1 Champion Novice Hurdle at Punchestown – he was one of eight winners at the Festival for his trainer – when he beat a high quality field which contained two previous Grade 1 winners, namely Finian's Oscar and Death Duty. Once again, Bacardys's stamina was key as he became the first horse to beat Colin Tizzard's Aintree winner, wearing him down in the shadows of the post.

A nine lengths winner of his second Irish point over three miles in testing ground, he should improve for a step up to three miles and may well provide Ireland's champion trainer with his fifth win in the RSA Chase following the victories of Florida Pearl (1998), Rule Supreme (2004), Cooldine (2009) and Don Poli (2015). Bacardys's record at Grade 1 level is 331P1.

**POINTS TO NOTE:**
Probable Best Distance — 2m 4f – 3 miles
Preferred Going — Good/Soft
Connection's Comments: "He was bought as a chasing prospect and that's what he'll be doing next season." Willie MULLINS at Punchestown (28/4/17)

| GOING: | R | W | P | | TRACK: | R | W | P |
|---|---|---|---|---|---|---|---|---|
| Heavy | 1 | 1 | 0 | | Left Handed | 6 | 4 | 1 |
| Soft/Heavy | 1 | 0 | 0 | | Right | 3 | 1 | 1 |
| Soft | 2 | 2 | 0 | | Galloping | 6 | 4 | 1 |
| Yield/Soft | 1 | 1 | 0 | | Stiff/Undul. | 2 | 0 | 1 |
| Yielding | 1 | 1 | 0 | | Tight | 1 | 1 | 0 |
| Good/Yield. | 2 | 1 | 1 | | | | | |
| Good/Soft | 1 | 0 | 0 | | | | | |
| Good | 2 | 0 | 1 | | | | | |

| TRIP: | R | W | P | | JOCKEY: | R | W | P |
|---|---|---|---|---|---|---|---|---|
| 2m | 5 | 2 | 2 | | R.Walsh | 3 | 1 | 1 |
| 2m 1f | 1 | 1 | 0 | | P.W.Mullins | 5 | 4 | 1 |
| 2m 2f | 1 | 1 | 0 | | P.Townend | 1 | 0 | 0 |
| 2m 4f | 1 | 1 | 0 | | D.O'Connor | 2 | 1 | 0 |
| 2m 5f | 1 | 0 | 0 | | | | | |
| 3m | 2 | 1 | 0 | | | | | |

# BATTLEOVERDOYEN (IRE)
4 b g Doyen (IRE) – Battle Over (FR) (Sillery (USA))
OWNER: GIGGINSTOWN HOUSE STUD
TRAINER: G.ELLIOTT. Longwood, Co.Meath.
CAREER FORM FIGURES: 1
CAREER WIN: 2017: Apr LOUGHANMORE Good 4YO Mdn PTP 3m

The Dennison Commercials four year old maiden point-to-point at Loughanmore in County Antrim, Northern Ireland on Easter Saturday was won in 2016 by Claimantakinforgan, who was featured in last year's *Top 40 Prospects*. Subsequently bought by Nicky Henderson, the Great Pretender went on to finish third in the Cheltenham Festival bumper last spring.

The 2017 renewal was won in impressive fashion by the Jerry Cosgrave trained Battleoverdoyen as Declan Phelan explains: **"The Easter maiden at Loughanmore (L) is traditionally a race noted for supplying high class future track material: the 2017 version was divided and this middle-sized bay gelding debuted in one of the divisions. The race was run at a slow to steady pace: entering the final half mile, seven were covered by around eight lengths and Battleoverdoyen sat last of those seven. He began to loom up on the scene between the third and second last fences. At the penultimate fence a couple of rivals fell in front of him, and he illustrated the race craft to neatly sidestep the casualties and, once rebalanced, he was brought with a telling challenge and leading on touching down over the final fence, galloped out to the line for a three lengths success at the expense of Court Liability. He enjoyed the good ground on offer that day at the County Antrim venue and the aspect of appearing to quicken approaching the final fence, made him a desirable object at the subsequent Cheltenham April Sale, where Gordon Elliott made a winning bid of £235,000 on behalf of Gigginstown House Stud. Given that his damline pedigree is mainly Flat racers (and moderate ones), this gelding is not a natural for jumping on bloodlines, though by dent of pointing evidence as an individual he may buck that trend. It is noteworthy that**

Gigginstown also stepped in and purchased his three year old full-brother at the 2017 Derby store sale for £80,000 in June. I would expect him to be above average as a bumper horse and of at least Grade 3 standard as a novice hurdler, and my gut feeling is that when hurdling he may be happiest at around the two and a half miles trip."

Doyen, who won the King George VI & Queen Elizabeth Diamond Stakes at Ascot in 2004 for Godolphin, has yet to produce a top-class jumper with the majority of his stock being instilled with speed rather than stamina. That theory is backed up by the fact the son of Sadler's Wells has been responsible for useful two mile chasers Dandridge and Valdez (back in training this season having been absent since October 2014) and Listed hurdle winner Pine Creek. Backoverdoyen has the potential to develop into one of his best offspring.

**POINTS TO NOTE:**
**Probable Best Distance**      -      2 miles
**Preferred Going**      -      Good/Soft
**Connection's Comments:** "For such a big horse, he really enjoyed the ground conditions and never put a foot wrong. He was unbelievable." Jerry COSGRAVE at Loughanmore (15/4/17)

| GOING: | R | W | P | TRACK: | R | W | P |
|---|---|---|---|---|---|---|---|
| Good | 1 | 1 | 0 | Left Handed | 1 | 1 | 0 |

| TRIP: | R | W | P | JOCKEY: | R | W | P |
|---|---|---|---|---|---|---|---|
| 3m | 1 | 1 | 0 | M.J.O'Hare | 1 | 1 | 0 |

# BLACK OP (IRE)
6 br g Sandmason – Afar Story (IRE) (Desert Story (IRE))
**OWNER: R.S.BROOKHOUSE**
**TRAINER: T.R.GEORGE. Slad, Gloucestershire.**
**CAREER FORM FIGURES: 1 – 19**
**CAREER WINS: 2016: Mar LOUGHANMORE Yielding/Soft 5YO Mdn PTP 3m: 2017: Feb DONCASTER Good NHF 2m**

Gloucestershire trainer Tom George was understandably delighted with his personal best season of 71 winners and total prize-money exceeding the million pounds mark. The Worlds End won the Grade 1 Sefton Novices' Hurdle at Aintree, while Sir Valentino landed the Grade 2 Haldon Gold Cup at Exeter. Stable jockey Adrian Heskin partnered 49 of those winners as the pair formed a very good alliance in their first season together. Despite a disappointing performance in the Grade 2 championship bumper at Aintree in April, the ex-Irish pointer Black Op appears to be one of the stable's most promising novice hurdle prospects.

A twenty five lengths winner of his only race 'between the flags' when handled by Rodney Ian Arthur, the Sandmason gelding was subsequently acquired by owner Roger Brookhouse for £210,000 at the Aintree Sale in April 2016. Declan Phelan wrote in last year's *OJA*: **"This is one of those oddball horses: he has little favouring him in terms of pedigree: he is a smashing almost jet black tall individual, so he has it in the "looks" department. He excited on his sole run, a winning debut at Loughanmore (Yielding/Soft) on Easter Monday. His jumping in the early part of that race was far from foot perfect and he tended to race freely: if you freeze-framed the race at halfway, his chances did not look bright: in that context, the fact that he spruced up his ideas in the second half of the race, in particular in the final half mile, which saw him gallop his rivals into the ground, is all the more remarkable. He won by 25 lengths, this margin was a tad flattering as nearest rival**

Lough Derg Jewel fell at the last when held (would have been beaten about ten lengths). The clock did not lie, and the time he posted was the fastest recorded over the two day Easter meeting at the northern venue, and given the depth of talent on show, this aspect bestowed a great deal of credit on this horse. He is a tricky horse to assess: he could indeed be top class and a proper Grade 1 horse or a one hit wonder. I would be prepared to risk the former verdict, as I loved the way he was galloping with relish through the winning line despite his keenness during the race."

Black Op made an instant impression on his first start for George in a bumper at Doncaster in February. Racing prominently throughout, he responded well inside the final quarter of a mile to fend off the challenge of Cheltenham Festival bumper third Claimtakinforgan and score by two and a quarter lengths with eleven lengths back to the third. His connections elected to miss Cheltenham and head to Aintree instead. Strong in the market beforehand, the six year old was sent off 100/30 favourite but, having led three out, he weakened inside the final couple of furlongs eventually finishing ninth.

Tom George's charge is a fine big imposing gelding who will jump fences in twelve months time, but it will be disappointing if he can't develop into a decent novice hurdler beforehand.

**POINTS TO NOTE:**

| **Probable Best Distance** | | | - | **2m 4f** | | | |
|---|---|---|---|---|---|---|---|
| **Preferred Going** | | | - | **Good/Soft** | | | |

| **GOING:** | **R** | **W** | **P** | **TRACK:** | **R** | **W** | **P** |
|---|---|---|---|---|---|---|---|
| Yield/Soft | 1 | 1 | 0 | Left Handed | 3 | 2 | 0 |
| Good | 2 | 1 | 0 | Galloping | 1 | 1 | 0 |
| | | | | Tight | 1 | 0 | 0 |

| **TRIP:** | **R** | **W** | **P** | **JOCKEY:** | **R** | **W** | **P** |
|---|---|---|---|---|---|---|---|
| 2m | 2 | 1 | 0 | A.P.Heskin | 2 | 1 | 0 |
| 3m | 1 | 1 | 0 | J.P.McKeown | 1 | 1 | 0 |

# BRIO CONTI (FR)
6 gr g Dom Alco (FR) – Cadoulie Wood (FR) (Cadoudal (FR))
OWNER: The GI GI SYNDICATE
TRAINER: P.F.NICHOLLS, Ditcheat, Somerset.
CAREER FORM FIGURES: 3 – 1F28115
CAREER WINS: 2016: May STRATFORD Good/Soft NHF 2m: 2017: DONCASTER Good MH 2m 3f; Mar KEMPTON Good HH 2m 5f

It was announced in April that seven times Grade 1 winner Silviniaco Conti had been retired. The Dom Alco, who was bought by Anthony Bromley out of Guillaume Macaire's yard in 2010, won 16 of his 36 races amassing £1,151,609 in prize-money. A dual winner of the King George (Kempton), *Betfair* Chase (Haydock) and Bowl (Aintree), he was ridden to victory on eight occasions by Noel Fehily and was officially rated 177 when at his peak in the spring of 2014. He was a top-class horse.

By the same sire, Brio Conti has a long way to go before he can be mentioned in the same breath as his former stablemate but he is a promising horse in his own right. Built and bred for fences, the six year old was a useful horse over hurdles last term winning impressively at Doncaster and Kempton. Appreciating the step up to two and a half miles, he was a ready nine lengths winner at Town Moor from Wenyerreadyfreddie. Paul Nicholls was aiming the grey at the Martin Pipe Conditional Jockeys' Hurdle at the Cheltenham Festival off an attractive looking mark of 134 but he failed to make the cut. Rerouted to Kempton for a valuable consolation prize, namely the Silver Plate Handicap Hurdle over two miles five, he moved strongly under Sean Bowen before bounding clear after the last to register an emphatic three and a half lengths win. Raised eleven pounds (145) as a result, Brio Conti was then stepped up in class and took his chance in the Grade 1 Mersey Novices' Hurdle at Aintree. Not disgraced in fifth behind Finian's Oscar, he was beaten around nine lengths. A future chaser, he lacked the gears on such a track from the penultimate flight.

Paul Nicholls and owner John Hales have tasted plenty of big race glory with horses sired by Dom Alco, most notably Grand National winner Neptune Collonges and also Cheltenham Festival victor Al Ferof. Whether Brio Conti reaches such lofty heights, time will tell, but he ought to make a smart staying chaser and win plenty of races. A further step up to three miles should bring about even more improvement.

**POINTS TO NOTE:**

| | | |
|---|---|---|
| **Probable Best Distance** | - | **2m 4f – 3 miles** |
| **Preferred Going** | - | **Good/Soft** |

| GOING: | R | W | P | | TRACK: | R | W | P |
|---|---|---|---|---|---|---|---|---|
| Soft | 1 | 0 | 1 | | Left Handed | 7 | 2 | 2 |
| Good/Soft | 2 | 1 | 0 | | Right | 1 | 1 | 0 |
| Good | 5 | 2 | 1 | | Galloping | 1 | 1 | 0 |
| | | | | | Stiff/Undul. | 1 | 0 | 0 |
| | | | | | Tight | 4 | 2 | 1 |
| | | | | | Tight/Undul. | 2 | 0 | 1 |

| TRIP: | R | W | P | | JOCKEY: | R | W | P |
|---|---|---|---|---|---|---|---|---|
| 2m | 3 | 1 | 1 | | S.Bowen | 4 | 2 | 0 |
| 2m 1f | 1 | 0 | 0 | | S.T-Davies | 3 | 1 | 1 |
| 2m 3f | 2 | 1 | 1 | | H.Cobden | 1 | 0 | 1 |
| 2m 4f | 1 | 0 | 0 | | | | | |
| 2m 5f | 1 | 1 | 0 | | | | | |

# CHACUN POUR SOI (FR)
**5 b g Policy Maker (IRE) – Kruscyna (FR) (Ultimately Lucky (IRE))**
**OWNER: Mrs S.RICCI**
**TRAINER: W.P.MULLINS. Bagenalstown, Co.Carlow.**
**CAREER FORM FIGURES: 1253**
**CAREER WIN: 2015: Aug DIEPPE Very Soft Hdle 2m 1f**

As discussed, French trainer Emmanuel Clayeux has been a tremendous source as far as a lot of his British and Irish counterparts are concerned. Willie Mullins has enjoyed his fair share of success with ex-Clayeux recruits, including his three times Grade 1 winner and dual Cheltenham Festival scorer Sir Des Champs and Grade 1 winning novice chaser from last season Great Field. The lightly raced Chacun Pour Soi hails from the same stable in France having been bought in the spring of last year on behalf of Rich and Susannah Ricci. Despite holding entries at the Cheltenham Festival last March, he has yet to race for his new connections, due to a setback. However, he is considered a high-class novice chase prospect for this winter.

The five year old raced four times over hurdles in his native France winning by fifteen lengths on his debut at Dieppe (fourth has won twice since). Runner-up at Auteuil next time, he then finished fifth at the same venue in a Listed hurdle. Switched to fences, Chacun Pour Soi was a staying on third behind King's Socks at Enghien in a conditions event in March 2016. Beaten two lengths, the winner subsequently finished runner-up in a Grade 1 four year old hurdle at Auteuil behind Footpad before being bought by David Pipe for €210,000.

Yet to race beyond two and a quarter miles, Chacun Pour Soi is expected to continue over fences this season and is the sort to develop into a leading contender for the JLT Novices' Chase at the Festival, a race Mullins has won four times in the last six years, including with the aforementioned Sir Des Champs in 2012.

**POINTS TO NOTE:**

| | | | |
|---|---|---|---|
| Probable Best Distance | - | 2m 4f | |
| Preferred Going | - | Good/Soft | |

| GOING: | R | W | P | TRACK: | R | W | P |
|---|---|---|---|---|---|---|---|
| Very Soft | 4 | 1 | 1 | Left Handed | 3 | 0 | 1 |
| | | | | Right | 1 | 1 | 0 |

| TRIP: | R | W | P | JOCKEY: | R | W | P |
|---|---|---|---|---|---|---|---|
| 2m 1f | 3 | 1 | 1 | F.De Giles | 4 | 1 | 1 |
| 2m 2f | 1 | 0 | 0 | | | | |

# DESTIN D'AJONC (FR)
4 b g Martaline – Fleur D'Ajonc (FR) (April Night (FR))
OWNER: J.P.McMANUS
TRAINER: G.ELLIOTT. Longwood, Co.Meath.
CAREER FORM FIGURES: 1
CAREER WIN: 2016: Oct AUTEUIL Very Soft Hdle 2m 2f

Despite being denied the Irish trainers' title on the final day of the season at the Punchestown Festival, Gordon Elliott enjoyed a magnificent campaign with 193 domestic winners earning £4,380,705. The stable were responsible for 10 Grade 1 winners with three of those at the Cheltenham Festival.

The Grand National winning trainer's string has been bolstered still further during the summer with some highly promising youngsters from the point-to-point field. Cullentra House Stables is now also the residence of two potentially top-class recruits from France. These include the former Yannick Fouin trained Destin D'Ajonc who was purchased by J.P.McManus in early December following a hugely impressive winning debut over hurdles at Auteuil two months earlier. The McManus team are reportedly very excited about the Martaline gelding having paid a substantial amount for him. Don't be surprised if he develops into a household name this winter.

Five lengths fourth of fourteen on his sole run on the Flat at Clairefontaine (1m 4f : Very Soft) in August last year, he switched to obstacles a couple of months later. Bought for €9,500 as a two year old, he destroyed his fifteen rivals by upwards of ten lengths in the Prix Pride of Kildare, a conditions hurdle at Auteuil. Partnered by Baptiste Meme, he took charge on the final circuit and quickened away on the home turn (the race is available to watch on *Youtube)* before recording a ten lengths success. Form wise, the third has won over fences since, while the fourth (Kapcorse) has also been bought by McManus and joined Paul Nicholls. Destin D'Ajonc appears to be a big, tall imposing gelding who will make some chaser one day. However, it will be interesting to see what direction he takes over hurdles this season because he is no longer a novice and will presumably contest conditions/Graded hurdles. Either way, he is a horse to really look forward to this season and beyond.

**POINTS TO NOTE:**

| | | | | | | | |
|---|---|---|---|---|---|---|---|
| **Probable Best Distance** | | | - | 2 miles – 2m 4f | | | |
| **Preferred Going** | | | - | Good/Soft | | | |

| **GOING:** | R | W | P | **TRACK:** | R | W | P |
|---|---|---|---|---|---|---|---|
| **Very Soft** | 1 | 1 | 0 | <u>Left Handed</u> | 1 | 1 | 0 |
| | | | | Galloping | 1 | 1 | 0 |

| **TRIP:** | R | W | P | **JOCKEY:** | R | W | P |
|---|---|---|---|---|---|---|---|
| **2m 2f** | 1 | 1 | 0 | B.Meme | 1 | 1 | 0 |

# DIESE DES BIEFFES (FR)
**4 gr g Martaline – Chanel Du Berlais (FR) (Saint Preuil (FR))**
**OWNER: SULLIVAN BLOODSTOCK Limited**
**TRAINER: N.J.HENDERSON. Lambourn, Berkshire.**
**CAREER FORM FIGURES: 5**

Dan Skelton's loss is very much Nicky Henderson's gain following the news owner Jared Sullivan has relocated the promising pair Charming Zen and Diese Des Bieffes to Seven Barrows during the summer.

The latter is chosen as a horse to follow on the basis that he reportedly impressed his rider Noel Fehily in his homework, prior to making his debut in a competitive bumper at Kempton towards the end of February. The Martaline gelding was bought by Warren Ewing and Barry Geraghty at the Goffs Land Rover Sale in Ireland for €45,000 as a three year old before presumably being sold privately to Sullivan. I was working for *Racing UK* at the Sunbury track on *Betbright* Chase day and Diese Des Bieffes is a good looking sort with plenty of scope. He was solid in the market, too, being sent off 4/1 in the nine runner field. Holding every chance turning for home, Fehily's mount failed to pick up and could only finish fifth, twelve and a half lengths behind Emma Lavelle's unbeaten four year old Irish Prophecy.

It will be interesting to see if Diese Des Bieffes has another run in a bumper for his new trainer. Hopefully, his homework will be transferred to the racecourse this season.

**POINTS TO NOTE:**

| | | | | | | | |
|---|---|---|---|---|---|---|---|
| **Probable Best Distance** | | | - | 2 miles – 2m 4f | | | |
| **Preferred Going** | | | - | Good/Soft | | | |

| **GOING:** | R | W | P | **TRACK:** | R | W | P |
|---|---|---|---|---|---|---|---|
| **Good** | 1 | 0 | 0 | <u>Right</u> | 1 | 0 | 0 |
| | | | | Tight | 1 | 0 | 0 |

| **TRIP:** | R | W | P | **JOCKEY:** | R | W | P |
|---|---|---|---|---|---|---|---|
| **2m** | 1 | 0 | 0 | N.Fehily | 1 | 0 | 0 |

# DORRELLS PIERJI (IRE)
**4 br g Coastal Path – Playa Pierji (FR) (Sleeping Car (FR))**
**OWNER: SHANAKIEL RACING SYNDICATE**
**TRAINER: W.P.MULLINS. Bagenalstown, Co.Carlow.**
**CAREER FORM FIGURES: 1**
**CAREER WIN: 2017: Feb BELHARBOUR Yielding 4YO Mdn PTP 3m**

"Tipperary handler Pat Doyle is noted for sending talented horses to contest the early season four year old maiden staged at Belharbour (L), with the likes of Ball D'Arc counting amongst many previous winners the yard have enjoyed in the race. Once again, Doyle saddled a well touted warm favourite, Dorrells Pierji. Only six runners faced the starter for the 2017 version and the Doyle representative headed the market an odds on jolly. Derek O'Connor partnering Dorrells Pierji elected to bowl along from the front and the combination set a fair pace and by the home turn had the opposition cooked. With closest rival Sangha River (has joined Dan Skelton) exiting nearing the last when held, the Doyle trained runner bolted up, winning by a distance. This bay gelding, with a white nose, clearly possesses a high cruising speed, what he may find if tested remains to be seen. Purchased privately by Willie Mullins (the second of the Coastal Path 2017 four year old point winners), this youngster looks set for graded success, possibly at the highest level over jumps and, if focussed on bumpers for the coming winter, could easily be one of the top ten in that discipline," believes expert Declan Phelan.

Bought for €26,000 as a three year old at the Tattersalls Derby Sale, the gelded son of Coastal Path looks another exciting prospect for Ireland's champion trainer.

**POINTS TO NOTE:**

| | | | | | |
|---|---|---|---|---|---|
| **Probable Best Distance** | | | - | 2 miles | |
| **Preferred Going** | | | - | Good/Soft | |

| **GOING:** | **R** | **W** | **P** | **TRACK:** | **R** | **W** | **P** |
|---|---|---|---|---|---|---|---|
| Yielding | 1 | 1 | 0 | Left Handed | 1 | 1 | 0 |

| **TRIP:** | **R** | **W** | **P** | **JOCKEY:** | **R** | **W** | **P** |
|---|---|---|---|---|---|---|---|
| 3m | 1 | 1 | 0 | D.O'Connor | 1 | 1 | 0 |

# DORTMUND PARK (FR)
**4 b g Great Pretender (IRE) – Qena (FR) (Le Balafre (FR))**
**OWNER: GIGGINSTOWN HOUSE STUD**
**TRAINER: G.ELLIOTT. Longwood, Co.Meath.**
**CAREER FORM FIGURES: 11**
**CAREER WINS: 2017: Apr LE LION-D'ANGERS Soft NHF 1m 3f; June NANTES Good NHF 1m 4f**

This is the other exciting recruit from France who is now under the guidance of Gordon Elliott having been bought by agent Mags O'Toole on behalf of the O'Leary's and Gigginstown House Stud at the Arqana Sale for €230,000 in July.

Previously owned by Bloodstock agent and trainer Richard Hobson, who purchased Hurricane Fly and Golden Silver amongst others for Willie Mullins, he is from the family of Valyssa Monterg and was handled in France by Fabrice Foucher and was unbeaten in two starts in APQS bumpers earlier this year. A three lengths winner of the Prix De Durval at Lion-D'Angers on testing ground in mid April (runner-up won next time), Dortmund Park then won by seven lengths in the Grand Prix Des APQS – the French champion bumper - at Nantes on decent ground.

The fact the Great Pretender gelding is proven on slow and good ground is a major plus and one can imagine him developing into a very smart two mile novice hurdler this season with Cheltenham Festival aspirations. Gordon Elliott won the Skybet Supreme Novices' Hurdle last March with the now sidelined Labaik and he may have a leading contender for the 2018 renewal, too.

**POINTS TO NOTE:**

**POINTS TO NOTE:**

| **Probable Best Distance** | - | 2 miles – 2m 4f |
|---|---|---|
| **Preferred Going** | - | Good/Soft |

Connection's Comments: "He is a lovely horse." Richard HOBSON, his former owner at the Arqana Sale (7/17)

| GOING: | R | W | P | | R | W | P |
|---|---|---|---|---|---|---|---|
| Soft | 1 | 1 | 0 | Good | 1 | 1 | 0 |

| TRIP: | R | W | P | JOCKEY: | R | W | P |
|---|---|---|---|---|---|---|---|
| 1m 3f | 1 | 1 | 0 | A.Bourgeais | 1 | 1 | 0 |
| 1m 4f | 1 | 1 | 0 | A.Roussel | 1 | 1 | 0 |

# DOSTAL PHIL (FR)

4 b g Coastal Path – Quiphile (FR) (Panoramic)
**OWNER: J.P.McMANUS**
**TRAINER: P.J.HOBBS. Minehead, Somerset.**
**CAREER FORM FIGURES: 1**
**CAREER WIN: 2016: Oct DEAUVILLE Good NHF 1m 4f**

Philip and Sarah Hobbs had a terrific 2016/2017 campaign with 111 winners at a strike-rate of 19%. The stable's total prize-money reached £1,502,991 and the highlight was provided by the unbeaten Defi Du Seuil, who won the Triumph Hurdle at Cheltenham in devastating fashion.

The Voix Du Nord gelding started his career in French bumpers and J.P.McManus and the Hobbs team will be hoping lightning strikes twice with their latest recruit from across the English Channel. Indeed, the Minehead stable have been sent two potentially exciting youngsters from France bought by the legendary owner during the summer. Demopolis is a three year old who won his only start over hurdles at Auteuil and this gelded son of Coastal Path is also unbeaten having landed an APQS bumper at Deauville in October (the race is available to watch on *Youtube*). A tall gelding who was trained by Yannick Fouin, he stayed on strongly to beat Demou D'Aunou (also bought by McManus) by a length and a half. It was a striking display and not surprisingly he attracted plenty of attention at the Arqana Sale less than a month later. Purchased by the champion owner for €295,000, the four year old joined Hobbs in late July and has reportedly settled in well.

Whether he develops into a Skybet Supreme Novices' Hurdle contender, time will tell but he possesses the size and scope to make a tremendous chaser one day. In the meantime, expect him to more than pay his way over hurdles this winter.

**POINTS TO NOTE:**

| **Probable Best Distance** | - | 2 miles |
|---|---|---|
| **Preferred Going** | - | Good/Soft |

| GOING: | R | W | P | TRACK: | R | W | P |
|---|---|---|---|---|---|---|---|
| Good | 1 | 1 | 0 | Right | 1 | 1 | 0 |
| | | | | Galloping | 1 | 1 | 0 |

| TRIP: | R | W | P | JOCKEY: | R | W | P |
|---|---|---|---|---|---|---|---|
| 1m 4f | 1 | 1 | 0 | P.Boudot | 1 | 1 | 0 |

# FELIX DESJY (FR)

4 ch g Maresca Sorrento (FR) – Lamadoun (FR) (Smadoun (FR))
OWNER: GIGGINSTOWN HOUSE STUD
TRAINER: G.ELLIOTT. Longwood, Co.Meath.
CAREER FORM FIGURES: 1
CAREER WIN: 2017: Mar DROMAHANE Soft Mdn PTP 3m

Bloodstock agent Mags O'Toole bought the unbeaten Felix Desjy on behalf of Gigginstown House Stud for €29,000 at the Goffs Land Rover Sale last year. By 22 year old stallion Maresca Sorrento, he was a fifteen lengths winner of his only Irish point at Dromahane in March when trained by Eddie Hales, who was sending out his first pointing winner of the season.

Irish expert Declan Phelan takes up the story: **"Arguably the most exciting Gigginstown House Stud own brand four year old pointer of 2017...by own brand, I imply one they owned when pointed rather than one they bought subsequent to pointing. Handled by Eddie Hales for pointing purposes, he launched his career in style at Dromahane (L) in March. Moving to lead after a mile, he set a fair tempo: leaving the backstraight he was given a breather and allowed the chasing pack to move onto his flanks. Once facing the downhill third last, he was given an inch of rein, and from that moment, he asserted, jumping the last five lengths clear, he was nudged out and sprinted away to win by fifteen lengths. Upon crossing the line, I marked him down as a surefire Graded track winner, at least Grade 3, and probably Grade 2 or higher. He is a middle sized athletic chestnut with a crisp jumping technique and he possesses that key ability to quicken. He has a pure French pedigree, his dam won over jumps as have others on his family tree. Picked up by Gigginstown for £29,000 as a store, he would have easily commanded a deep six figure trade following this point victory. Speaking to those involved with this horse, their verdict mentioned he would be as effective at two and a half as three miles, and he will perform to his optimum with cut in the ground."**

**POINTS TO NOTE:**
Probable Best Distance          -     2m 4f – 3 miles
Preferred Going                 -     Soft

| GOING: | R | W | P | TRACK: | R | W | P |
|--------|---|---|---|--------|---|---|---|
| Soft | 1 | 1 | 0 | Left Handed | 1 | 1 | 0 |

| TRIP: | R | W | P | JOCKEY: | R | W | P |
|-------|---|---|---|---------|---|---|---|
| 3m | 1 | 1 | 0 | D.L.Queally | 1 | 1 | 0 |

# FINIAN'S OSCAR (IRE)

5 b g Oscar (IRE) – Trinity Allen (IRE) (Taipan (IRE))
OWNER: ALAN POTTS
TRAINER: C.TIZZARD. Milborne Port, Dorset.
CAREER FORM FIGURES: 111112
CAREER WINS: 2016: Oct PORTRUSH Good/Yielding 4YO Mdn PTP 3m; Dec HEREFORD Soft NH 2m 5f: 2017: Jan SANDOWN Soft Grade 1 NH 2m; Feb EXETER Soft Listed NH 2m 1f; Apr AINTREE Good Grade 1 NH 2m 4f

Despite the loss of expensive purchase Flemenshill (£480,000), who died of a heart attack in the summer, owner Alan Potts and Colin Tizzard have one of the most exciting horses in training in the UK in the shape of another ex-Irish pointer, Finian's Oscar. Rated 151 over hurdles, there is every reason to believe the five year old will be even better over fences.

Following an eight lengths win in his only point at Portrush in October for Denis Murphy, he went through the sales ring the following month at Cheltenham and was purchased for £250,000. **"He did a piece of work up the Old Vic gallop on the Curragh about a month before he won his point-to-point and he looked like he was something special then. Down the line I think he could be a Gold Cup horse,"** believes his former trainer.

From the family of Champion Chase winner Finian's Rainbow, Colin Tizzard's latest star made an instant impression when slamming previous winner Acting Lass by seven lengths at Hereford in mid December. Immediately promoted in class, he beat six rivals by upwards of five lengths in the Grade 1 Tolworth Hurdle at Sandown early in the New Year. **"He's getting towards one of the best I've ridden. He could be anything, and he'll be a lovely chaser,"** remarked Tom O'Brien. Finian's Oscar was then workmanlike in victory in a Listed novices' hurdle at Exeter before a bruised foot ruled him out of the Cheltenham Festival. However, the Oscar gelding gained ample compensation when beating the likes of Captain Forez and Grade 1 winner Messire Des Obeaux by three lengths or more under Robbie Power at Aintree in April. **"He's a beautiful horse. He's the horse we were all hoping he would be. When they had to race in earnest off the bend he came through. He had to ask him, but goodness me didn't he find. He's a gorgeous young horse and has everything in front of him,"** enthused Tizzard afterwards. He was sent off 13/8 favourite to follow suit in another Grade 1 contest at the Punchestown Festival only to be headed on the line by the aforementioned Bacardys with seven lengths back to the third Death Duty, another Grade 1 winner. He nearly provided his stable with their fourth winner of the Festival.

The return to two and a half miles in the spring appeared to be to the five year old's liking and with his connections electing to go chasing, Finian's Oscar looks a major contender for the JLT Novice Chase at Cheltenham in March. He jumps, travels, handles any ground and is a Grade 1 winner over two and two and a half miles. He looks faultless.

**POINTS TO NOTE:**

| | | |
|---|---|---|
| Probable Best Distance | - | 2m 4f |
| Preferred Going | - | Good/Soft |

Connection's Comments: **"It was just raw ability that got Finian's Oscar through today. He was unbelievably green. He was jumping up in the air a little bit, and he had never gone that pace in a competitive race before. Trying to get him to travel and hold his position wasn't easy, but halfway down the back the penny dropped and I knew when I straightened up he would always win. When he got to the front he had a good look at the stands and idled, but he's just very, very good."** Robbie POWER at Aintree (8/4/17)

| GOING: | R | W | P | TRACK: | R | W | P |
|---|---|---|---|---|---|---|---|
| Soft | 3 | 3 | 0 | Left Handed | 2 | 2 | 0 |
| Good/Yield. | 2 | 1 | 1 | Right | 4 | 3 | 1 |
| Good | 1 | 1 | 0 | Galloping | 2 | 1 | 1 |
| | | | | Stiff/Undul. | 1 | 1 | 0 |
| | | | | Tight | 2 | 2 | 0 |

| TRIP: | R | W | P | JOCKEY: | R | W | P |
|---|---|---|---|---|---|---|---|
| 2m | 1 | 1 | 0 | R.M.Power | 2 | 1 | 1 |
| 2m 1f | 1 | 1 | 0 | T.O'Brien | 3 | 3 | 0 |
| 2m 4f | 2 | 1 | 1 | J.J.Codd | 1 | 1 | 0 |
| 2m 5f | 1 | 1 | 0 | | | | |
| 3m | 1 | 1 | 0 | | | | |

# FIXE LE CAP (FR)

5 gr g Kapgarde (FR – Lady Fix (FR) (Turgeon (FR))
OWNER: SIMON MUNIR & ISAAC SOUEDE
TRAINER: N.J.HENDERSON. Lambourn, Berkshire.
CAREER FORM FIGURES: 52 – 41128 – 2 - 1
CAREER WINS: 2015: Dec NEWBURY Soft NH 2m: 2016: Jan WARWICK Soft NH 2m: 2017: May COMPIEGNE Very Soft Listed Hdle 2m 3f

Champion trainer Nicky Henderson appears to have a strong hand when it comes to novice chasers for this season. The likes of Brain Power, Constantine Bay, Lough Derg Spirit and River Wylde (tailormade for the Wayward Lad Novices' Chase at Kempton on the 27th December – his stable have won it nine times) are all set to jump fences for the first time and ought to prove above average.

Fixe Le Cap is another Seven Barrows inmate who will embark on a chasing career and, given his size and scope, the five year old ought to excel. The ex-French gelding, who had three runs over hurdles at Auteuil before joining Henderson, was a smart juvenile during the 2015/2016 campaign winning twice at Newbury and Warwick before finishing runner-up behind Frodon in the Victor Ludorum Hurdle at Haydock. Only eighth in the Fred Winter Juvenile Hurdle at the Festival on unsuitably quick ground in March 2016, the Kapgarde gelding was off the track for nearly a year until returning in the Imperial Cup at Sandown last spring. Despite an absence of 360 days and shouldering top weight, Fixe Le Kap was sent off 5/1 favourite and he ran a cracker only being denied by a length behind the Ian Williams trained London Prize. He was then stepped up to two miles three for the first time in a Listed hurdle at Compiegne in France in early May. Daryl Jacob's mount made virtually all the running before fending off Fafintadenient to prevail by a length and a quarter with the pair seven lengths clear of the third.

Owned by Simon Munir and Isaac Suede, who enjoyed dual Grade 1 success at Auteuil on the 11th June with L'Ami Serge and Prince Ali, Fixe Le Kap has the physique of a chaser and, granted soft/heavy ground, he will take some beating over fences this winter. Races such as the Henry VIII Novices' Chase (9th December) and Scilly Isles Novices' Chase (February), both at Sandown, could feature on his agenda. Two and a half miles in testing ground may prove to be his optimum conditions.

## POINTS TO NOTE:
Probable Best Distance  -  2m 4f
Preferred Going  -  Soft
Connection's Comments: "Fixe Le Kap has run a very good race, unfortunately he loves soft ground so we'll have to try and find somewhere suitable to run, but he's all about chasing next year anyway." Nicky HENDERSON at Sandown (11/3/17)

| GOING: | R | W | P | TRACK: | R | W | P |
|---|---|---|---|---|---|---|---|
| Heavy | 3 | 0 | 2 | Left Handed | 8 | 3 | 1 |
| Very Soft | 2 | 1 | 0 | Right | 1 | 0 | 1 |
| Soft | 3 | 2 | 1 | Galloping | 6 | 2 | 2 |
| Good | 1 | 0 | 0 | Stiff/Undul. | 1 | 0 | 0 |
| | | | | Tight | 1 | 0 | 1 |
| | | | | Tight/Undul. | 1 | 1 | 0 |

| TRIP: | R | W | P | JOCKEY: | R | W | P |
|---|---|---|---|---|---|---|---|
| 2m | 7 | 2 | 3 | D.Jacob | 4 | 2 | 1 |
| 2m 1f | 1 | 0 | 0 | J.McGrath | 1 | 1 | 0 |
| 2m 3f | 1 | 1 | 0 | D.Bass | 1 | 0 | 1 |
| | | | | A.Acker | 3 | 0 | 1 |

# HELLO BERTIE

5 b g Kayf Tara – I'm Delilah (Overbury (IRE))
OWNER: C.S.JOHNSTON & T.AMBLER
TRAINER: J.M.JEFFERSON. Norton, Malton, North Yorkshire.
CAREER FORM FIGURES: 33

With a personal best 40 winners and total prize-money of £504,073, Malcolm Jefferson had a season to remember and has plenty to look forward to this winter, too. Exciting novice chasers from last year Cloudy Dream, Double W's and Waiting Patiently spearhead his challenge, while Grade 1 runner-up Mount Mews will test the water in the Champion Hurdle division by contesting the Fighting Fifth Hurdle at Newcastle (2nd December). Newstead Cottage Stables on the outskirts of Malton is also the home of a number of promising and highly regarded youngsters.

The twice raced and well bred Hello Bertie falls into that bracket having run with plenty of encouragement in a couple of bumpers last spring. By Kayf Tara out of I'm Delilah (all four of her career wins came on good ground), his dam provided Nicky Richards with his first winner at Cheltenham in April 2007 before joining Ferdy Murphy. She went on to be Grade 2 and 3 placed over fences (rated 137), including in the Red Rum Chase at Aintree in 2011. Hello Bertie is therefore related to another decent chaser who Murphy handled, namely Watch My Back (rated 150), a six times winner (all his wins were also gained on good or faster ground).

Three and three parts of a length third on his racecourse debut at Perth's spring Festival in April, the five year old stayed on well under Brian Hughes having been outpaced two out. The race was won by Rose Dobbin's Planet Nine, who scored under a penalty on his British debut having already won a bumper at Thurles for Timmy Hyde. Hello Bertie headed to Southwell less than a month later and was sent off 6/5 favourite. Taken wide, he was unsuited by the steady early gallop and was tapped for speed in the sprint to the line. Beaten three lengths by Whoshotwho (has won a maiden hurdle at Newton Abbot by 23 lengths since before being sold for £26,000), he will benefit from stepping up to two and a half miles over hurdles.

Malcolm Jefferson has indicated Hello Bertie may have another run in a bumper before sent jumping and, speaking to him in August, he clearly thinks the five year old is capable of winning one. His family were at their best on decent ground and this gelded son of Kayf Tara has yet to race on anything worse than good. It is possible he will follow suit and hopefully develop into a useful performer.

**POINTS TO NOTE:**

| | | | | | |
|---|---|---|---|---|---|
| Probable Best Distance | | - | 2m 4f | | |
| Preferred Going | | - | Good | | |

| GOING: | R | W | P | TRACK: | R | W | P |
|---|---|---|---|---|---|---|---|
| Good | 2 | 0 | 2 | Left Handed | 1 | 0 | 1 |
| | | | | Right | 1 | 0 | 1 |
| | | | | Tight | 2 | 0 | 2 |

| TRIP: | R | W | P | JOCKEY: | R | W | P |
|---|---|---|---|---|---|---|---|
| 2m | 2 | 0 | 2 | B.Hughes | 2 | 0 | 2 |

# INVINCIBLE CAVE (IRE)

4 b g Court Cave (IRE) – Bespoke Baby (IRE) (Invincible Spirit (IRE))
OWNER: GIGGINSTOWN HOUSE STUD Ltd
TRAINER: G.ELLIOTT. Longwood, Co.Meath.
CAREER FORM FIGURES: 1
CAREER WIN: 2017: May BARTLEMY Good Mdn PTP 3m

Another exciting unbeaten pointer who has joined Gordon Elliott, he was a seven lengths winner of his only start 'between the flags' at Bartlemy in May. Not surprisingly, he attracted plenty of interest when going through the sales ring at the Goffs UK Spring Horses In Training Sale at Doncaster a week after his victory. Eddie and Michael O'Leary of Gigginstown House Stud paid £210,000 for the gelded son of Court Cave. His sire was responsible for last season's Neptune Investments Novices' Hurdle winner Willoughby Court.

"Posted one of the most polished displays of the spring when taking the spoils in one of the divisions of the four year old maiden at Bartlemy (R). Led home a 1-2-3 for the Monbeg syndicate, his superiority was evident. On a rare Derek O'Connor ride for this yard, the multiple point champion jockey was happy to cut out the running on this slick jumper: motionless and holding a two lengths lead approaching the second last, the race was soon wrapped up, and his mount eased away for minimum pressure to win by seven lengths: with the fourth, Another Barney, winning since, the form has a solid look about it. By an increasingly popular sire of jumpers, Court Cave, this gelding has a real physical presence and loads of scope for the future. The family is light on back form, his dam was useless, though as a daughter of Invincible Spirit, she may inject some speed from her genepool. When he turned up at the Doncaster Spring sales, he became a desirable object, and with team McManus, Willie Mullins and Gigginstown all getting involved, the latter landed him at £210,000 as he topped that sale. He already has the talent to achieve graded success as a hurdler and chaser, and during his career he may be capable of mixing it at Grade 1 level," believes Declan Phelan.

POINTS TO NOTE:

| Probable Best Distance | - | 2 miles |
| Preferred Going | - | Good/Soft |

| GOING: | R | W | P | TRACK: | R | W | P |
|---|---|---|---|---|---|---|---|
| Good | 1 | 1 | 0 | Right | 1 | 1 | 0 |

| TRIP: | R | W | P | JOCKEY: | R | W | P |
|---|---|---|---|---|---|---|---|
| 3m | 1 | 1 | 0 | D.O'Connor | 1 | 1 | 0 |

# JERRYSBACK (IRE)

5 b g Jeremy (USA) – Get A Few Bob Back (IRE) (Bob Back (USA))
OWNER: J.P.McMANUS
TRAINER: P.J.HOBBS. Minehead, Somerset.
CAREER FORM FIGURES: 42 - F111
CAREER WINS: 2016: Oct LOUGHANMORE Soft 4YO Mdn PTP 3m: 2017: Jan PLUMPTON Heavy NH 2m 4f; Feb WETHERBY Good/Soft NH 2m 3f

Unbeaten in two starts under Rules for J.P.McManus and Philip Hobbs, the former Irish pointer Jerrysback is one of the horses I am most looking forward to seeing this year. The gelded son of Jeremy sauntered to success in two modest novice hurdles at Plumpton and Wetherby during the early part of this year before a minor cut below his knee ruled him out of the rest of the campaign. We are in the dark as to how good he really is but there is no doubting his immense potential.

Trained in Ireland by Colin McKeever, he raced in four point-to-points and was an early faller on his reappearance at Tinahely in October. Returning to the fray a week later at Loughanmore, he was an easy ten lengths winner with his handler saying afterwards: **"In the springtime the penny hadn't dropped with him as he was still a baby, but over the summer he has grown up and improved."** Acquired soon afterwards, Jerrysback was sent off 1/2 favourite for his Rules debut at Plumpton in late January. While his jumping was far from fluent on occasions, he ploughed through the mud to win hard held by four and a half lengths. His rider Barry Geraghty remarked: **"Jerrysback is a big baby. He jumped well and big at times. He was clumsy at the second last. He did as much as he had to."** The five year old then made short work of nine opponents under a penalty at Wetherby less than a month later with Geraghty sitting motionless throughout. A winning margin of a length and a half grossly flattered the runner-up Plus One with previous winner Eaton Hill (had beaten Mount Mews at the same track) back in third. I was working that day for *Racing UK* and speaking to Geraghty afterwards it was evident that he feels the gelding has a big future.

Yet to be given an official rating, it will be interesting to see if he is tested in a valuable handicap hurdle before going chasing. His future lies over the larger obstacles and, regardless of which route he takes during the early part of this season, Jerrysback is very much a horse to follow.

**POINTS TO NOTE:**
**Probable Best Distance**      -      2m 4f – 3 miles
**Preferred Going**      -      Good/Soft
**Connection's Comments: "Jerrysback is a gorgeous horse who did that very well. I would say he wouldn't go to Cheltenham this year, he'll probably go over fences next season." Barry GERAGHTY at Wetherby (21/2/17)**

| GOING: | R | W | P | TRACK: | R | W | P |
|---|---|---|---|---|---|---|---|
| Heavy | 2 | 1 | 0 | Left Handed | 3 | 3 | 0 |
| Soft/Heavy | 1 | 0 | 1 | Right | 3 | 0 | 1 |
| Soft | 1 | 1 | 0 | Galloping | 1 | 1 | 0 |
| Good/Soft | 1 | 1 | 0 | Tight/Undul. | 1 | 1 | 0 |
| Good | 1 | 0 | 0 | | | | |
| | | | | | | | |
| TRIP: | R | W | P | JOCKEY: | R | W | P |
| 2m 3f | 1 | 1 | 0 | B.Geraghty | 2 | 2 | 0 |
| 2m 4f | 1 | 1 | 0 | D.O'Connor | 4 | 1 | 1 |
| 3m | 4 | 1 | 1 | | | | |

# LAD OF LUCK (FR)
**4 b g Soldier of Fortune (IRE) – Baraka Du Berlais (FR) (Bonnet Rouge (FR))**
**OWNER: Mrs STEPHANIE HOFFMAN**
**TRAINER: J.J.O'NEILL. Temple Guiting, Gloucestershire.**
**CAREER FORM FIGURES: 1**
**CAREER WIN: 2017: Feb CHEPSTOW Soft NHF 2m**

John Joseph O'Neill, the son of former dual champion jockey and now head of Jackdaws Castle, Jonjo O'Neill, has made an impressive start to his riding career booting home four winners in the UK last season and another one in the famous J.P.McManus silks at the

Punchestown Festival in the spring. Indeed the victory aboard the Neil Mulholland trained Dead Right must have provided his young rider with the biggest thrill of his short career thus far. Due to spend the summer in France gaining more experience, Jonjo O'Neill jnr looks a jockey with a bright future.

He partnered his father's Lad of Luck to an impressive winning debut in a Chepstow bumper in late February. The Soldier of Fortune gelding was the subject of good support beforehand and justified it in no uncertain terms winning by eleven lengths. Making smooth headway inside the final half a mile, the four year old quickened away in the manner of a smart performer to beat former Irish pointer Hidden Impact easily. The third has won over hurdles since giving the form some substance. Not seen again, Lad of Luck will presumably go straight over hurdles this Autumn. He is bred to be useful, too, being a half-brother to Willie Mullins' Cheltenham Festival winning mare Let's Dance, who captured the Grade 2 Dawn Run Novices' Hurdle in March.

While he may start off over the minimum trip over hurdles, one would expect Lad of Luck to come into his own over two and a half miles. He looks an exciting prospect for this and many seasons to come.

**POINTS TO NOTE:**

| | | |
|---|---|---|
| Probable Best Distance | - | 2m 4f |
| Preferred Going | - | Good/Soft |

| GOING: | R | W | P | TRACK: | R | W | P |
|---|---|---|---|---|---|---|---|
| Soft | 1 | 1 | 0 | Left Handed | 1 | 1 | 0 |
| | | | | Stiff/Undul. | 1 | 1 | 0 |

| TRIP: | R | W | P | JOCKEY: | R | W | P |
|---|---|---|---|---|---|---|---|
| 2m | 1 | 1 | 0 | J.J.O'Neill | 1 | 1 | 0 |

# LALOR (GER)

5 b g It's Gino (GER) – Laviola (GER) (Waky Nao)
OWNER: D.G.STADDON
TRAINER: P.WOOLLACOTT. South Molton, Devon.
CAREER FORM FIGURES: 1211
CAREER WINS: 2016: Dec WINCANTON Soft NHF 2m: 2017: Mar WINCANTON Heavy NHF 2m; Apr AINTREE Good Grade 2 NHF 2m 1f

Despite being sent off 33/1, there was no fluke about Lalor's two and a half lengths win in the Grade 2 championship bumper at Aintree's Grand National meeting. Beating fifteen previous winners in a nineteen strong field, Richard Woollacott's stable star accounted for the likes of Western Ryder (Listed winner) and Claimantakinforgan (third in the Cheltenham Festival bumper) and established himself as one of the best in the division.

Bought for €16,000 at the Tattersalls Derby Sale in Ireland as a three year old, he comes from a German family which has a blend of speed and stamina. Lalor crossed the line in second on his debut at Wincanton on Boxing Day, three lengths behind Victor Dartnall's Run To Milan but was later awarded the race. He then found the unbeaten Sam Brown a length and a quarter too strong over the same course and distance in early February. However, the It's Gino gelding made no mistake on his third visit to the West Country five weeks later justifying strong market support with a powerful display. Partnered by Daryl Jacob for the first time, he revelled in the testing conditions and put his seven rivals to the sword winning by thirteen lengths. That victory booked his ticket to Aintree and champion jockey Richard Johnson took the ride in the

Grade 2 event. If the drying ground was a concern beforehand, it certainly wasn't reflected in Lalor's performance as he loomed up travelling strongly with two furlongs to run. Pushed out for a comfortable success, he readily accounted for a whole host of promising youngsters.

I contacted his trainer in early September and Lalor has reportedly done well during the summer and is all set to embark on a hurdling campaign. The Woollacott stable sent out 13 winners last term and, in this five year old, they have a horse capable of taking them to some of the biggest meetings in the calendar.

**POINTS TO NOTE:**
Probable Best Distance     -     2m 4f
Preferred Going     -     Good/Soft
Connection's Comments: "Lalor is a lovely horse. As soon as I saw him I fell in love with him. We'll take him home, give him a cuddle and then turn him out." Richard WOOLLACOTT at Aintree (7/4/17)

| GOING: | R | W | P | TRACK: | R | W | P |
|---|---|---|---|---|---|---|---|
| Heavy | 2 | 1 | 1 | Left Handed | 1 | 1 | 0 |
| Soft | 1 | 1 | 0 | Right | 3 | 2 | 1 |
| Good | 1 | 1 | 0 | Galloping | 3 | 2 | 1 |
| | | | | Tight | 1 | 1 | 0 |

| TRIP: | R | W | P | JOCKEY: | R | W | P |
|---|---|---|---|---|---|---|---|
| 2m | 3 | 2 | 1 | D.Jacob | 1 | 1 | 0 |
| 2m 1f | 1 | 1 | 0 | R.Johnson | 1 | 1 | 0 |
| | | | | S.Houlihan | 1 | 1 | 0 |
| | | | | T.O'Brien | 1 | 0 | 1 |

# MINELLA AWARDS (IRE)
6 b g Oscar (IRE) – Montys Miss (IRE) (Presenting)
OWNER: MASTERSON HOLDINGS Limited
TRAINER: H.FRY. Seaborough, Dorset.
CAREER FORM FIGURES: 2 - 25 - 211
CAREER WINS: 2017: Mar SANDOWN Soft NHH 2m 4f; Apr PUNCHESTOWN Good/ Yielding HH 3m

Sad news broke in August when Harry Fry announced that his Cheltenham Festival runner-up Neon Wolf had been put down following a freak accident at home. Found to have a complete laceration of his right hindlimb deep digital flexor tendon, the former Irish pointer had won his first three starts for Fry and owners Masterson Holdings Limited before failing by a head to reel in Willoughby Court in the Neptune Investments Novices' Hurdle in March. The Vinnie Roe gelding was viewed as an outstanding chasing prospect and is a major loss to his connections and National Hunt racing.

On a more positive note, Harry Fry has sent out 4 winners at the Punchestown Festival in his short training career, including two on the same card last April. Unowhatimeanharry won his third Grade 1 in the Ladbrokes Champion Stayers Hurdle at 5.30 on the 27th April and then Minella Awards took a typically competitive twenty five runner three miles handicap hurdle at 6.05. The latter has only had three runs for Fry and progressed from an official mark of 128 to 145 over timber.

Runner-up in his only Irish point for John Nallen, he was subsequently bought by Potensis Bloodstock Ltd and Chris Giles for £120,000 in March 2015 and joined Nicky Henderson.

Runner-up behind Champers On Ice at Newbury's Hennessy meeting, he then disappointed in the Listed Sidney Banks Memorial Hurdle at Huntingdon in February last year. Purchased privately by Masterson Holdings Limited and transferred to Dorset, the Oscar gelding didn't reappear until January finding No Comment two lengths too strong in a novices' hurdle at Plumpton. However, Minella Awards thrived thereafter and won the EBF Final at Sandown over two months later. The six year old looked to be in trouble leaving the back straight but Noel Fehily's mount responded to pressure before running out a comfortable one and a quarter lengths winner. Raised six pounds to a rating of 134, he relished the step up to three miles and turned the tables on his old rival No Comment at Punchestown. Despite being eight pounds worse off compared to their first meeting at the Sussex track in January, the Fry runner emerged out on top recording a length victory over Philip Hobbs' charge. It was a measure of the improvement he made last spring.

There are few better 'target trainers' than Harry Fry and Paul Nicholls' former assistant has his eye on the valuable fixed brush handicap hurdle at Haydock (25th November). His performance there will determine whether he continues over the smaller obstacles or goes chasing. Either way, he is a fine prospect who couldn't be in better hands. Unexposed over three miles, it is not beyond the realms of possibility he could develop into a live threat to stablemate Unowhatimeanharry in the top staying hurdles.

**POINTS TO NOTE:**

| Probable Best Distance | - | 3 miles |
|---|---|---|
| Preferred Going | - | Good/Soft |

| GOING: | R | W | P | TRACK: | R | W | P |
|---|---|---|---|---|---|---|---|
| Soft | 3 | 1 | 2 | Left Handed | 3 | 0 | 3 |
| Good/Soft | 1 | 0 | 0 | Right | 3 | 2 | 0 |
| Good/Yield | 1 | 1 | 0 | Galloping | 4 | 2 | 1 |
| Yielding | 1 | 0 | 1 | Tight/Undul. | 1 | 0 | 1 |

| TRIP: | R | W | P | JOCKEY: | R | W | P |
|---|---|---|---|---|---|---|---|
| 2m 3f | 1 | 0 | 0 | N.Fehily | 5 | 2 | 2 |
| 2m 4f | 3 | 1 | 2 | J.T.Carroll | 1 | 0 | 1 |
| 3m | 2 | 1 | 1 | | | | |

# MR BIG SHOT (IRE)
6 br g Flemensfirth (USA) – Une Etoile (IRE) (Un Desperado (FR)
OWNER: Prof CAROLINE TISDALL
TRAINER: D.E.PIPE, Nicholashayne, Somerset.
CAREER FORM FIGURES: 1 - 11
CAREER WINS: 2016: Mar UTTOXETER Soft NHF 2m: 2017: Jan WETHERBY Good/Soft NH 2m; Apr CARLISLE Good/Soft NH 2m 1f

Owner Professor Caroline Tisdall tasted more Cheltenham Festival glory in March when £450,000 purchase Un Temps Pour Tout won the Ultima Handicap Chase for the second consecutive year. The same owner also witnessed Vieux Lion Rouge take the Becher Chase at Aintree in December and the Grand National Trial at Haydock over two months later.

With former Festival bumper winner Moon Racer currently sidelined following a bout of colic during the summer, Tisdall's most promising youngster at Pond House is the unbeaten Mr Big Shot. Rated 138 over hurdles following two bloodless victories at Wetherby and Carlisle, he remains unexposed and is expected to show further improvement when stepping up in distance this season. Indeed, he looks tailormade for the 0-140 Intermediate handicap hurdle at Cheltenham's November meeting (18th) over two miles five, a race David Pipe won with subsequent Grade 1 winning chaser and World Hurdle runner-up Grands Crus in 2010 off a lenient looking 126.

Considered backward both mentally and physically, the Flemensfirth gelding was an eight lengths winner of a Uttoxeter bumper in March 2016 with his trainer saying afterwards: **"Mr Big Shot is massive and doesn't show much at home. It was a fantastic introduction for him, he was as green as grass so should come on a lot for this. Conor (O'Farrell) gave him a great ride, he took his time with him and hit the front approaching the final furlong. He's been backward, a big baby but that was a nice debut."** The six year old didn't make his hurdles debut until the end of January but ran out a ready thirteen lengths winner from a dozen opponents at Wetherby with the runner-up winning his next two starts. Mr Big Shot had no trouble defying his penalty at Carlisle in early April trouncing Skipthescales by seventeen lengths at odds of 1/8. The handicapper hasn't taken too many chances allocating such a rating but he could progress significantly with experience and longer distances.

**POINTS TO NOTE:**
Probable Best Distance      -      **2m 4f – 3 miles**
Preferred Going      -      **Good/Soft**
Connection's Comments: **"Mr Big Shot is still very raw but he's a fine prospect. We've always held him in decent regard and we hope there's more to come." Tom SCUDAMORE at Wetherby (24/1/17)**

| GOING: | R | W | P | TRACK: | R | W | P |
|---|---|---|---|---|---|---|---|
| Soft | 1 | 1 | 0 | Left Handed | 2 | 2 | 0 |
| Good/Soft | 2 | 2 | 0 | Right | 1 | 1 | 0 |
| | | | | Galloping | 1 | 1 | 0 |
| | | | | Stiff/Undul. | 1 | 1 | 0 |
| | | | | Tight/Undul. | 1 | 1 | 0 |

| TRIP: | R | W | P | JOCKEY: | R | W | P |
|---|---|---|---|---|---|---|---|
| 2m | 2 | 2 | 0 | T.Scudamore | 2 | 2 | 0 |
| 2m 1f | 1 | 1 | 0 | C.O'Farrell | 1 | 1 | 0 |

# MR LINGO (IRE)
4 b g Curtain Time (IRE) – Pharlingo (IRE) (Phardante (FR))
OWNER: GIGGINSTOWN HOUSE STUD
TRAINER: G.ELLIOTT. Longwood, Co.Meath
CAREER FORM FIGURES: 1
CAREER WIN: 2017: Apr DROMAHANE Good Mdn PTP 3m

**"One of the star turns of the four year old academy of 2017: a half-brother to 2012 Galway Plate winner Bob Lingo, he lined up for his maiden at Dromahane (L) in April with rumours circulating that he had beaten a number of Willie Mullins horses in a schooling bumper at Thurles as preparation for his point. He did not disappoint as he eased to the front inside the first mile and making the jumping seem effortless, he soon had all the others in trouble and simply flew home over the closing line of three fences to win by eight lengths with his jockey James Hannon not moving a muscle. The display reeked of sheer class. A solid bay with a white face, in his manner of movement and appearance he reminds me greatly of former Grade 1 horse Direct Route. A trip to Cheltenham Sales in April resulted in a £250,000 transfer to Gordon Elliott, and of all the horses in the four year age group, he looks the sure fire bet to slot into Grade 1 company on the track. The only minor worry is that he was pointed by Joe Ryan in Clare and said handler has produced many promising**

looking pointers in past years, unfortunately most have not trained on afterwards on the track proper. I am happy to believe Mr Lingo will buck that trend," enthused Declan Phelan about this gelded son of Curtain Time (best horse over jumps he has produced is dual Grade 2 winner Texas Jack). Likely to make his Rules debut in a bumper, the four year old's first start for his new connections is eagerly anticipated.

**POINTS TO NOTE:**

| Probable Best Distance | - | 2 miles – 2m 4f |
| Preferred Going | - | Good/Soft |

| GOING: | R | W | P | TRACK: | R | W | P |
|---|---|---|---|---|---|---|---|
| Good | 1 | 1 | 0 | Left Handed | 1 | 1 | 0 |

| TRIP: | R | W | P | JOCKEY: | R | W | P |
|---|---|---|---|---|---|---|---|
| 3m | 1 | 1 | 0 | J.Hannon | 1 | 1 | 0 |

# MUSICAL SLAVE (IRE)
**4 b g Getaway (GER) – Inghwung (Kayf Tara)**
**OWNER: J.P.McMANUS**
**TRAINER: P.J.HOBBS. Minehead, Somerset.**
**CAREER FORM FIGURES: 6**

Getaway, who was a dual Group 1 winner on the Flat and fourth behind Dylan Thomas in the Prix de L'Arc de Triomphe ten years ago, has produced a couple of promising youngsters during the early part of his stallion career. Unbeaten winning pointer Getabird would almost certainly have been sent off favourite for the Cheltenham Festival bumper last spring only to be denied a run due to injury, while Nicky Henderson trains the talented mare Verdana Blue, who finished fourth in the inaugural running of the Grade 2 Dawn Run Novices' Hurdle in March and is rated 136.

The same sire is responsible for the once raced Musical Slave. Rather like stablemate No Comment, the J.P.McManus owned four year old ran in a bumper at the Punchestown Festival in April. While he was unable to replicate his success from twelve months earlier, Philip Hobbs' charge ran an encouraging race finishing sixth only four lengths behind the winner Roaring Bull. Leading amateur Derek O'Connor did the steering and he reportedly liked the gelding and the form has worked out well, too. Both the third and fourth (twice) have scored subsequently.

Musical Slave is likely to go straight over hurdles this Autumn and will benefit from stepping up to two and a half miles. The Getaway gelding moved like an above average horse for the majority of his debut in Ireland and should have no trouble winning races.

**POINTS TO NOTE:**

| Probable Best Distance | - | 2m 4f |
| Preferred Going | - | Good/Soft |

| GOING: | R | W | P | TRACK: | R | W | P |
|---|---|---|---|---|---|---|---|
| Good/Yield | 1 | 0 | 0 | Right | 1 | 0 | 0 |
| | | | | Galloping | 1 | 0 | 0 |

| TRIP: | R | W | P | JOCKEY: | R | W | P |
|---|---|---|---|---|---|---|---|
| 2m | 1 | 0 | 0 | D.O'Connor | 1 | 0 | 0 |

# NOT THAT FUISSE (FR)

**4 b g Fuisse (FR) – Edelmina (FR) (Kahyasi)**
**OWNER: COLM DONLON**
**TRAINER: D.SKELTON. Shelfield Green, Alcester.**
**CAREER FORM FIGURES: 1**
**CAREER WIN: 2017: Apr WARWICK Good NHF 2m**

Bought at the Land Rover Sale as a three year old for €20,000, Not That Fuisse was one of his stable's ten bumper winners last season. A four lengths winner at his local track, Harry Skelton's mount always appeared to be in control and only had to be pushed out to record an emphatic success.

Sent off 9/2 favourite, the winning time was slow in comparison to the second division won by World Premier (subsequently bought by J.P.McManus) but the manner of his win was striking with Dan Skelton's charge displaying a high cruising speed. The form received a boost, too, with the third Equus Amadeus winning easily at Exeter on his next start. Only four, Not That Fuisse has been well schooled over hurdles and jumps well at home. Not short of speed, he is likely to start off over two miles and shouldn't have any trouble handling easier ground than he encountered on his debut.

**POINTS TO NOTE:**
**Probable Best Distance          -          2 miles – 2m 4f**
**Preferred Going          -          Good/Soft**
**Connection's Comments:** "Not That Fuisse is a lovely horse who we think quite a bit of. He travelled well and quickened up nicely when given a squeeze." Dan SKELTON at Warwick (24/4/17)

| GOING: | R | W | P | TRACK: | R | W | P |
|--------|---|---|---|--------|---|---|---|
| Good | 1 | 1 | 0 | Left Handed | 1 | 1 | 0 |
| | | | | Tight/Undul. | 1 | 1 | 0 |
| | | | | | | | |
| TRIP: | R | W | P | JOCKEY: | R | W | P |
| 2m | 1 | 1 | 0 | H.Skelton | 1 | 1 | 0 |

# PLOUIOS (IRE)

**4 b g Milan – Garlucy (IRE) (Un Desperado (FR))**
**OWNER: J.P.McMANUS**
**TRAINER: H.DE BROMHEAD. Knockeen, Co.Waterford.**
**CAREER FORM FIGURES: 1**
**CAREER WIN: 2017: Apr LOUGHANMORE Good Mdn PTP 3m**

One of the chief beneficiaries of Gigginstown House Stud's decision to remove their horses from Willie Mullins last Autumn, County Waterford based trainer Henry De Bromhead had a tremendous season in 2016/2017 with 68 domestic winners, including Grade 1 victories for Petit Mouchoir (twice), Some Plan, Special Tiara (Queen Mother Champion Chase) and Valseur Lido. With Balko Des Flos winning the Galway Plate in August, he has already made a telling start to the new campaign as well.

De Bromhead trained Home Farm to win a Listed chase and was placed in the Irish National. It is therefore appropriate he has taken charge of unbeaten winning pointer Plouios, who hails from the same family. **"Posted a very professional winning debut at Loughanmore (L) on**

Easter Saturday: a loose moving athlete and efficient jumper, he made the running, tested on the run to the final fence, he responded to a nudge from rider Rob James, pinged the last and stamped his authority on proceedings to win by a non flattering four lengths. He looked very sharp on the day and was a step or two above his rivals in terms of class. A €52,000 purchase at the 2016 Derby Sale, the Monbeg syndicate sold him privately to J.P.McManus for a sum involving six figures, permitting a handsome profit on the nine months turnaround. He is the horse I like most amongst the McManus shopping spree in the four year old division. He signalled speed in this race and he should be versatile to move from trips between two and a half and three miles in comfort. He can win a bumper and would have reasonable claims of securing graded novice hurdles and chases and could be a 140 + horse at some stage in his future," believes Declan Phelan.

POINTS TO NOTE:

| | | |
|---|---|---|
| Probable Best Distance | - | 2m 4f – 3 miles |
| Preferred Going | - | Good/Soft |

Connection's Comments: "He's a lovely big horse and jumped great. He's an easy going, very straightforward horse." Donnchadh DOYLE at Loughanmore (15/4/17)

| GOING: | R | W | P | TRACK: | R | W | P |
|---|---|---|---|---|---|---|---|
| Good | 1 | 1 | 0 | Left Handed | 1 | 1 | 0 |

| TRIP: | R | W | P | JOCKEY: | R | W | P |
|---|---|---|---|---|---|---|---|
| 3m | 1 | 1 | 0 | R.James | 1 | 1 | 0 |

# POLI ROI (FR)

5 b g Poliglote – Belle Du Roi (FR)
OWNER: GIGGINSTOWN HOUSE STUD
TRAINER: G.ELLIOTT. Longwood, Co.Meath.
CAREER FORM FIGURES: 113
CAREER WINS: 2016: Nov ROCKFIELD Yielding/Soft 4YO Mdn PTP 3m: 2017: Feb NAVAN Soft/Heavy NHF 2m

Gigginstown House Stud have won the Grade 1 Albert Bartlett Novices' Hurdle at the Cheltenham Festival twice thanks to Weapon's Amnesty (2009) and Very Wood (2014). There is every possibility Poli Roi will emerge as their main contender for the 2018 version. A half-brother to Grade 1 Finale Hurdle winner Le Rocher, he was bought as a three year old for £46,000 at the Doncaster Spring Sales before joining Denis Murphy in Ireland.

A ten lengths winning pointer in November, he was sold a few days later at the Cheltenham Sale for £300,000. A two lengths winner of a bumper at Navan on his first start for Gordon Elliott, he wasn't disgraced last time when around twelve lengths in arrears of stablemate and Cheltenham Festival bumper winner Fayonagh in the championship event at Punchestown in late April. Conceding seven pounds to the winning mare, he will appreciate a stiffer test of stamina over hurdles. Point expert Declan Phelan comments: **"Apart from Finian's Oscar this athletic bay gelding (with white face and socks), was the best maiden winner seen in the run up to Christmas from the autumn session in the Irish pointing world. Alike Finian's, he also represented trainer Denis Murphy. He contested the four year old maiden at Rockfield (L) in November: that race was distinguished by the hot pace from the start and proved a good test of the participants. Poli Roi was tightened for room climbing for home with two to jump as he sat in sixth/seventh place. Jamie Codd navigated him into a clear passage jumping the second last: and gave him a squeeze and with an immediate response, he really quickened up smartly and drove away for a ten lengths win in a commendable time.**

Coupling that memorable display with a pedigree rich in French Graded jumps winners, a high sales prices was anticipated when he came under the hammer at Cheltenham Tattersalls sales five days later. Gigginstown House Stud and Gordon Elliott won the bidding war at £300,000. He had two bumper runs for new connections in the spring, winning an ordinary seven runner race at Navan at his leisure, which earned him a crack at the Champion bumper at the Punchestown Festival and, given the steep rise in class, he covered himself in glory with an acceptable third behind stablemate Fayonagh. There is plenty to admire about this five year old: he has speed, stamina and a bit of character (showed at Rockfield as he wasn't bothered when baulked): he has also form to his name on good and heavy ground: in summary, he will certainly win graded races this winter over hurdles and Grade 1s may be within his range. I fancy he would enjoy the hill at Cheltenham and he could be one of the 2016/17 Irish pointers with the potential to entertain aspirations of winning at the March Festival in 2018."

**POINTS TO NOTE:**

| | | |
|---|---|---|
| Probable Best Distance | - | 2m 4f – 3 miles |
| Preferred Going | - | Good/Soft |

Connection's Comments: "This is a well bred horse. His work at home has always been very good and he showed that there." Denis MURPHY at Rockfield (6/11/16)

| GOING: | R | W | P | TRACK: | R | W | P |
|---|---|---|---|---|---|---|---|
| Soft/Heavy | 1 | 1 | 0 | Left Handed | 2 | 2 | 0 |
| Yield/Soft | 1 | 1 | 0 | Right | 1 | 0 | 1 |
| Good/Yield | 1 | 0 | 1 | Galloping | 2 | 1 | 1 |

| TRIP: | R | W | P | JOCKEY: | R | W | P |
|---|---|---|---|---|---|---|---|
| 2m | 2 | 1 | 1 | J.J.Codd | 2 | 2 | 0 |
| 3m | 1 | 1 | 0 | K.Walsh | 1 | 0 | 1 |

# POTTERMAN

4 b g Sulamani (IRE) – Polly Potter (Kayf Tara)
OWNER: JAMES & JEAN POTTER
TRAINER: A.KING. Barbury Castle, Wiltshire.
CAREER FORM FIGURES: 1
CAREER WIN: 2017: May HUNTINGDON Good NHF 2m

Numerically and financially, Alan King had his best season for eight years last winter with an impressive tally of 104 winners and prize-money exceeding £1.3m. Messire Des Obeaux and Yanworth (twice) provided Barbury Castle with Grade 1 victories, while Sceau Royal (Elite Hurdle) and Master Blueyes (Adonis) were Grade 2 victors.

King is understandably excited about the season ahead having assembled a particularly strong team of juvenile and novice hurdlers. Recruitments from France include the potentially high-class pair Desiremoi D'Authie and Melody of Scotland, while the yard sent out some eyecatching bumpers winners during the spring and none more so than the well bred Potterman. From the family of Denman and Kayf Grace, the Sulamani gelding didn't surprise his connections when making a winning debut in a six runner event at Huntingdon in late May. Wayne Hutchinson's mount moved strongly throughout and, having taken charge with a furlong to run, he pulled clear to beat market leader Raising The Bar by ten lengths.

Speaking to his trainer in August, the four year old may have another run in a bumper before sent jumping. Not short of speed, he looks one to follow in two mile novice hurdles.

**POINTS TO NOTE:**

| Probable Best Distance | - | 2 miles |
| Preferred Going | - | Good/Soft |

| GOING: | R | W | P | | TRACK: | R | W | P |
|---|---|---|---|---|---|---|---|---|
| Good | 1 | 1 | 0 | | Right | 1 | 1 | 0 |
| | | | | | Galloping | 1 | 1 | 0 |

| TRIP: | R | W | P | | JOCKEY: | R | W | P |
|---|---|---|---|---|---|---|---|---|
| 2m | 1 | 1 | 0 | | W.Hutchinson | 1 | 1 | 0 |

# PYM (IRE)

**4 b g Stowaway – Liss Rua (IRE) (Bob Back (USA))**
**OWNER: Mrs PATRICIA PUGH**
**TRAINER: N.J.HENDERSON. Lambourn, Berkshire.**
**CAREER FORM FIGURES: 1**
**CAREER WIN: 2017: Apr AYR Good/Soft NHF 2m**

Patricia Pugh owns arguably the hottest property in National Hunt racing at present, Altior. The High Chaparral gelding has won 12 of his 14 races earning £365,736 in prize-money in the process and providing his connections with two Cheltenham Festival successes. The seven year old, who won the Skybet Supreme Novices' Hurdle in 2016, is unbeaten in half a dozen races over fences, including a six lengths victory in the Arkle Trophy last March. Not surprisingly, Nicky Henderson's charge is a short price ante-post favourite for the Queen Mother Champion Chase next spring.

The same owner is also responsible for the once raced Pym, who ensured the Lambourn trainer's monopoly of the bumper on Scottish National day at Ayr in April continued. Henderson was winning it for the fifth time since Sprinter Sacre took the race in 2010 (Fourth Estate (2011), River Maigue (2012) and William Henry (2015)). A big scopey gelding by Stowaway, who cost €35,000 at the Land Rover Sale in Ireland as a three year old, he is a half-brother to hurdle winners Beneagles and Minella Aris. In a race which was run at a sound gallop from the outset, Pym was shaken up with two furlongs to run by Jerry McGrath and soon responded to quicken up in good style before taking over inside the final 200 yards to win going away by four lengths. The third, Ballyvic Boru, had won an Irish point and a bumper at Musselburgh beforehand and subsequently scored over hurdles at Perth.

Held in high regard, Pym may prove quick enough to be effective over two miles but a step up to two and a half miles is expected to suit and he looks to have the potential to develop into a Graded novice hurdler this season with the Neptune Investments Novice Hurdle at the Festival a realistic goal.

**POINTS TO NOTE:**

| Probable Best Distance | - | 2m – 2m 4f |
| Preferred Going | - | Good/Soft |

| GOING: | R | W | P | | TRACK: | R | W | P |
|---|---|---|---|---|---|---|---|---|
| Good/Soft | 1 | 1 | 0 | | Left Handed | 1 | 1 | 0 |
| | | | | | Galloping | 1 | 1 | 0 |

| TRIP: | R | W | P | | JOCKEY: | R | W | P |
|---|---|---|---|---|---|---|---|---|
| 2m | 1 | 1 | 0 | | J.McGrath | 1 | 1 | 0 |

# RAVENHILL ROAD (IRE)

6 ch g Exit To Nowhere (USA) – Zaffarella (IRE) (Zaffaran (USA))
OWNER: P.J.MARTIN
TRAINER: B.ELLISON. Norton, Malton, North Yorkshire.
CAREER FORM FIGURES: 111
CAREER WINS: 2016: May BROUGHSHANE Good Mdn PTP 3m; Oct MARKET RASEN
Good NHF 2m; Nov DONCASTER Good NHF 2m

With the assistance of leading patron Phil Martin, Brian Ellison has built up a terrific team of jumpers and is understandably looking forward to the winter ahead. Definitly Red was a three times winner last season, including victories in the Rowland Meyrick Chase at Wetherby and Grimthorpe Chase at Doncaster, with his rating over fences rising from 142 to 159. The Charlie Hall Chase at Wetherby (4th November) has already been pencilled in for his likely reappearance, while the same owner's Forest Bihan will be targeted at the top two mile chases having been narrowly denied Grade 1 glory at Aintree on Grand National day last spring.

However, arguably the most exciting prospect at Spring Cottage Stables is the unbeaten Ravenhill Road. A fifteen lengths winner of his only Irish point for the Crawford family, the Exit To Nowhere gelding was acquired for £100,000 eleven days later at the Doncaster Spring Sales last year. The gelding was the subject of a strong word prior to his first start for Ellison in a bumper at Market Rasen last Autumn with reports of him working well with the aforementioned Definitly Red. Making virtually all the running, the even money favourite showed signs of greenness but it didn't prevent him from destroying his eight rivals by upwards of fourteen lengths with a powerful display of galloping. He ran his opponents into submission under conditional Kaine Wood. The same rider was on board at Doncaster over a month later and, while the winning margin wasn't quite so substantial, Ravenhill Road gave another authoritative display under a penalty. He conceded twelve pounds to the runner-up Molly Childers (subsequently fifth in a Listed bumper at Sandown) beating Stuart Edmunds mare by four and a half lengths.

Absent since, the plan was for him to be aimed at the Cheltenham Festival bumper but he incurred an injury to his hock, which may explain why he hung to his left at both Market Rasen and Doncaster. A brilliant jumper, according to his trainer, he will go novice hurdling over two and a half miles and is undoubtedly one of the brightest prospects in the North. Brian Ellison believes he is out of the top drawer.

## POINTS TO NOTE:

| | | |
|---|---|---|
| Probable Best Distance | - | 2m 4f |
| Preferred Going | - | Good |

Connection's Comments: "Ravenhill Road is very good, he's done everything we've asked of him." Kaine WOOD at Doncaster (25/11/16)

| GOING: | R | W | P | | TRACK: | R | W | P |
|---|---|---|---|---|---|---|---|---|
| Good | 3 | 3 | 0 | | Left Handed | 2 | 2 | 0 |
| | | | | | Right | 1 | 1 | 0 |
| | | | | | Galloping | 1 | 1 | 0 |
| | | | | | Tight/Undul. | 1 | 1 | 0 |

| TRIP: | R | W | P | | JOCKEY: | R | W | P |
|---|---|---|---|---|---|---|---|---|
| 2m | 2 | 2 | 0 | | K.Wood | 2 | 2 | 0 |
| 3m | 1 | 1 | 0 | | B.Crawford | 1 | 1 | 0 |

# SALSARETTA (FR)

4 b f Kingsalsa (USA) – Kendoretta (FR) (Kendor (FR))
OWNER: Mrs S.RICCI
TRAINER: W.P.MULLINS. Bagenalstown, Co.Carlow.
CAREER FORM FIGURES: 392

The Ricci's and Willie Mullins captured the first running of the Trull House Stud Mares' Novices' Hurdle (Dawn Run) at the Cheltenham Festival last March when the heavily supported Let's Dance got the better of compatriot Barra. The two miles one event is expected to be the ultimate target for another ex-French trained filly who will be sporting the same silks this season.

Salsaretta was acquired privately out of Francois Nicolle's yard last Autumn following three runs over hurdles at Auteuil. A half-sister to new stablemate Breaken, she filled third position on her debut in the Listed Prix Wild Monarch in May 2016. Beaten two and a half lengths by Dans La Foulee, she was then a disappointing ninth over an extra couple of furlongs at the same track over three weeks later. However, the Kingsalsa filly returned to form four months later when only losing out by a short neck behind D'Vina (runner-up twice since in Grade 3 company) in another Listed hurdle for fillies at the Parisian track.

Reported to have pleased her new connections, hopes are high Salsaretta can develop into a smart filly this season and mix it at the highest level against her own sex.

**POINTS TO NOTE:**

| | | | |
|---|---|---|---|
| Probable Best Distance | - | 2 miles – 2m 4f | |
| Preferred Going | - | Soft | |

| GOING: | R | W | P | TRACK: | R | W | P |
|---|---|---|---|---|---|---|---|
| Very Soft | 3 | 0 | 2 | Left Handed | 3 | 0 | 2 |
| | | | | Galloping | 3 | 0 | 2 |

| TRIP: | R | W | P | JOCKEY: | R | W | P |
|---|---|---|---|---|---|---|---|
| 1m 7f | 1 | 0 | 1 | T.Chevillard | 2 | 0 | 2 |
| 2m 1f | 1 | 0 | 0 | R.Schmidlin | 1 | 0 | 0 |
| 2m 2f | 1 | 0 | 1 | | | | |

# SAMCRO (IRE)

5 ch g Germany (USA) – Dun Dun (IRE) (Saddlers' Hall (IRE))
OWNER: GIGGINSTOWN HOUSE STUD
TRAINER: G.ELLIOTT. Longwood, Co.Meath.
CAREER FORM FIGURES: 1 - 111
CAREER WINS: 2016: Apr MONKSGRANGE Heavy 4YO Mdn PTP 3m; Nov PUNCHESTOWN Soft NHF 2m; Dec NAVAN Soft/Heavy Listed NHF 2m: 2017: Apr FAIRYHOUSE Good/Yielding NHF 2m

Gigginstown House Stud and Gordon Elliott won the Cheltenham Gold Cup in 2016 with Don Cossack and, while the unbeaten Samcro has a long way to go before he matches his former stablemate's acheivements, there is no doubting his unlimited potential. It is very easy to make comparisions between the pair – both won the same bumpers at Navan (December) and Fairyhouse (Easter Monday).

Featured in last year's *Top 40* having won his only Irish point-to-point for Colin Bowe and subsequently bought for £335,000 at the Aintree Sale in April 2016, Samcro won all three of his bumpers last season for Elliott including a nine and a half lengths victory on his Rules debut at Punchestown in November. He was more workmanlike next time in a Listed contest at Navan (Don Cossack won the same race in 2011) in mid December when beating Willie Mullins' mare Good Thyne Tara by half a length. Making all under Jamie Codd, his trainer said afterwards: **"He is a lovely horse and we really like him a lot. Jamie [Codd] said it was a game of cat and mouse and he would do a lot more in a gallop at home but, in fairness to Katie [Walsh], she did the right thing to try and beat us and came with one run but Jamie did not even hit him. He might just have one more run for the rest of the year, we will mind him now."** That proved the case as the Germany gelding didn't reappear until Easter Monday at Fairyhouse, where he produced his most impressive performance to date. Partnered by Cheltenham Festival winning rider Lisa O'Neill, Samcro destroyed his six rivals with an awesome display. Leading two out, the five year old quickly pulled clear to win by seventeen lengths with Elliott saying: **"He's a proper horse. Lisa (O'Neill) said that he felt like he was asleep the whole way round but that when she gave him a squeeze turning in he just came alive."**

Set to go novice hurdling this season, one would expect him to follow a similar route to the one stablemate Death Duty took last year, namely a maiden hurdle followed by the Grade 3 Monksfield Novices' Hurdle at Navan (26th November). The stable have won it with Mount Benbulben (2011), Free Expression (2014), plus Death Duty last year. Then, all being well, the Grade 2 Navan Hurdle (17th December) – No More Heroes (2014) and Death Duty (2016) were both successful in the two and a half miles event for Elliott. Interestingly, while interviewing Olly Murphy in August, I asked Gordon Elliott's former assistant about Samcro and he feels the gelding is the best horse in Gordon's yard, which is high praise considering the talent on offer throughout the whole stable. The Neptune Investments Novices' Hurdle at Cheltenham in March may prove to be his ultimate goal this season and the 16/1 currently available in the ante-post markets is tempting.

I will leave the final word to point expert Declan Phelan who wrote in last year's *One Jump Ahead*: **"A big, strong bodied chestnut son of Germany, similar in make up to Faugheen, another offspring of that sire. He coasted through the mud at Monksgrange (Heavy) to account for Elegant Escape: he was worth much more than his one length winning margin: he was not fluent at times jumping in what were hostile weather conditions. He did, however, give a swagger of real class, as in a few strides he opened up a five lengths margin over his opponents between the last two fences: his jockey Barry O'Neill had to actually slow him down into the last to find a stride and this checked his momentum, yet he kept on to win cosily. It was an above average performance."**

**POINTS TO NOTE:**

| | | |
|---|---|---|
| Probable Best Distance | - | 2m 4f – 3 miles |
| Preferred Going | - | Good/Soft |

Connection's Comments: **"He's a good one and he's one to look forward to further down the road when he goes hurdling and chasing." Gordon ELLIOTT at Punchestown (20/11/16)**

| GOING: | R | W | P | TRACK: | R | W | P |
|---|---|---|---|---|---|---|---|
| Heavy | 1 | 1 | 0 | Left Handed | 2 | 2 | 0 |
| Soft/Heavy | 1 | 1 | 0 | Right | 2 | 2 | 0 |
| Soft | 1 | 1 | 0 | Galloping | 3 | 3 | 0 |
| Good/Yield. | 1 | 1 | 0 | | | | |

| TRIP: | R | W | P | JOCKEY: | R | W | P |
|---|---|---|---|---|---|---|---|
| 2m | 3 | 3 | 0 | J.J.Codd | 2 | 2 | 0 |
| 3m | 1 | 1 | 0 | B.O'Neill | 1 | 1 | 0 |
| | | | | Ms L.O'Neill | 1 | 1 | 0 |

# SANGHA RIVER (IRE)
4 br g Arcadio (GER) – Hidden Reserve (IRE) (Heron Island (IRE)
OWNER: MRS BARBARA HESTER
TRAINER: D.SKELTON. Shelfield Green, Alcester.
CAREER FORM FIGURES: U

One of the biggest disappointments of the 2016/2017 National Hunt campaign was the season and possibly career ending fall suffered by the potentially top-class Robin Roe in the Grade 1 Challow Hurdle at Newbury on New Year's Eve. The Robin Des Champs gelding had created such a favourable impression when annihilating the highly regarded No Comment by a dozen lengths at Aintree in late October. Sent off 7/4 favourite at the Berkshire track next time, he was beginning to mount his challenge when coming to grief at the third last.

The six year old belongs to Barbara Hester who has invested large amounts of money into stable recently and she returned to the same source, the Irish pointing field, to acquire the Timmy Hyde trained Sangha River. A four year old by Arcadio, point expert Declan Phelan comments: **"Dan Skelton has enjoyed plenty of success with his purchases from the Hyde team in Tipperary, Cause Toujours, one such example. He stepped in quickly to snap up this once raced pointer in February. A bay gelding and full brother to winning Gigginstown pointer Hardline, he had one pointing experience in early February at Belharbour (L): he was receiving a tender educational ride and appearing to be ready to claim the runners-up spot when he collided with a marker/bale after jumping the second last and unseated rider. He would not have troubled the easy winner Dorrells Pierji, though the run was full of promise. If he continues the family habits, then two to two and a half miles will be his preferred distance range."** Since arriving in Warwickshire, the four year old has impressed his work riders and is considered a good prospect for bumpers/novice hurdles.

POINTS TO NOTE:
| | | |
|---|---|---|
| Probable Best Distance | - | 2 miles - 2m 4f |
| Preferred Going | - | Good/Soft |

| GOING: | R | W | P | TRACK: | R | W | P |
|---|---|---|---|---|---|---|---|
| Yielding | 1 | 0 | 0 | Left Handed | 1 | 0 | 0 |

| TRIP: | R | W | P | JOCKEY: | R | W | P |
|---|---|---|---|---|---|---|---|
| 3m | 1 | 0 | 0 | S.Connor | 1 | 0 | 0 |

# STAY HUMBLE (IRE)
4 b g Beat Hollow – Rosy De Cyborg (FR) (Cyborg (FR)
OWNER: ANDREA & GRAHAM WYLIE
TRAINER: W.P.MULLINS. Bagenalstown, Co.Carlow.
CAREER FORM FIGURES: 1
CAREER WIN: 2017: Apr BALLYNOE Good/Yielding Mdn PTP 3m

Irish point expert Declan Phelan is in no doubt the once raced Stay Humble is a high-class prospect in the making saying: **"A tall, well muscled bay gelding, home bred by renowned jumps breeder/vet Walter Connors. He posted a high ranking effort when making a winning** debut at Ballynoe (R) in April. Trained for this point by Pat Doyle, he was relaxed by Derek O'Connor off a very strong gallop, cruising into contention on the climb towards the second last fence, he soon asserted and drew clear to win by five lengths with something still left in his locker. There were plenty of positives from the performance: jumping, cruising speed, temperament, and the ability to finish the job were all boxes getting a generous ticking. His half-brother Smuggler's Blue (at 5, a year older) won his maiden point a fortnight later in April: he is not a patch on this youngster. Willie Mullins is more than happy to deal with owner Connors and he has had much success with previous purchases from this source, including of late Bacardys. I gather a private deal in the region north of £250,000 saw him transfer to Mullins. His style of racing reminds me of a young Florida Pearl: I fully expect him to feature very high up the pecking order of Mullins bumper horses this winter, could even be a possible Cheltenham Festival bumper winner and thereafter a career mixing with top class horses in graded races over hurdles and primarily fences beckons." Interestingly, Pat Doyle reportedly indicated afterwards that the Beat Hollow gelding is the best four year old he has trained, which is high praise considering he has handled the likes of Grade 1 winning hurdler Death Duty amongst others.

Indeed, I contacted Stay Humble's new owner Graham Wylie in August and he highlighted the four year old as one to watch out for in bumpers this season. The North East based owner won the Festival bumper with Briar Hill four years ago and he may have another prime contender here as Mullins seeks a record ninth win in the championship event. Stay Humble could be top-class.

**POINTS TO NOTE:**

| | | | | | | | |
|---|---|---|---|---|---|---|---|
| **Probable Best Distance** | | | - | 2 miles | | | |
| **Preferred Going** | | | - | Good/Soft | | | |

| GOING: | R | W | P | TRACK: | R | W | P |
|---|---|---|---|---|---|---|---|
| Good/Yield | 1 | 1 | 0 | Right | 1 | 1 | 0 |

| TRIP: | R | W | P | JOCKEY: | R | W | P |
|---|---|---|---|---|---|---|---|
| 2m | 1 | 1 | 0 | D.O'Connor | 1 | 1 | 0 |

# STEELY ADDITION (IRE)

5 b g Craigsteel – Blond's Addition (IRE) (Lord Americo)
OWNER: STEP BY STEP
TRAINER: P.J.HOBBS. Minehead, Somerset
CAREER FORM FIGURES: 1334
CAREER WIN: 2016: May HEXHAM Good Mdn PTP 2m 4f

The lightly raced former English pointer Steely Addition looks a well handicapped young hurdler, especially following the news that he had been transferred to Philip Hobbs during the summer. The Craigsteel gelding has only raced three times over timber and it will be disappointing if he can't make a significant impact off a rating of 116.

A fifteen lengths winner of a six runner two and a half miles open maiden point-to-point at Hexham in May 2016 (only 2 finished) when trained by Chris Dawson, he was purchased by Somerset based Hugo Froud for £45,000 eleven days later at the Cheltenham Premier Horses In Training Sale. Steely Addition made his hurdling debut for his new connections in a two mile novices' hurdle at Wincanton in mid December and produced a fine effort finishing four and a half lengths third behind subsequent *Betfair* Hurdle runner-up Movewiththetimes (rated 146). Stepped up to two miles three at Taunton less than a month later, the five year old bumped into another decent novice, namely Bags Groove (rated 133), and again was placed. Disappointing when dropping back to the minimum trip at Market Rasen in late April, he was sent off 13/8 favourite but could only fill fourth position over thirteen lengths behind the winner Gris De Pron.

Now qualified for handicaps and residing in a different part of Somerset, Steely Addition will appreciate the return to two and a half miles and is likely to be found an opportunity in a novices' handicap hurdle. It is hoped his official rating will be considerably higher by the spring.

POINTS TO NOTE:

| Probable Best Distance | - | 2m 4f |
|---|---|---|
| Preferred Going | - | Good/Soft |

| GOING: | R | W | P | TRACK: | R | W | P |
|---|---|---|---|---|---|---|---|
| Good/Soft | 1 | 0 | 1 | Left Handed | 1 | 1 | 0 |
| Good | 3 | 1 | 1 | Right | 3 | 0 | 2 |
| | | | | Galloping | 1 | 0 | 1 |
| | | | | Stiff/Undul. | 1 | 1 | 0 |
| | | | | Tight | 1 | 0 | 1 |
| | | | | Tight/Undul. | 1 | 0 | 0 |

| TRIP: | R | W | P | JOCKEY: | R | W | P |
|---|---|---|---|---|---|---|---|
| 2m | 2 | 0 | 1 | J.Dawson | 1 | 1 | 0 |
| 2m 3f | 1 | 0 | 1 | N.De Boinville | 1 | 0 | 0 |
| 2m 4f | 1 | 1 | 0 | D.Jacob | 2 | 0 | 2 |

# THE BIG LENSE (IRE)

4 b g Court Cave (IRE) – Megans Joy (IRE) (Supreme Leader)
OWNER: GIGGINSTOWN HOUSE STUD
TRAINER: G.ELLIOTT. Longwood, Co.Meath.
CAREER FORM FIGURES: 1
CAREER WIN: 2017: Feb CRAGMORE Good/Yielding Mdn PTP 2m 4f

"He could be one of the star four year olds to emerge from the 2017 spring campaign. His dam, Megans Joy was a quality race mare, she won two bumpers and scored four times over hurdles, including at Grade 2 level, all her wins at the two mile trip, though she won on a variety of grounds (heavy to firm): she peaked with a mark of 137 over hurdles. She has already produced a dual winner, in the guise of the tough and consistent 133 rated mare Happy Diva. In hindsight, when The Big Lense came under the hammer at the 2016 Derby Store Sale, he was bought at a bargain price of €24,000. Simon McGonagle was the main stakeholder in the syndicate who pointed him. Simon had soldiered together with Gordon Elliott back in their days riding as amateurs attached to Tony Martin. Since Gordon set up as a trainer, Simon has been his long-term trusty right hand man, and it is safe to say that he is a vital intelligent cog in the Elliott machine. Simon travelled down with The Big Lense to Limerick for his pointing debut. Cragmore (L) stages its fixture on land owned by the Costello family and the four year old point is run over two and a half miles. Eight faced the starter, with three to jump The Big Lense began to take control, he was already ten lengths in front when his nearest pursuer fell two out and, without coming under any pressure, he extended away to win by twenty lengths: the second won next time out to frank the form. The Big Lense was entered for the Cheltenham Festival sale in March, he did not travel as apparently a private sale materialised and he will remain in house with Elliott under new ownership. He is a solid bay gelding with three white socks and a flick of grey in his hair, very similar markings to his mother. **He has loads of speed and I think he will operate at a very high level at trips between two and two and a half miles, and one day you might see him win a Ryanair or Champion Chase at a Cheltenham Festival,"** believes Irish expert Declan Phelan.

**POINTS TO NOTE:**

| | | |
|---|---|---|
| Probable Best Distance | - | 2 miles – 2m 4f |
| Preferred Going | - | Good/Soft |

Connection's Comments: **"That's great, he did it nicely. He jumped well and travelled well so we couldn't be happier. He'll go for a bumper next as he's a horse who's not short of speed."** Simon McGONAGLE at Cragmore (19/2/17)

| GOING: | R | W | P | TRACK: | R | W | P |
|---|---|---|---|---|---|---|---|
| Good/Yield | 1 | 1 | 0 | Left Handed | 1 | 1 | 0 |
| | | | | | | | |
| TRIP: | R | W | P | JOCKEY: | R | W | P |
| 2m 4f | 1 | 1 | 0 | A.J.Fox | 1 | 1 | 0 |

# TOPOFTHEGAME (IRE)

**5 ch g Flemensfirth (USA) – Derry Vale (IRE) (Mister Lord (USA))**
**OWNER: CHRIS GILES**
**TRAINER: P.F.NICHOLLS. Ditcheat, Somerset**
**CAREER FORM FIGURES: 1 - 142**
**CAREER WINS: 2016: Mar BELCLARE Yielding/Soft Mdn PTP 3m; Dec ASCOT Good/Soft MH 2m 5f**

Paul Nicholls' former Irish pointer retains his place in the *Top 40 Prospects* because the five year old remains a horse of tremendous potential, especially now his attentions are turned to fences. A nine lengths winner of his only race 'between the flags' when accounting for No Hassle Hoff (Graded placed and rated 134 over hurdles for Dan Skelton), he was subsequently bought for £120,000.

The Flemensfirth gelding was given a relatively easy time over hurdles last season with a view to sending him chasing this time around. Restricted to three outings, he was a short head scorer on his Rules debut in a two miles five maiden hurdle at Ascot in mid December. Topofthegame looked set to win easily approaching the last but made heavy weather of it thereafter and was all out to hold the late thrust of Criq Rock. However, he had moved through the majority of the race like a high-class horse. That high cruising speed was once again in evidence when stepped up in class at Cheltenham's 'Trials' meeting in late January. Although beaten eleven lengths by Wholestone in the Grade 2 contest, having raced keenly early on, he held every chance at the second last (took a false step) but was unable to pick up once turning for home. Narrowly denied on his third and final start over timber at Ascot, he was outsprinted after the last by the ex-Flat racer Beyond Conceit going down by a neck to Nicky Henderson's eight year old.

Rated 139 over hurdles, the former champion trainer purposely swerved the end of season Festivals with the giant five year old and he was turned away for the summer. With age very much on his side, Topofthegame could take high rank amongst this season's staying novice chasers. Expect him to start his fencing career over two and a half miles but come into his own over further. Remember what pointing expert Declan Phelan wrote about the gelding in last year's edition of *One Jump Ahead*: **"A chunky chestnut son of Flemensfirth with an engine: he bounced out in front at Belclare (Yielding/Soft) and, whilst initially controlling a slow** pace, he gradually went through the gears and stretched clear from the second last at his leisure. He was exquisite in the jumping department. Amongst those found in his family are the stayer Merry Masquerade and the current top class two miler Identity Thief, suggesting speed and stamina are to be found amongst his kin. He has an attacking style reminiscent of a former Nicholls star Denman: More than likely, he may be campaigned in novice hurdles and he may be marking time before his true vocation of chasing." Paul Nicholls may have another chasing star on his hands.

POINTS TO NOTE:
Probable Best Distance      -      3 miles
Preferred Going      -      Good/Soft
Connection's Comments: "Topofthegame won his Irish point-to-point without coming off the bridle. He is big and green. He sauntered to the front then idled. He will improve and improve." Paul NICHOLLS at Ascot (16/12/16)

| GOING: | R | W | P | TRACK: | R | W | P |
|---|---|---|---|---|---|---|---|
| Soft | 2 | 0 | 1 | Left Handed | 1 | 0 | 0 |
| Yield/Soft | 1 | 1 | 0 | Right | 3 | 2 | 1 |
| Good/Soft | 1 | 1 | 0 | Galloping | 2 | 1 | 1 |
| | | | | Stiff/Undul. | 1 | 0 | 0 |

| TRIP: | R | W | P | JOCKEY: | R | W | P |
|---|---|---|---|---|---|---|---|
| 2m 3f | 1 | 0 | 1 | S.T-Davies | 1 | 1 | 0 |
| 2m 4f | 1 | 0 | 0 | S.Bowen | 1 | 0 | 1 |
| 2m 5f | 1 | 1 | 0 | N.Fehily | 1 | 0 | 0 |
| 3m | 1 | 1 | 0 | R.James | 1 | 1 | 0 |

# WHISKEY IN THE JAR (IRE)
5 b g Oscar (IRE) – Baie Barbara (IRE) (Heron Island (IRE))
OWNER: Mrs BARBARA HESTER
TRAINER: D.SKELTON. Shelfield Green, Alcester.
CAREER FORM FIGURES: 21
CAREER WIN: 2017: Mar WARWICK Soft NHF 2m

Dan Skelton has an impressive record with his bumper runners at his local track Warwick. Paul Nicholls' former assistant has sent out 6 winners from 21 runners (29%) in that division since taking out a licence, and 3 winners from only 8 runners (38%) during 2016/2017. One of those victories last spring was provided by ex-Irish trained gelding Whiskey In The Jar who looks a smart prospect for novice hurdles.

Rather like the aforementioned stablemate Sangha River, the Oscar gelding was handled in Ireland by Timmy Hyde before being bought privately on behalf of Barbara Hester. Five and a half lengths runner-up behind the unbeaten Gordon Elliott trained Monbeg Worldwide (won twice since) in a bumper at Roscommon in October, he stayed on well under his inexperienced rider.

The five year old joined Skelton soon afterwards and was sent off 2/1 favourite for his new connections at the Midlands venue in late March. Whiskey In The Jar's supporters never had an anxious moment as he sauntered to an easy seven lengths victory. The form may not amount to much but it confirmed the promise he had shown in Ireland. Time will tell whether soft or heavy ground is a requisite but one can imagine him developing into a candidate for something like the Grade 2 Leamington Spa Novices' Hurdle at the same track in January. The stable won it with Three Musketeers a couple of years ago. As discussed, Timmy Hyde has been a good source for his owner and trainer with Knockgraffon and the ill-fated Walking In The Air also starting their careers at Cashel in County Tipperary. Whiskey In The Jar looks another very good acquisition.

**POINTS TO NOTE:**

| | | |
|---|---|---|
| **Probable Best Distance** | - | **2m 4f – 3 miles** |
| **Preferred Going** | - | **Soft** |

Connection's Comments: "Whiskey In The Jar is a proper nice horse, but has needed time. He's understated - typical of Oscar - and doesn't make you ring any bells, but he's genuine and will go hurdling in the autumn. I've got a nice bunch of bumper horses and he's high enough up the pecking order." Dan SKELTON at Warwick (30/3/17)

| GOING: | R | W | P | TRACK: | R | W | P |
|---|---|---|---|---|---|---|---|
| Heavy | 1 | 0 | 1 | Left Handed | 1 | 1 | 0 |
| Soft | 1 | 1 | 0 | Right | 1 | 0 | 1 |
| | | | | Tight | 1 | 0 | 1 |
| | | | | Tight/Undul. | 1 | 1 | 0 |

| TRIP: | R | W | P | JOCKEY: | R | W | P |
|---|---|---|---|---|---|---|---|
| 2m | 2 | 1 | 1 | H.Skelton | 1 | 1 | 0 |
| | | | | Mr S.Connor | 1 | 0 | 1 |

---

## *MY HORSE TO FOLLOW FOR 2017/2018*

### Leading Owner
# RICH RICCI
## CHACUN POUR SOI

### Racing Manager
# JOE CHAMBERS
## MIN

---

# TALKING TRAINERS
## Brian ELLISON
Stables: Spring Cottage Stables, Langton Road, Norton, North Yorkshire.
2016/2017: 45 Winners / 230 Runners 20% Prize-Money £432,337
www.brianellisonracing.co.uk

### ALWAYS RESOLUTE 6 b g Refuse To Bend (IRE) – Mad Annie (USA)
He incurred an injury in the Cesarewitch last year and was therefore forced to miss last season. Given plenty of time, he finished fourth on the Flat at Carlisle in August and we are considering sending him novice chasing. We haven't schooled him over fences yet but I don't envisage any problems. Rated 132 over hurdles, he was progressive on the Flat prior to the injury and we will give him another spin on the level before going back over jumps.

### APTERIX (FR) 7 b g Day Flight – Ohe Les Aulmes (FR)
Despite the fact he is inclined to get low at his fences, he took well to chasing last season winning three times at Sedgefield, Wetherby and Doncaster. With a rating of 141, it won't be easy this time around but I am sure he will pay his way in two and two and a half mile handicap chases.

### BAL DE RIO (FR) 4 b g Vertigineux (FR) – Baldoranic (FR)
Twice a winner on the Flat in France, he was bought with a view to going jumping and he was unlucky not to win on his hurdles debut at Sedgefield at the end of August. Beaten a neck, he was headed close home over two and a half miles. Prior to that, he had a couple of races on the Flat during the summer, including when a staying on third at Carlisle earlier the same month. I will be disappointed if he doesn't win races over hurdles.

### BALLYCRYSTAL (IRE) 6 b g Oscar (IRE) – Musical Madam (IRE)
A winning Irish pointer, he goes novice chasing. He had a good season over hurdles winning a couple of times at Sedgefield and Newcastle. Two and a half to two miles six is ideal but he doesn't want soft ground. Good ground brings out the best in him.

### BALLYVIC BORU (IRE) 5 b g Brian Boru – Thedoublede (IRE)
He won a point-to-point in Ireland for Shark Hanlon before we bought him last Autumn. A bumper winner at Musselburgh in February, he also won on his hurdles debut at Perth during the summer and remains a novice for this season. Unfortunately, he was suffering with a kissing spine and has therefore undergone surgery on his back. It means he won't be running until after Christmas but he is a very nice horse who will make a lovely chaser one day. He works well at home and is certainly quick enough for two miles.

### BORDEAUX BILL (IRE) 6 b g Craigsteel – Laura Croft (IRE)
We acquired him at the Cheltenham November Sale having won the second of his two Irish points. Having finished third in a bumper at Wetherby, he won twice over hurdles at Sedgefield before we stepped him up in class at Aintree. Pulled up in Grade 1 company, he didn't fire on the day and had probably had enough by that stage of the season anyway. He will go novice chasing over two and a half miles and is a nice prospect.

### CONTRE TOUS (FR) 5 b g Forestier (FR) – Orphee De Vonnas (FR)
A lovely horse we bought out of Paul Nicholls' yard at the Doncaster May Sales as part of the Million In Mind dispersal, we may start him off over hurdles because he is still a novice. He won twice over fences at Market Rasen last season for his previous connections and there is every chance he will go chasing later on. Two miles appears to be his trip at the moment.

## CRACKDELOUST (FR) 5 b g Daramsar (FR) – Magic Rose (FR)

He is a nice horse who will come good one day. A French bumper winner, he won over hurdles at Sedgefield but I think he will benefit from being ridden with more restraint in future. Third at Hexham and Kelso in May, he is quick enough for two miles but will stay further. The plan is for him to go novice chasing and he jumps brilliantly.

## DEFINITLY RED (IRE) 8 ch g Definite Article – The Red Wench (IRE)

He has done very well during the summer and looks fantastic. He enjoyed a very good season last winter winning three times, including the Rowland Meyrick and Grimthorpe Chases at Wetherby and Doncaster respectively. Pulled up in the Grand National having been badly hampered at Becher's Brook first time around, his saddle slipped. We won't be aiming him at the National this season though. His first target is the Charlie Hall Chase at Wetherby (4th November) and then we will have an idea of where we are going for the rest of the campaign. He handles most types of ground but is very effective on an easy surface.

## FOREST BIHAN (FR) 6 ch g Forestier (FR) – Katell Bihan (FR)

Looks amazing and I think he is top-class. He would win on the Flat if he ever went down that route but we will be aiming him at the top two mile chases. A three times winner over fences last season, including the Grade 2 Lightning Novices' Chase at Doncaster in January, he was unlucky not to win the Grade 1 Maghull Novices' Chase at Aintree on Grand National day. Left in the lead at the final fence following the departure of Politologue, he pulled himself up in front and was collared on the line. He has really thickened out during the summer and I couldn't be happier with him.

## IT'S YOUR MOVE (IRE) 5 b g Flemensfirth (USA) – Jeruflo (IRE)

Third in his only point-to-point for Colin Bowe in Ireland, we purchased him at the Cheltenham December Sale. Still very backward last year, he finished third in a couple of bumpers for us at Wetherby and Doncaster. He has done well physically since, and I would expect him to want two and a half to three miles over hurdles this winter.

## KID VALENTINE (IRE) 7 b g Scorpion (IRE) – Supreme Nova

Yet to run for us, we haven't done much with him since he arrived from Michael Smith's. A leg problem has sidelined him since the summer of last year but we know he has ability having won twice over hurdles and is officially rated 130. A winning Irish pointer, too, he has done some steady cantering but we haven't made any plans.

## MAHLERDRAMATIC (IRE) 7 br g Mahler – Image of Vermont (IRE)

A dual bumper winner, he scored on his hurdles debut at Doncaster in November before being placed in his next two races at Sedgefield. However, he came back with a knee injury last time and it has been operated on since. Yet to race beyond two miles under Rules, he ran in a handful of Irish points over three miles at the start of his career so will have no trouble staying further. He is another set to go novice chasing.

## MANITOWOC COUNTY (IRE) 5 b g Darsi (FR) – Murphys Appeal (IRE)

A six lengths winner of an Irish point for Denis Murphy during the Autumn, we bought him at the Cheltenham November Sale. However, he went wrong shortly afterwards and had problems with ulcers. We therefore gave him time to come right and he is fine now. He looks well and I would think he will run in a bumper before going novice hurdling.

## MIDAS GOLD (IRE) 5 b g Rip Van Winkle (IRE) – Hespera

Another horse we acquired last November who has yet to run for us due to a setback. He was an easy winner of a bumper at Southwell for David Loder and we bought him as a result. Injured soon afterwards, we have done very little with him and it will be the second half of the season before he is in action.

### NIETZSCHE 4 ch g Poet's Voice – Ganga (IRE)

He is a grand horse who has won four times on the Flat and another three over hurdles since he joined us towards the end of 2015. Having won at Catterick (twice) and Market Rasen, he was only beaten half a length in third in the Fred Winter Juvenile Hurdle at the Cheltenham Festival in March. Hitting the front between the final two flights, he was headed on the run-in and narrowly denied. He looks very well following his summer break and we will give him a run on the Flat before his first big target, the Greatwood Hurdle at Cheltenham (19th November). We will then continue to aim him at the top two mile handicap hurdles. He likes soft ground.

### NORDIC COMBINED (IRE) 3 b g Haafhd – Chilly Filly (IRE)

A winner on the Flat over a mile as a two year old, he finished runner-up over twelve furlongs at Haydock this summer. Not the quickest, he stays well and has schooled nicely over hurdles. He will go juvenile hurdling.

### PISTOL PARK (FR) 6 b g Poliglote – Pistolera (GER)

He is a smashing horse who had a good season over fences winning at Hexham and Newcastle (twice) and finishing runner-up on three other occasions. Suited by heavy ground, he has benefited from a break and will win more races. Even though his three wins were gained over the minimum trip, he ran very well over two and a half miles on heavy ground at Uttoxeter on New Year's Eve. That might turn out to be his ideal trip this season.

### POINT THE WAY (IRE) 6 br g Brian Boru – Caslain Og (IRE)

A three times winner over hurdles the previous season, he failed to get his head in front last winter. I would expect him to improve over fences this time though being an ex-pointer. The plan therefore is to send him novice chasing. We will start him off over two and a half but three miles is his trip.

### RAVENHILL ROAD (IRE) 6 ch g Exit To Nowhere (USA) – Zaffarella (IRE)

He looks fantastic and I think he is top drawer. An impressive winner of his two bumpers at Market Rasen and Doncaster, we were aiming him at the championship bumper at the Cheltenham Festival but he injured his hock and therefore missed the rest of the season. Back cantering, he is fine now and we are looking forward to sending him hurdling. He is a brilliant jumper and we will start him off over two and a half miles. All three of his career wins, including his Irish point, have been gained on good ground but he is a big horse and I am sure he will handle it on the easy side. We knew from an early stage he was a very good horse. Funnily enough, he never worked well on the all-weather but as soon as we switched him to the grass he had no trouble lying up with the likes of Definitly Red and Seamour. He will be in action in late October/early November.

### SAM'S ADVENTURE 5 b g Black Sam Bellamy (IRE) – My Adventure (IRE)

He has done nothing wrong winning three of his four bumpers, including at Ayr last time. We haven't schooled him yet but he will be going novice hurdling and will want a trip. I would imagine he will start over two and a half but three miles will suit him eventually. He likes soft ground and ought to develop into a nice staying novice hurdler.

### SEAMOUR (IRE) 6 b g Azamour (IRE) – Chifney Rush (IRE)

In all likelihood, he will be going jumping this winter. Rated 131, he won both his starts as a juvenile hurdler in 2014 but has raced exclusively on the Flat since. He looks to be on a good mark (131) considering he is rated 101 on the Flat. Third in a Listed event at York in May, he wasn't suited by the steady early gallop in the Northumberland Plate before running creditably in the Ebor at York in August. Two and a half miles will be his trip over hurdles.

## SHEARLING 4 b f Rail Link – Casual

Bought at the Newmarket July Sales last year, she is a very good filly who won three of her five bumpers. Fourth in the Grade 2 mares' bumper at Aintree in the spring, she has run well on the Flat since. Third in a Listed event at Pontefract during the summer, she has been running over a mile and a half but will be suited by further. She has schooled very well over hurdles but her owners aren't overly keen to go jumping.

## SMART TALK (IRE) 7 b m Hubbly Bubbly (USA) – Belon Breeze (IRE)

A very good mare who won Grade 2 and Listed mares' hurdles a couple of seasons ago, she unfortunately missed last winter having banged her tendon. However, all being well, she will be back in action after Christmas and the plan is to send her chasing. She is a classy mare who has schooled brilliantly over fences. Two or two and a half miles is ideal.

## TOMNGERRY (IRE) 7 b g Craigsteel – Lady Vic (IRE)

Another who was forced to miss last season due to injury, he is back in work and chasing is also on his agenda. A winning pointer, he won both his bumpers, plus twice over hurdles before incurring an injury at Aintree in the Grade 1 Sefton Novices' Hurdle last year. I think he will do well in novice chases over two and a half to three miles.

## ZAIDIYN (FR) 7 b g Zamindar (USA) – Zainta (IRE)

Absent last season following an injury, he made an encouraging return to action on the Flat at Ascot during the summer. The plan is for him to continue in handicap hurdles. We tried him over fences a couple of seasons ago and he was in the process of running well behind Fox Norton at Market Rasen when falling. It is possible he will go chasing again at some stage. He isn't a bad jumper but he tends to be clumsy. A strongly run two miles suits him over hurdles.

---

**TRAINER'S HORSE TO FOLLOW: RAVENHILL ROAD**

---

# Harry FRY
### Stables: Manor Farm, Seaborough, Beaminster, Dorset.
### 2016/2017: 67 Winners / 286 Runners 23% Prize-Money £886,752
### www.harryfryracing.com

## ACTING LASS (IRE) 6 b g King's Theatre (IRE) – Darrens Lass (IRE)

A big horse who delighted us when winning on his debut over hurdles at Hereford. He then finished runner-up behind subsequent dual Grade 1 winner Finian's Oscar under a penalty at the same track, which obviously represents very good form. However, he was never quite right thereafter and below par when running at Ascot in February. He was a big immature horse last year who has benefited from another summer behind him and we are looking forward to sending him novice chasing. Two and a half miles appears to be his ideal trip.

## AIR HORSE ONE 6 gr g Mountain High (IRE) – Whisky Rose (IRE)

Very progressive last season winning three times at Exeter, Taunton and Ascot before producing a career best performance in the County Hurdle at Cheltenham when finishing fourth. The plan is for him to continue over hurdles and we will consider races such as the Elite Hurdle at Wincanton (11th November) and Greatwood Hurdle at Cheltenham (19th November). Although he stays further, a strongly run two miles on a stiff track such as Cheltenham suits him very well. Life is obviously going to be tougher this year off his higher mark but his run in the County Hurdle proved he can be competitive off it.

**AMERICAN (FR) 7 b g Malinas (GER) – Grande Sultane (FR)**
Unbeaten as a novice chaser last season, including a Listed event at Warwick in January, he was forced to miss the Cheltenham Festival owing to the drying ground. However, he won impressively at Uttoxeter a few days later and we are very much looking forward to his second season over fences. His first big target is the Ladbrokes Gold Cup (formerly the Hennessy Gold Cup) at Newbury (2nd December) and he appears to have the ideal profile. We have to decide whether to give him a run beforehand though. Due to the fact he is fragile, he ideally wants around eight weeks between his races, which means he would need to be running in October. The ground is important to him because he has struggled with his knees in the past. He wants good to soft or slower conditions. His run at Newbury will dictate his plans for the second half of the season. I have been very pleased with him during the summer and he looks well.

**ANY DRAMA (IRE) 6 b g Gamut (IRE) – Oak Lodge (IRE)**
A wide margin winner at Market Rasen and Exeter last winter when the mud was flying, he didn't stay three miles in the Albert Bartlett Hurdle at the Cheltenham Festival. The intention is for him to remain over hurdles this season and start him off in a suitable handicap. If he proves good enough, we may then consider races such as the Relkeel Hurdle at Cheltenham (1st January) and National Spirit Hurdle at Fontwell (February). Two and a half miles on soft ground are his optimum conditions.

**ART OF PAYROLL (GER) 8 b g Shirocco (GER) – Anna Maria (GER)**
He arrived from Ireland following the retirement of Sandra Hughes. We were aiming him at the Summer Plate at Market Rasen in July but he suffered a bout of colic, which was frustrating. However, he gained compensation by winning a decent prize at Southwell the following month. Having won over fences at Down Royal in May, he remains a novice which gives us plenty of options. However, he prefers decent ground so he will continue to race into the Autumn before having a winter break.

**AS I SEE IT 5 b g King's Theatre (IRE) – Chomba Womba (IRE)**
Bought at the Doncaster May Sales, he won his only point-to-point over two and a half miles at Buckfastleigh in February. The English pointing scene has been a very good source for us over the years. From a good family, he may start off in a bumper before going novice hurdling.

**BAGS GROOVE (IRE) 6 b g Oscar (IRE) – Golden Moment (IRE)**
Twice a winner at Taunton last season, he will stay over hurdles and we will see how far he can progress. Rated 133, his mark looks fair and we will be looking towards the valuable handicap hurdles over two and a half miles. We always have the option of going chasing later on.

**BEHIND TIME (IRE) 6 b g Stowaway – She's Got To Go (IRE)**
He is well named because it has taken a long time for the penny to drop. I was very pleased with his win at Cheltenham in November but then we rode him wrong at Newbury's Hennessy meeting when racing under a penalty. Still raw, he didn't seem to handle the very testing ground at Sandown last time. We were going to run him at Haydock in the spring but Barry (Geraghty) wasn't happy with the ground so we put him away for the summer. The time off won't have done him any harm and hopefully he will come into his own over fences this season. Rated 127, he will contest a suitable novices' handicap chase. Three miles is his trip.

**BLACK MISCHIEF 5 b g Black Sam Bellamy (IRE) – Miss Mitch (IRE)**
We were disappointed he didn't manage to win a bumper finishing third in all three of his starts. Switched to hurdling in Wincanton in January, he was all set to win easily when falling at the last. It proved to be a blessing in disguise because we didn't run him again until May in order to preserve his novice status for this season. Reappearing at Warwick in a maiden hurdle, he won emphatically and is the sort to progress. Suited by some cut in the ground, he has yet to race beyond two miles but will have no trouble staying two and a half.

### BULLIONAIRE (IRE) 4 b g Gold Well – Dontcallerthat (IRE)
A very exciting horse who won the Goffs UK Spring Sales Bumper at Newbury in March on his only start last season. He had pleased us at home beforehand and we were hoping he may finish in the first four but feared he could be too green to win. However, his sheer ability got him through and he won very well. Noel (Fehily) said he was still green at Newbury and physically he has done well during the summer. The plan is to aim him at the Listed bumper at Cheltenham (18th November). Only four, we will then decide whether to continue in bumpers and target the championship events or go over hurdles.

### CARIBERT (FR) 4 b g Ballingarry (IRE) – Cardamine (FR)
A big unraced horse who I have been pleased with. He produced some good homework during the spring and ought to go well in a bumper in the Autumn.

### CHALONNIAL (FR) 5 ch g Protektor (GER) – Kissmirial (FR)
He showed a useful level of form over hurdles last season winning at Bangor before finishing third in the Grade 1 Tolworth Hurdle at Sandown. I shouldn't have run him in the Grade 2 at Kelso because the ground was bad. Given a long break since, we have always viewed him as a chaser in the making and he will go over fences in the Autumn over two or two and a half miles.

### COCKNEY WREN 4 b f Cockney Rebel (IRE) – Compose
A full-sister to Scottish Champion Hurdle winner Cockney Sparrow, she was placed on her first three starts in bumpers. It was therefore good to see her get her head in front at Taunton last time. Suited by better ground, she will be aimed at mares' only novice hurdles and will be in action early on. We will start her off over two miles.

### DASHING OSCAR (IRE) 7 b g Oscar (IRE) – Be My Leader (IRE)
Had a good season winning at Bangor and Sandown and was placed on two other occasions. He will stay over hurdles and hopefully do well in the decent handicap hurdles. I think two and a half miles is his trip, although he is effective over a strongly run two miles. In terms of ground, he wouldn't want extremes.

### DESERT QUEEN 9 b m Desert King (IRE) – Priscilla
I was delighted with her last year winning two Listed mares' chases at Market Rasen and Leicester. Ironically, her owner toyed with the idea of sending her to stud at the start of last season but thankfully we persuaded him to keep her in training. There is such a valuable programme for mares and she will follow a similar route over fences. Two and a half to three miles suits her.

### DRUMCLIFF (IRE) 6 b g Presenting – Dusty Too
He didn't have much luck last season being very unfortunate not to win at Kempton over Christmas. Not right when he ran next time at Musselburgh, we thought we had him spot on for Punchestown but he got brought down at the second flight. Still a maiden, we feel a step up to two and a half miles will suit him and the Silver Trophy at Chepstow (14th October) is a likely starting point. He is suited by better ground.

### ELEANOROFAQUITANE (IRE) 4 b f Flemensfirth (USA) – Misty Heather (IRE)
From the family of Rock On Ruby, she didn't run during the spring due to weakness. She has strengthened up since and will make her debut in a mares' only bumper in the Autumn.

### EMPEROR RENARD (IRE) 6 b g Scorpion (IRE) – Lirfox (FR)
A winning English pointer, he was also fourth in a bumper at Exeter and joined us during the summer. We are still learning about him but I would expect him to be campaigned in two and a half mile novice hurdles.

## FLETCHERS FLYER (IRE) 9 b g Winged Love (IRE) – Crystal Chord (IRE)

His whole season was geared around the Irish National last term but he paid the price for trying to go with the winner (Our Duke), who is obviously a very good horse. Earlier on in the season, he ran well to finish third in the Grade 2 Reynoldstown Novices' Chase at Ascot. His main target this season is the three miles six handicap chase at the Punchestown Festival, which he won in 2016. In the meantime, he could contest something like the Sodexo Gold Cup at Ascot (4th November) or the Badger Ales at Wincanton a week later. Versatile in terms of ground, he must go right-handed and his mark of 143 over fences is about right.

## HELL'S KITCHEN 6 b g Robin Des Champs (FR) – Mille Et Une (FR)

Unfortunately, it was a case of hold up after hold up last season hence he was restricted to one outing. Third on his chasing debut at Ascot in November, he ran well considering he was very keen throughout. Absent since, he is a huge horse and the time off won't have done him any harm. He has always promised a lot and hopefully he will deliver this season. When Barry (Geraghty) rode him at Ascot, he said he wouldn't be against dropping him back to two miles, which may help him settle. Therefore he could start in a two mile beginners/novice chase.

## IF THE CAP FITS (IRE) 5 b g Milan – Derravaragh Sayra (IRE)

Initially, we didn't think he was a bumper horse but suddenly the penny dropped and he won his first two at Plumpton and Taunton. We then ran him in the Grade 2 championship event at Aintree's Grand National and, even though he got lit up beforehand, he ran well in fourth. We are therefore hoping he will develop into one of our leading novice hurdlers. I would think he will start off over two miles but will have no trouble staying two and a half miles.

## JUST A STING (IRE) 5 b g Scorpion (IRE) – Shanann Lady (IRE)

A lovely big horse who is unbeaten following wins in bumpers at Bangor and Exeter. I must admit he surprised me a bit but you could see the penny dropping during his debut and then he did well to follow up under a penalty. A galloper, he will go over hurdles starting off over two and a half miles and I hope he will be a nice staying novice. He will go chasing next season.

## JUSTAPUZZLE 5 ch m Apple Tree (FR) – Gaelic Gold (IRE)

An unraced half-sister to our Grade 1 winning mare Bitofapuzzle, we were keen to run her in a bumper in the spring but the ground wasn't suitable. She has done plenty of work and is a galloper who will be suited by soft ground. We will start her off in a mares' bumper.

## KYLEMORE LOUGH 8 b g Revoque (IRE) – One of The Last

His owners have kindly asked me to train him and I am delighted to have him because he is an exciting horse. A Grade 1 winner over fences, Kerry Lee did a very good job with him. The Grade 2 1965 Chase at Ascot is a possible starting point (25th November), a race in which he finished second last year. Other options include the Old Roan Chase at Aintree (29th October) or the BetVictor Gold Cup at Cheltenham (18th November). There is also the Peterborough Chase at Huntingdon (10th December) to consider later on.

## LADY OF LAMANVER 7 b m Lucarno (USA) – Lamanver Homerun

She missed the whole of last season but is back now and, while still a maiden over hurdles, we are hoping to make the most of her mark in handicaps. Unfortunately, she finished first in the mares' final at Newbury a couple of seasons ago but was later disqualified hence she is still qualified for novices' hurdles.

## LITTERALE CI (FR) 4 b f Soldier of Fortune (IRE) – Cigalia

She is also a maiden over hurdles having finished runner-up twice in three starts last season. Second at Exeter and Bangor, she is still only four and it may prove a blessing in disguise because it gives us more options this year. We are likely to mix between novice events and handicaps and I will be disappointed if she can't win races. She will stay further in time but we will keep her at two miles for the moment.

## MELROSE BOY (FR) 5 b g Saint Des Saints (FR) – Pollypink (FR)

Placed in all three of his races over hurdles last winter, I am not sure how he didn't manage to win. Having said that, he had the misfortune to bump into the likes of River Wylde and Mount Mews who were smart novices. Still a maiden, he is another who could be aimed at handicaps because he doesn't look badly treated off 123 considering the horses he raced against last season.

## MINELLA AWARDS (IRE) 6 b g Oscar (IRE) – Montys Miss (IRE)

We had to be patient with him last season because he took time to come to himself but we were rewarded in the spring. He seemed to enjoy the better weather and really came good winning the EBF Final at Sandown and then followed up in a three mile handicap hurdle at the Punchestown Festival. The time was good, too, on the latter occasion only being a second slower than Unowhatimeanharry's win in the Grade 1 staying hurdle. He is an exciting horse and we now need him to reproduce the same level of form during the first half of the season. The race I have in mind for him is the fixed brush handicap hurdle at Haydock (25th November). Strong at the finish at Punchestown, he stays very well.

## MISTERTON 6 gr g Sagamix (FR) – Mighty Splash

A bumper winner at Newton Abbot on his reappearance, he also won two of his four races over hurdles last season. We have a number of second season hurdlers who will hopefully be contesting the valuable handicaps this winter and he is another one. Suited by the step up to two and a half miles at Wincanton last time, he is another likely to be targeted at the Silver Trophy at Chepstow (14th October).

## MR ONE MORE (IRE) 5 b g Asian Heights – Norah's Quay (IRE)

We thought he would run well having shown ability at home prior to making a winning debut in a bumper at Bangor in October. A three and three quarters of a length winner, he was forced to miss the rest of the season due to minor niggles. We decided to give him time rather than rush him back in the spring. The form of his race has worked out extremely well with the second, third, fourth, sixth and seventh all winning since. He will go novice hurdling in the Autumn.

## ONEFORTHEROADTOM 4 gr g Fair Mix (IRE) – Ifni Du Luc (FR)

J.P.McManus kindly sent him to us during the summer and we are delighted to be training him. A three lengths winner of his only Irish point for Brian Hamilton, he stayed on well that day and gave the impression he will be suited by two and a half miles plus over hurdles. He was subsequently bought at the Cheltenham April Sale.

## ONEOFTHESENIGHTS (IRE) 6 b m Milan – Alfreeze

Acquired at the Cheltenham December Sale, she won her sole Irish point the previous month but took a while to settle in when she first arrived. We are still learning about her but, in all likelihood, she will start off in a mares' bumper before going hurdling.

## OUTOFTHISWORLD (IRE) 4 b f Shantou (USA) – Mystic Masie (IRE)

She surprised us when winning by eleven lengths at Market Rasen on her debut in the spring. I have been pleased with her since having filled out during the summer, and there is every chance we could run her in another mares' bumper under a penalty. Alternatively, she could head straight to Cheltenham in November (18th) and contest the Listed mares' bumper. Only four, we will then decide whether to keep her to bumpers or send her jumping. She has plenty of speed for two miles.

## OVER TO SAM 6 b g Black Sam Bellamy (IRE) – Lady Brig

A lovely horse who took time to come to hand last season. He won well though on his first run for us at Exeter in January but then I ran him too soon at Bangor the following month. A winning English pointer, he will go chasing in the Autumn and is a horse with plenty of ability. He stays well and is a three mile chaser in the making.

## ROSEMARY RUSSET 5 b m Midnight Legend – Apple Days

She won at Southwell in March on her third start and has improved over the summer. A galloper who wants soft ground, she will be running in mares' only novice hurdles over two and a half miles.

## SECRET DOOR (IRE) 6 b m Stowaway – Cellar Door (IRE)

She did well winning twice, including the valuable Challenger Mares' Handicap Hurdle Series Final at Haydock on Easter Saturday. Third last time against the boys at Market Rasen, she will be aimed at the two mile six mares' handicap hurdle at Wincanton (11th November). A former pointer, she could go chasing later in the season.

## SEROSEVSKY (IRE) 4 b g Morozov (USA) – Be My Rainbow (IRE)

He won an English point for Philip Rowley before we bought him at the Doncaster May Sales. I have been pleased with him since arriving because he has done well physically. Still only a four year old, we will decide whether to start him off in a bumper or go straight over hurdles once he has done some fast work.

## SHALL WE GO NOW 4 b g Midnight Legend – Suave Shot

Unraced, we were targeting him at the sales bumper at Newbury in the spring, which Bullionaire won, but he was balloted out. Then, the ground wasn't suitable so we roughed him off for the summer. He will run in a bumper in the spring and should hold his own.

## SPACE ODDITY (FR) 6 b g Al Namix (FR) – Schoune (FR)

Twice a winner over hurdles at Exeter and Taunton in January, he made a good start to his chasing career when winning well at Uttoxeter in May. An exuberant horse who likes to bowl along, he looks capable of winning under a penalty but doesn't want it too soft. He will be in action in early Autumn and could be one for the first Cheltenham meeting (27th & 28th October) before returning in the spring. He is effective over two and two and a half miles.

## TANGLEY 5 b m Black Sam Bellamy (IRE) – All Rise (GER)

A winning pointer, she had a couple of runs in bumpers before making a successful start to her hurdles career at Wincanton in March. Only a novice until the 1st November, we will run her in another mares' novice during October before going handicapping. She could be one for the Challenger Series, which Secret Door won last season. Two or two and a half miles will be her trip.

## THOMAS BROWN 8 b g Sir Harry Lewis (USA) – Tentsmuir

In keeping with every previous season, he won on his reappearance at Aintree last November. His final run came in the Topham Chase over the National fences but he found the trip too sharp. We are going to campaign him in the Cross Country races at Cheltenham this season but first time out is the time to catch him.

## UNOWHATIMEANHARRY 9 b g Sir Harry Lewis (USA) – Red Nose Lady

It is hugely exciting to be training a horse of his ability. Cheltenham was obviously disappointing only finishing third in the Stayers' Hurdle but he bounced back at Punchestown to win the Ladbrokes Champion Stayers' Hurdle and turn the tables on Nichols Canyon. I don't think he was at his best at Cheltenham but he still had a fantastic season winning four of his five races, including two Grade 1s. He started last season on an official mark of 149 and is now rated 167. Given the fact he is nine years old, he is going to stick to what he is good at and remain over hurdles. I would imagine he will follow an identical route, namely the Long Distance Hurdle at Newbury (1st December), Long Walk Hurdle at Ascot (23rd December), Cleeve Hurdle (January) and World Hurdle at the Festival.

**WOTZIZNAME (IRE) 7 b g Fruits of Love (USA) – Native Beau (IRE)**

He endured a frustrating season having looked such a promising horse the previous campaign. We sent him chasing and he made his debut at Aintree but his wind stopped him. He underwent a breathing operation but we decided to keep him as a novice over fences until this season. We therefore qualified him for the Pertemps Final at Cheltenham when finishing fourth at Musselburgh in February. Unfortunately, another horse galloped into the back of him that day which sidelined him for the rest of the season. Hopefully, he will make up for lost time over fences this time around.

> **TRAINER'S HORSE TO FOLLOW: AMERICAN**

# Philip HOBBS

**Stables: Sandhill, Bilbrook, Minehead, Somerset.**
**2016/2017: 111 Winners / 593 Runners 19% Prize-Money £1,502,991**
**www.pjhobbs.com**

**ACTION REPLAY (IRE) 6 b g Milan – Mary Connors (IRE)**

A big strong horse who has shown ability, including when finishing second at Plumpton in January. He is the sort to progress with time and when tackling fences but we will keep him over hurdles for the moment. Yet to race beyond two miles, he will stay further but isn't devoid of speed.

**ALLEE BLEUE (IRE) 7 ch g Mount Nelson – Murrieta**

A genuine horse, although his form was something of a mixed bag last season. An easy winner at Leicester in February, we are likely to give him a run on the Flat at some stage because he is only rated 69. Then he will have another run over hurdles before we decide whether to send him novice chasing. Suited by soft ground, he stays two and a half miles very well and may get further.

**BALLYGOWN BAY (IRE) 4 b g Flemensfirth (IRE) – Star Shuil (IRE)**

Ran well in his two bumpers last season, including a very promising debut at Warwick. He has grown during the summer and, in all likelihood, he will go straight over hurdles over two and a half miles.

**BOOK DIRECT (IRE) 6 b g Kayf Tara – Sinnaja**

Placed in an Irish point, he ran well on his first start for us over hurdles at Newton Abbot last Autumn finishing second. Runner-up again next time at Hereford, he missed the remainder of the season due to a pelvic injury. Back in work, he has plenty more to offer and ought to win over hurdles before going chasing later on. I think two and a half miles will be his trip.

**CASTERLY ROCK (IRE) 5 b g King's Theatre (IRE) – Alderbrook Girl (IRE)**

He was very disappointing on his debut in a bumper at Taunton and we don't know why. Thankfully, he ran much better next time over hurdles finishing fourth at Kempton. Still green, he will improve for the experience and will continue in two mile novice hurdles.

**CIGARISI (IRE) 5 b g Kalanisi (IRE) – Eileens Dream (IRE)**

A winner over hurdles at Plumpton in February, he remains lightly raced and is open to further improvement. While his future lies over fences, he is likely to have another run over hurdles. He will stay further but we will keep him to two miles for the time being.

**CONTENTED (IRE) 4 gr g Dalakhani (IRE) – Leo's Spirit (IRE)**
Previously trained by Johnny Hurley in Ireland, he finished third in his only bumper at Thurles in March. Subsequently bought by Highclere Thoroughbred Racing at the Aintree April Sale, he will hopefully develop into a nice novice hurdle prospect.

**COPPER KAY 7 b m Kayf Tara – Presenting Copper (IRE)**
She has done very well winning three times over hurdles last season and finishing runner-up in the mares' final at Newbury in the spring. Yet to finish out of the third three over jumps, we will aim her at a handicap hurdle before possibly switching to mares' novice chases. Rated 135 over hurdles, she ought to do well over fences in mares' only events. Two and a half miles is her trip and she appears to handle any ground.

**COSTLY DREAM (IRE) 5 b g Yeats (IRE) – What Price Love (USA)**
He is a big strong horse who disappointed us on his debut in a bumper at Haydock last November. However, the ground was atrocious and we have done some work on his wind since, which will hopefully make a difference. I would expect him to go straight over hurdles.

**DEFI DU SEUIL (FR) 4 b g Voix Du Nord (FR) – Quarvine Du Seuil (FR)**
He arrived back in the yard on the 1st August and looks fantastic. We were obviously delighted with him last season winning three Grade 1 events, including the Triumph Hurdle at Cheltenham in March. It is a long time since I trained a horse to win seven races on the trot and he is an exciting prospect for the future. Ever since he won on his debut for us at Ffos Las in October we had a fair idea he was a very good horse, although it is difficult to tell on some occasions. Unbeaten, the plan is for him to remain over hurdles and the obvious starting point is the four year old hurdle at Cheltenham (28th October), where he will be forced to carry an eight pounds penalty. In all likelihood, he will then head to Newcastle for the Fighting Fifth Hurdle (2nd December) rather than the International Hurdle at Cheltenham because he won't have to carry a penalty in the former. Alternatively, we could consider the Greatwood Hurdle at Cheltenham (19th November). It is a race we have done well in and, if he is going to develop into a Champion Hurdle contender, he ought to go close off his mark of 157. Effective on any ground, he has certainly got enough speed for two miles.

**DEMOPOLIS (FR) 3 b g Poliglote – Princess Demut (GER)**
A potentially exciting prospect for juvenile hurdles who arrived in August. Owned by J.P.McManus, he won his only start over hurdles at Auteuil in late May when trained by Guy Cherel.

**DOSTAL PHIL (FR) 4 b g Coastal Path – Quiphile (FR)**
He is another interesting horse who belongs to J.P.McManus having been bought at the Arqana Sale in France last November. A length and a quarter winner of an APQS Flat race at Deauville in October for Yannick Fouin, he will hopefully develop into a very nice novice hurdle prospect.

**DRUMLEE SUNSET (IRE) 7 br g Royal Anthem (USA) – Be My Sunset (IRE)**
A consistent horse, he won over hurdles and fences at Exeter last season and I am sure he will win more races in the future. Still relatively lightly raced, he is suited by two and a half miles. Not over big, both his wins last term were gained on decent ground, although he handles an easier surface.

**DUKE DES CHAMPS (IRE) 7 b g Robin Des Champs (FR) – Ballycowan Lady (IRE)**
Unfortunately, he was forced to miss last season due to a tendon injury and is unlikely to be in action before Christmas. However, he is a big strong horse who we have always held high hopes for over fences. Twice a winner over hurdles, he will hopefully develop into a very nice novice chaser.

### FOR GOOD MEASURE (IRE) 6 b g King's Theatre (IRE) – Afdala (IRE)

A full-brother to Balthazar King, he is the same size as him and has a very similar constitution in that he is tough and genuine. He has already proved to be a better hurdler than his brother. Despite not winning last season, he ran some very good races in defeat, including when finishing runner-up twice at Cheltenham. He will go novice chasing this season which will hopefully bring about further improvement.

### GAELIC PRINCE (FR) 5 b g Martaline (FR) – Gaelic Jane (FR)

An enormous unraced horse, he has the potential to be very nice. He has been very good in everything he has done at home but has been big and backward. Unhealthy in the spring, he has been likened to Captain Chris at home, who didn't start his racing career until he was six years old.

### GALA BALL (IRE) 7 b g Flemensfirth (USA) – Nuit Des Chartreux (FR)

A big strong horse who showed a good level of form over fences last season winning at Exeter and finishing in the first three on his four other runs. Two miles suits him and I am hoping he will do well in those decent handicap chases off his mark of 145. He handles plenty of cut in the ground.

### GARDE LA VICTOIRE (FR) 8 b g Kapgarde (FR) – Next Victory (FR)

Twice a winner last season, including the Welsh Champion Hurdle at Ffos Las, he isn't the easiest horse to place off his mark. He is a lovely horse though who has done very well for us over the years winning the Greatwood Hurdle in 2014, plus four times over fences. Unhealthy in the spring after his run in the Queen Mother Champion Chase, we may aim him at a conditions hurdle over two and a quarter miles at Auteuil in October. Alternatively, he could return to Ffos Las for the Welsh Champion Hurdle (21st October) once again because he is only two pounds higher than last year. Then, we have the option of going back over fences for the Haldon Gold Cup at Exeter (7th November), a race in which he finished a short head second last year. Two miles is probably his optimum trip because there remain doubts about him staying two and a half miles.

### GUMBALL (FR) 3 gr g No Risk At All (FR) – Good Time Girl (FR)

An interesting recruit from France who was bought by Claude Charlet on behalf of Terry Warner. Third on his only start over hurdles at Dieppe in late April, he will go juvenile hurdling.

### HARDNESS (IRE) 4 b g Makfi – Hideaway (FR)

Yet to race for us, he was bought at the Arqana Sale in France during the summer of last year. Despite the fact he raced half a dozen times on the Flat, finishing third twice at Strasbourg, he has been a backward horse who we have given plenty of time. Gelded since arriving, we quite like him and will be aiming him at novice hurdles.

### HELLO GEORGE (IRE) 8 b g Westerner – Top Ar Aghaidh (IRE)

A talented horse, he has been quite fragile but was an easy winner over hurdles at Newbury last spring. We then took him to Perth in April but withdrew him because the ground was too quick. Suited by soft ground, he is effective over two and a half miles but may stay three in time. He is likely to go novice chasing.

### ICE COOL CHAMPS (IRE) 6 ch g Robin Des Champs (FR) – Last of Many (IRE)

Lightly raced, he produced a very good first run when a couple of lengths runner-up in a bumper at Warwick on New Year's Eve. He confirmed the promise when winning over hurdles next time at Hereford before finishing third at the same track. A big horse who can only improve, he is officially rated 122 and will probably go over fences and we will look for a suitable novices' handicap chase. I think two and a half to three miles will be his trip.

**IF IN DOUBT (IRE) 9 b g Heron Island (IRE) – Catchers Day (IRE)**
Unfortunately, he suffered a tendon injury following his run at Wetherby last October. Back now, he doesn't really enjoy jumping fences so he will probably continue over hurdles, although he isn't the easiest to place off 153. Conditions hurdles could be on his agenda once again.

**I'M A GAME CHANGER (IRE) 5 b g Arcadio (GER) – Drinadaly (IRE)**
He looks very well following his summer break and we are hoping he will improve again. Progressive last season, he won twice at Bangor and Ludlow but was inclined to be free and keen during his races. With that in mind, we will keep him to two miles. There is every chance he will go novice chasing, although he is likely to have a run over hurdles beforehand.

**JERRYSBACK (IRE) 5 b g Jeremy (USA) – Get A Few Bob Back (IRE)**
A horse with a lovely attitude, he is potentially very nice. Held in high regard by Wilson Dennison in Ireland, for whom he ran in four point-to-points before joining us, he won both his starts over hurdles at Plumpton and Wetherby in impressive fashion. The intention was to run him again during the spring but he incurred a minor cut below his knee. Back in, he looks fantastic but we haven't decided whether to continue over hurdles or go chasing. He is a big strong horse whose future lies over fences but we could have a look at something like the Silver Trophy at Chepstow (14th October), depending on what mark he is allocated. He appears to be well suited by slow ground.

**KAYF ADVENTURE 6 b g Kayf Tara – My Adventure (IRE)**
He has loads of potential and was an impressive winner over hurdles at Fontwell in February. Placed on his other three runs, he is a very big horse so we have taken our time with him. The plan is to send him chasing and, with a rating of 128, we will go down the novice handicap route to start with. He likes soft ground.

**KRUZHLININ (GER) 10 ch g Sholokhov (IRE) – Karuma (GER)**
Successful in the fixed brush handicap hurdle at Haydock last season, he is ten years old now and not the easiest to place. We are therefore going to send him hunter chasing and hopefully he will do well in that sphere.

**LITTLE MISS POET 5 b m Yeats (IRE) – R De Rien Sivola (FR)**
A model of consistency, she won twice over hurdles at Market Rasen and Newton Abbot last term and finished runner-up on her three other starts. I think there is room for improvement, too, off her mark of 121. She handles soft ground and, while she has the speed for two miles, she stays further.

**LONGTOWN (IRE) 6 b g Scorpion (IRE) – Desirable Asset (IRE)**
He is a fine big strong horse with a very good temperament. Runner-up on his hurdles debut at Uttoxeter, he won well on his final start at Warwick in March. I would expect him to go chasing and we will be looking towards a novices' handicap off his rating of 123. There is no doubt he has got ability.

**LOUIS' VAC POUCH (IRE) 5 b g Oscar (IRE) – Coming Home (FR)**
Showed progressive form during the second half of last season winning three times. I hope he will improve again this time around because he has only had half a dozen races over hurdles. He will continue in handicap hurdles and we are hoping he may stay further. I don't think the ground matters to him.

**MAJESTIC TOUCH (IRE) 6 br g Kalanisi (IRE) – Alexander Divine**
A five lengths winner at Uttoxeter last time, it wasn't the strongest of races but he remains lightly raced and ought to improve again this season. Still eligible for novice hurdles, he will jump fences in time but hopefully there are more races to be won with him over hurdles beforehand. He has the speed for two miles.

### MANCE RAYDER (IRE) 4 b g Flemensfirth (USA) – J'y Viens (FR)

An enormous horse who was still very green last season. Indeed, he did well to make a winning debut in testing conditions in a bumper at Warwick during the spring. He therefore should improve and will go novice hurdling over two and a half to three miles.

### MCNAMARAS BAND (IRE) 4 b g Getaway (GER) – Katies Pet (IRE)

For sale, he overcame greenness to win on his debut at Worcester during the summer. He appears to have improved since and will start off over two and a half miles over hurdles.

### MIDNIGHT GLORY 5 b m Midnight Legend – Land of Glory

A nice mare who I like and one with a very good attitude. She won at Newbury in January and was placed on her final start at the same track. I will be disappointed if she can't win a handicap hurdle off her current mark.

### MULTICULTURE (IRE) 5 b g Mount Nelson – Gracious Melange

He joined us from Ireland last season and showed progressive form over hurdles winning three times at Uttoxeter, Wincanton and Warwick. I thought he would run well in the Swinton Hurdle at Haydock but he was very disappointing and I don't know why. I am sure he is a lot better than he showed that day. More of a hurdling type, we will continue to aim him at the decent two mile handicap hurdles.

### MUSICAL SLAVE (IRE) 4 b g Getaway (GER) – Inghwung

A horse I like very much, he is a big strong staying horse in the making who will hopefully do well in two and a half mile novice hurdles this season. Only a four year old, he made his debut in a bumper at the Punchestown Festival and, while I was hoping he would finish in the first four, he still ran well in sixth. Very green that day, Derek O'Connor liked him a lot and is one to look forward to.

### NEW MILLENNIUM (IRE) 4 b c Galileo (IRE) Banquise (IRE)

Originally trained on the Flat by Aidan O'Brien, he had one run over hurdles for John Halley in Ireland before joining us. He has taken time to strengthen but looks a lot better now and we are hopeful he will improve this season. Fourth at Kempton last time, he has only had three races over hurdles and is seemingly on a good mark. Inclined to be keen, we will be aiming him at a novices' handicap hurdle.

### NO COMMENT 6 br g Kayf Tara – Dizzy Frizzy

Very consistent over hurdles last season, he is a horse I like a lot. A three times winner last term, he ran well at both Aintree and Punchestown during the spring finishing second on both occasions. Although he has the speed for two and a half miles, he stays three and, while we may start him off in a handicap hurdle, it probably won't be long before he goes novice chasing. He is a very nice horse.

### ONEFITZALL (IRE) 7 b g Indian Danehill (IRE) – Company Credit (IRE)

Even though he isn't the most robust, he is a likeable horse who won at Newbury's Hennessy meeting last year. Off since Boxing Day, he is back in work now and it is possible he will have another run over hurdles before embarking on a chasing career.

### OZZIE THE OSCAR (IRE) 6 b g Oscar (IRE) – Private Official (IRE)

A winner at Wetherby in October, he produced a career best in the County Hurdle at the Cheltenham Festival. Only beaten half a length in third, he disappointed last time in the Scottish Champion Hurdle at Ayr. Given a break, he is a horse with plenty of ability and I hope he will develop into a decent two mile novice chaser.

## PERFORM (IRE) 8 b g King's Theatre (IRE) – Famous Lady (IRE)
A talented horse but one who has proved frustrating. A winner over hurdles at Aintree a couple of years ago, he has been held up by so many silly little problems since and has only raced four times during his career. He ran OK in his two starts last season but really wants to be going over fences.

## POPPY KAY 7 b m Kayf Tara – Double Red (IRE)
A dual winner over hurdles at Uttoxeter, she ran well last time when a neck runner-up in the Challenger Mares' Handicap Hurdle Series Final at Haydock on Easter Saturday. Despite a six pounds rise to a mark of 129, I hope she will progress again over hurdles before running in mares' novice chases.

## ROBBIN'HANNON (IRE) 6 ch g Robin Des Champs (FR) – Culleen Lady (IRE)
He won his only Irish point before we bought him at the Cheltenham December Sale. A ready winner over hurdles on his first start for us at Warwick in March, he then finished runner-up in a Listed novices' event at Perth the following month. Granted a mark of 142, he remains a novice until the end of October. Therefore we will aim him at the Grade 2 Persian War Novices' Hurdle at Chepstow (15th October) but he is ground dependent – he wants soft conditions. He stays three miles and is potentially a very nice horse.

## ROCK THE KASBAH (IRE) 7 ch g Shirocco (GER) – Impudent (IRE)
He looked very good on occasions over fences last season winning twice at Chepstow and finishing sixth in the Bet365 Gold Cup at Sandown last time. In between, he lost his confidence on occasions, including at Cheltenham in November when ballooning his fences. I am hoping he is an improver and we will be looking to target him at races such as the Badger Ales Handicap Chase at Wincanton (11th November) and the Ladbrokes Gold Cup (formerly known as the Hennessy Gold Cup) at Newbury (2nd December). He needs to relax during his races.

## ROLLING DYLAN (IRE) 6 ch g Indian River (FR) – Easter Saturday (IRE)
Successful over hurdles at Uttoxeter in November, he finished runner-up on three other occasions. He is a horse we have always liked and, being a former Irish pointer, we will send him chasing this season and start him off in a novices' handicap off his rating of 132.

## ROYAL REGATTA (IRE) 9 b g King's Theatre (IRE) – Friendly Craic (IRE)
A Grade 2 winner at Ascot last November, his form tended to be in and out. Two and a half miles is his trip and the obvious starting point is the Old Roan Chase at Aintree (29th October), a race he finished fifth in last year. He isn't the easiest horse to place off his mark of 154.

## SAMBURU SHUJAA (FR) 4 b g Poliglote – Girelle (FR)
Named after a Kenyan tribe, he is a very big horse who ran well on his second start in a bumper at Warwick during the spring. Runner-up on that occasion, he will improve and be suited by two and a half miles over hurdles.

## SGROPPINO (IRE) 5 b g Getaway (GER) – Boadicea
He is named after an Italian ice cream and I was very pleased with his first run when finishing a close second in a bumper at Newton Abbot in October. The form has worked out well, too, but he disappointed next time at Newbury five months later. However, he scoped badly afterwards. I think he is a nice horse who could run in another bumper before going hurdling.

## SNEAKY FEELING (IRE) 5 b g Oscar (IRE) – Shuil Aris (IRE)
Potentially a good horse who finished fourth in his only Irish point-to-point before joining us. Twice a winner over hurdles at Newbury and Sandown, he is inclined to get stressed and wound up. Indeed, he sweated up before the start at Sandown. Rated 135, he is likely to continue over hurdles for now but his long-term future lies over fences. He will stay further but two and a half miles suits him at present.

### SPRINGTOWN LAKE (IRE) 5 b g Gamut (IRE) – Sprightly Gal (IRE)
We bought him at the Cheltenham December Sale having finished runner-up in his sole Irish point the previous month. Following a disappointing Rules debut at Kempton in a bumper, he ran much better over hurdles at Ascot next time when a close second. Rather like Sneaky Feeling, he can get stressed and needs to learn to relax. He will hopefully improve.

### STEELY ADDITION (IRE) 5 b g Craigsteel – Blond's Addition (IRE)
A new addition to the yard, he won an English point-to-point prior to running three times over hurdles for Hugo Froud last season. Officially rated 116, I hope he will make an impact in novice handicap hurdles.

### STERNRUBIN (GER) 6 b g Authorized (IRE) – Sworn Mum (GER)
A former Ladbroke Hurdle winner, he finished fifth in the Greatwood Hurdle at Cheltenham last season. He has been running on the Flat during the summer winning at Windsor and Ffos Las. He has schooled well over fences but has a tendency to go to his right. We may therefore aim him at a novice chase at Exeter in October.

### STRONG PURSUIT (IRE) 7 ch g Flemensfirth (USA) – Loughaderra (IRE)
He is another who can get stressed and race keenly during his races. However, he is a big strong horse with plenty of ability. Twice a winner at Wincanton and Hereford last season, he may have another run over hurdles before going chasing. He is a former winning Irish pointer.

### TAPACULO 6 b g Kayf Tara – Aniston (IRE)
A very big horse, he is back having missed the whole of last season due to a tendon injury. He did well the previous campaign winning twice at Chepstow and finishing second at Kempton. His future undoubtedly lies over fences but he is likely to reappear over hurdles.

### TEN SIXTY (IRE) 7 br g Presenting – Senora Snoopy (IRE)
We rated him highly as a youngster but he has proved inconsistent. Despite winning over fences at Newbury in the spring, his jumping has been in and out. If he gets his jumping together, he isn't badly handicapped.

### THREE FACES WEST (IRE) 9 b g Dr Massini (IRE) – Ardnataggle (IRE)
Absent since winning a Graduation chase at Newbury in December, he had an issue which has been sorted out. He had also won at Haydock prior to that and is a talented horse. However, he also has temperament issues which we will hopefully keep in check this season. Effective on any ground, we will be targeting the decent three mile handicap chases off his mark of 147.

### TIDAL FLOW 4 b g Black Sam Bellamy (IRE) – Mrs Philip
Bred by Richard Johnson, he is a very nice unraced four year old. A half-brother to Kayf Willow, he would have run during the spring but the ground wasn't suitable. However, he has benefited from the time off and will make his debut in a bumper during the Autumn.

### VERNI (FR) 8 ch g Sabrehill (USA) – Nobless D'Aron (FR)
Has done very well since joining us winning three times over hurdles and finishing runner-up in the Martin Pipe Conditional Jockeys' Handicap Hurdle at the Cheltenham Festival in March. Suited by soft ground, he will stay hurdling for the time being but will go chasing later on.

### VICTARION (IRE) 5 b g Scorpion (IRE) – Gaye Preskina (IRE)
Apparently he is named after a character in *Game of Thrones*. I thought he was unlucky not to win a bumper last season. Runner-up at Uttoxeter last time, he copes well with testing ground and will be suited by two and a half miles plus over hurdles. It is possible he will have another run in a bumper beforehand though.

### VIEUX LILLE (IRE) 7 b g Robin Des Champs (FR) – Park Athlete (IRE)
Still a novice over fences, he has ability but needs to brush up his jumping. If he does, he could have a good season and is capable of winning a decent staying chase. Runner-up in the Tommy Whittle Chase at Haydock in December, we have the option of running in novice and handicap chases.

### VILLAGE VIC (IRE) 10 b g Old Vic – Etoile Margot (FR)
He ran some very good races during the first half of the season being placed three times at Cheltenham, including runner-up in the BetVictor Gold Cup in November. His form tailed off in the spring though and he isn't easy to place off 158. I would imagine he will reappear in the BetVictor Gold Cup (18th November) once again.

### WAIT FOR ME (FR) 7 b g Saint Des Saints (FR) – Aulne River (FR)
It was great to see him come good on the final day of the season at Sandown. Prior to that, his form had been in and out and he has had breathing issues in the past. However, he won very easily at Sandown and appeared to be suited by the step up to two and a half miles and being held up. Runner-up in a decent handicap hurdle at Newton Abbot in early September, he was badly hampered by a faller down the back straight before staying on. He will have another run over hurdles before we decide whether to send him chasing.

### WAR SOUND 8 b g Kayf Tara – Come The Dawn
Forced to miss the whole of last season due to a joint problem, he is a former Swinton Hurdle winner and very talented. However, he has been fragile. The plan is for him to go novice chasing.

### WESTEND STORY (IRE) 6 b g Westerner – Sarahall (IRE)
A high-class bumper horse a couple of seasons ago, I thought he would be our best novice hurdler last winter. However, he disappointed in three starts and remains a maiden over jumps. A former Irish pointer, he ought to stay well and I hope he will do better this time around.

### WHO'S MY JOCKEY (IRE) 4 b g Yeats (IRE) – Scandisk (IRE)
Well bred being a half-brother to Hurricane Fly, we have always liked him and he made a winning debut in a bumper at Market Rasen in April. He will go straight over hurdles and is likely to start off over a stiff two miles.

---

**TRAINER'S HORSE TO FOLLOW: SNEAKY FEELING**

---

# Malcolm JEFFERSON
**Stables: Newstead Cottage Stables, Norton, Malton, North Yorkshire.**
**2016/2017: 40 Winners / 202 Runners 20%  Prize-Money £504,073**
**www.malcolmjefferson.co.uk**

### BALLY CONOR (IRE) 4 b g Presenting – Soliya (FR)
We have some nice young unraced bumper horses who nearly ran in the spring but the ground dried up so we gave them time and this is one of them. Out of a decent mare who David Pipe trained, he has pleased me in his work and we will start him off in a bumper in the Autumn.

### BLACK IVORY 5 b g Revoque (IRE) – Annie's Gift (IRE)
He had a good season winning a bumper at Hexham last summer and then twice over hurdles, at Hexham again and Uttoxeter. Suited by two and a half miles, I think he will stay three miles eventually but we will keep him to shorter trips for the time being. An athletic horse, he will stay over hurdles for the time being and I hope there is more improvement to come.

**CATHAL'S STAR 4 ch g Malinas (GER) – Hand Inn Glove**
Another nice unraced four year old, we bought him at the Tattersalls Derby Sale last year. From the family of Henry Daly's Grade 1 winning chaser Hand Inn Hand, he nearly ran last season but the ground wasn't suitable. He will have a run in a bumper in the Autumn.

**CLOUDY DREAM (IRE) 7 gr g Cloudings (IRE) – Run Away Dream (IRE)**
He enjoyed a very good first season over fences winning three times, including the Grade 2 Future Champions Novices' Chase at Ayr in the spring. Runner-up in the Arkle Trophy at Cheltenham and the Grade 1 novice over two and a half miles at Aintree, he looks tremendous following his summer holiday. We will keep him to two and a half miles for the time being but he may stay three because he is settling better now. He certainly wasn't stopping over two and a half miles at Ayr last time. The Betvictor Gold Cup at Cheltenham (18th November) is a possible target for him and there is also the Colin Parker Memorial Chase at Carlisle (5th November). Although he handles soft ground, I think he is at his best on better ground.

**CYRUS DARIUS 8 b g Overbury (IRE) – Barton Belle**
Returned from injury last season and won the Morebattle Hurdle at Kelso before taking his chance in the Champion Hurdle last time. I am keen to send him back over fences having won his only novice chase at Perth a couple of years ago before he suffered his injury. That win was gained over two and a half miles and I think he wants a trip nowadays. In fact, it wouldn't surprise me if he ended up being a three miler. The handicapper hasn't given him a mark over fences having only raced once but he is a very good horse who likes give in the ground.

**DOUBLE W'S (IRE) 7 ch g Fruits of Love (USA) – Zaffre (IRE)**
He had a good season over fences winning the Red Rum Chase at Aintree's Grand National meeting off a mark of 139. We ran him in the novices' handicap chase at the Cheltenham Festival and, having travelled strongly, he didn't get home over two and a half miles hence we dropped him back to two miles at Aintree. He also won at Carlisle and Wetherby and the plan is to start him off in a decent two miles one handicap chase at Kelso (8th October). Provided he runs well, he could then go to Exeter for the Haldon Gold Cup (7th November). A strongly run two miles is ideal but he doesn't want it too soft.

**DUBAI ANGEL (IRE) 6 b g Dubai Destination (USA) – Just Another Penny (IRE)**
A nice horse who I am keen to send novice chasing this year. An easy winner of a bumper at Carlisle last Autumn, he won two of his four races over hurdles at Sedgefield and Newcastle and finished runner-up on the other two occasions. I was pleased with his performance at Newcastle because he settled better than on some of his previous starts. He has been green in front and we might fit him with a hood at some stage. I think two and a half is his trip at the moment, although we know he stays further.

**FERNAN (IRE) 5 br g Robin Des Champs (FR) – Rosa Rugosa (IRE)**
He is a good sort who had three runs in bumpers finishing second at Southwell on his penultimate start. We rode him prominently at Wetherby last time but it didn't suit him. Therefore we will be looking to drop him in over hurdles. He has been keen but is learning to settle now. I must say he has come back from his summer break looking tremendous having really strengthened up. Flat bred on the dam's side of his pedigree, he isn't slow and we will start him off in a National Hunt novice hurdle at the likes of Carlisle or Hexham.

**FINGAREETA 4 b f Schiaparelli (GER) – Annie's Answer (IRE)**
A full-sister to Schiaparannie, she is a nice big strong mare. Runner-up on her debut in a bumper at Uttoxeter in June, she won well at Southwell next time. We will aim her at mares' novice hurdles and I am expecting her to stay well because her mother was effective over three miles. Quite a heavy topped mare, she will be suited by some ease in the ground.

### HELLO BERTIE 5 b g Kayf Tara – I'm Delilah

Out of a good mare, he is a lovely horse who I like a lot. Third in both his bumpers at Perth and Southwell in the spring, he raced wide on the latter occasion. We may give him another run in a bumper before going hurdling. He should have no trouble staying two and a half miles over jumps.

### HELMSLEY LAD 6 gr g Fair Mix (IRE) – Wuchowsen (IRE)

Despite winning a bumper at Sedgefield and being placed over hurdles at Kelso, he was still weak last year. Still a novice over hurdles, he will have another couple of runs before we decide whether to send him chasing. I think two and a half miles is as far as he wants to go.

### KELKA 5 b m Exit To Nowhere (USA) – Scarvagh Diamond (IRE)

She is a decent mare who won three over hurdles last season at Hexham, Kelso and Newcastle. Fourth at Ayr on her final start, she suffered a horrible over reach which scratched the tendon. Thankfully, it has healed and she will go novice chasing. She loves soft ground and I think two miles is her best trip. Making all the running suits her because she has a good cruising speed. I hope she will do well in mares' events over fences.

### MAYO STAR (IRE) 5 b g Stowaway – Western Whisper (IRE)

A nice sort, he had three runs last season winning a bumper at Newcastle and was third on his hurdles debut at Kelso in the spring. A big backward horse, he was inclined to race keenly and needs to learn to settle. If he does, I think he has the potential to be a nice horse. Eventually, he ought to stay three miles but we will keep him to shorter distances for the time being.

### MOUNT MEWS (IRE) 6 b g Presenting – Kneeland Lass (IRE)

He is in great nick following his summer break and looks fantastic. Successful in three of his five races over hurdles, including a Grade 2 race at Kelso. Runner-up at Aintree in Grade 1 company last time, he ran well but they didn't go quick enough for him. Effective on any ground, I think the key to him is a strong gallop. He is still green and loses concentration and is inclined to look at everything. We will probably school him over fences because I think he could be an Arkle horse but the plan at the moment is to see if he is a Champion Hurdle horse. Therefore his first main target will be the Fighting Fifth Hurdle at Newcastle (2nd December) with one run beforehand.

### MR MONOCHROME 6 br g Indian Danehill (IRE) – Our Ethel

A half-brother to Attaglance, he had a funny season suffering a few niggles which held him up. He is a nice horse though who appreciates better ground. A bumper winner at Hexham and over hurdles at Ayr, his family were at their best over two and a half miles and I think that will prove to be his trip, too. He looks fantastic at the moment and I am keen to send him novice chasing.

### NORTHERN SOUL 4 ch g Presenting – Our Ethel

A lovely unraced horse, he is a half-brother to Attaglance and Mr Monochrome. He is a big strong four year old who was close to a run last spring but the ground was too quick. We will start him off in a bumper. I like him a lot.

### OSCAR ROCK (IRE) 9 b g Oscar (IRE) – Cash And New (IRE)

He won a handicap hurdle at Market Rasen in November on his reappearance but then suffered a suspensory injury and missed the rest of the season. A grand horse, he is back in work and his main target is the Scottish National. Rated 147 over fences, he wouldn't want to be going up much more so we may run him over hurdles at some stage during the year. I thought he ran a blinder in the Bet365 Gold Cup at Sandown the previous season and proved he stays well. He is a grand horse but doesn't want it too soft.

### RYEDALE RACER 6 b g Indian Danehill (IRE) – Jontys'lass
A grand horse who is very tough, he won over hurdles at Carlisle and Hexham and has provided his owners with a lot of pleasure. Two and a half miles on soft ground is ideal and we are going to send him novice chasing.

### SCHIAPARANNIE 5 b m Schiaparelli (GER) – Annie's Answer (IRE)
A full-sister to Fingareeta, she joined us from Mark Walford last season and won a bumper at Hexham before finishing a close third at Bangor. She is a nice mare who is strong and looks like a gelding. We may give her another run in a bumper before going for mares' novice hurdles. Her mother stayed three miles and this mare will jump fences one day.

### SECRETE STREAM (IRE) 8 ch g Fruits of Love (USA) – Bonny River (IRE)
Had been off the track for nearly two years when making a winning return at Uttoxeter last November. Fourth at Wetherby next time, he suffered another setback soon afterwards and missed the rest of the season. Back cantering, he is another who will go novice chasing over two and a half miles. Long-term, I think he will stay three miles as well.

### SPECIAL CATCH (IRE) 10 b g Catcher In The Rye (IRE) – Top Quality
Another grand horse who has done nothing wrong since joining us at the start of this year. A winner at Sedgefield, he was also runner-up a couple of times at Newcastle and Perth. High enough in the handicap off a mark of 139, he wants a stiff two miles or easy two and a half. Soft ground suits him well.

### TEMPLE MAN 5 b g Sulamani (IRE) – Altogether Now (IRE)
From the family of Mac Aeda, he ran OK in three bumpers last season but needs to settle in his races. Still weak last year, we have given him time and he is a lot stronger now. He will go straight over hurdles.

### WAITING PATIENTLY (IRE) 6 b g Flemensfirth (USA) – Rossavon (IRE)
Back cantering, he looks tremendous and we are looking forward to seeing him run again. Unbeaten in three races over fences, including a Grade 2 novice chase at Haydock in January, he then suffered an injury and missed the end of the season. We found some heat in his front joint and when the vet looked at him he found a chip which has been removed. He was never lame but we weren't going to take any chances with him. As far as his future is concerned, I think he is a two miler but his owner Richard Collins is keen to aim him at the Colin Parker Memorial Chase at Carlisle (5th November) over two and a half miles and believes he will be a three miler eventually. Although he won over two and a half miles at Haydock, I thought he was running out of petrol at the end. He is such a good jumper, I would love to take on the top two milers in something like the Tingle Creek Chase at Sandown. Admittedly, he needs to improve again to be competitive in the big races but he has only had three runs over fences. The softer the ground the better, I think he is a Dato Star type horse.

## Alan KING
**Stables: Barbury Castle Stables, Wroughton, Wiltshire.**
**2016/2017:  104 Winners / 490 Runners 21% Prize-Money £1,373,270**
**www.alankingracing.co.uk**

### AMADEUS ROX (FR) 3 b g Falco (USA) – Vittoria Vetra
A maiden on the Flat, he made an encouraging start to his hurdling career when finishing a close second at Newton Abbot during the summer. I will be disappointed if he doesn't win races.

### AZZERTI (FR) 5 b g Voix Du Nord (FR) – Zalagarry (FR)

He was progressive last season winning at Towcester and Sandown. Inclined to be quite hot, he got worked up beforehand at the latter track because there was a band playing and it upset him. We therefore fitted him with a hood at Cheltenham next time and he was more relaxed before finishing third. If we can keep a lid on him, he is a useful horse who will hopefully improve again this year. Only five, we will keep him over hurdles.

### BASTIEN (FR) 6 b g Panoramic – Que Du Charmil (FR)

A winner of his first two starts over hurdles at Fontwell and Plumpton, he disappointed at Market Rasen next time but was sick afterwards hence he never ran again. We have given him a good break since and he has summered well. Having only had three races over hurdles, he will continue over timber and go down the handicap route. I think two and a half miles will suit him.

### BENEAGLES (IRE) 5 b g Milan – Liss Rua (IRE)

A former Irish pointer, he was marking time over hurdles last winter but ran consistently, winning at Huntingdon and finishing second on a couple of occasions. Rated 127, he will go novice handicap chasing over trips around two miles six plus.

### CANELLO (IRE) 4 ch g Mahler – Nobody's Darling (IRE)

Owned by Million In Mind, he ran in two English point-to-points finishing second on his latest start. The winner of the race was subsequently sold for £150,000 to Willie Mullins and this fellow wasn't far behind him and cost a lot less at the Cheltenham April Sale. We haven't done a lot with him yet but I would expect him to go novice hurdling over two and a half miles plus.

### CHOSEN PATH (IRE) 4 b g Well Chosen – Karsulu (IRE)

Bought at the Cheltenham March sale, he finished third in his only Irish point over two and a half miles. He looks a promising sort to go novice hurdling.

### COEUR DE LION 4 b g Pour Moi (IRE) – Hora

Twice a winner at Wetherby and Sandown, he then finished seventh in the Triumph Hurdle at Cheltenham but paid the price because the handicapper raised him eleven pounds. I don't think there is a lot of leeway now with a mark of 144 but he may benefit from a step up to two and a half miles. In the meantime, he will have another run or two on the Flat having won in good style at Nottingham during the spring.

### COGBURN 5 ch g Black Sam Bellamy (IRE) – Realms of Gold (USA)

Partially sighted in one eye, we fitted him with an eyeshield after his first couple of runs in bumpers and it transformed him both at home and on the track. Runner-up at Huntingdon and Warwick on his next two starts, he is a full brother to Board of Trade. He will go novice hurdling.

### COSMEAPOLITAN 4 b g Mawatheeq (USA) – Cosmea

He won on his hurdles debut at Newbury in mid December but then suffered a fracture and didn't race again last season. Returning on the Flat during the spring/summer, he finished third at Bath in August but Fergus Sweeney was adamant he doesn't want soft ground. He lacks experience over jumps so we will be looking towards one of those Introductory hurdles. If we can get him back to him best, he isn't on a bad mark.

### CRIQ ROCK (FR) 6 ch g Kap Rock (FR) – Criquetot (FR)

A useful bumper horse a couple of seasons ago, he finished second three times over hurdles last year but wasn't at his best. Despite the fact he remains a maiden over hurdles, I am inclined to send him chasing because it may help him settle better.

## DESIRABLE COURT (IRE) 4 b f Court Cave (IRE) – Desirable Rhythm (IRE)

A big strong filly who won her only Irish point by eight lengths in the spring. We subsequently bought her on behalf of Simon Munir and Isaac Souede and she looks a very good prospect. Mares' novice hurdles are likely to be the plan.

## DESIREMOI D'AUTHIE (FR) 4 b g Cachet Noir (USA) – Toietmoi D'Authie (FR)

An impressive winner of his only APQS Flat race in France, he only arrived in August. I would think he will go straight over hurdles and is an exciting prospect.

## DEYRANN DE CARJAC (FR) 4 b g Balko (FR) – Queyrann (FR)

He is a horse I like a lot. He suffered a stress fracture during the winter and it was a rush to get him ready for the sales bumper at Newbury in March. I have been very pleased with him since because he has really strengthened and I think he is a smart horse. We may give him another run in a bumper before going hurdling. He will start off over two miles over jumps.

## DINGO DOLLAR (IRE) 5 ch g Golden Lariat (USA) – Social Society (IRE)

Rather like Beneagles, he is an ex-Irish pointer who will hopefully improve again once switched to fences. He is a likeable horse who won over hurdles at Bangor and Fontwell last season. He made all on the latter occasion and is suited by two miles five plus. It was too dry in the spring to school him over fences but being a former pointer I wouldn't envisage any problems.

## DINO VELVET (FR) 4 b g Naaqoos – Matgil (FR)

A winner at Sandown, he was unlucky in the Fred Winter Juvenile Hurdle at Cheltenham because he all but fell at the top of the hill. I think he would have been placed otherwise. He likes soft ground and, being only a four year old, he will continue over hurdles and go handicapping. We will start him off over two miles but he ought to stay further.

## DUSKY LEGEND 7 b m Midnight Legend – Tinagoodnight (FR)

She is fresh and well and in good form at home. Twice a winner over hurdles last season, she ran very well at the Cheltenham Festival finishing third in the Dawn Run Mares' Novices' Hurdle. She was then only beaten a neck in a Listed mares' novice hurdle at the same track the following month. The plan is to send her novice chasing and she could be exciting. I think two and a half miles is her optimum trip.

## ELGIN 5 b g Duke of Marmalade (IRE) – China Tea (USA)

He had a good season winning at Newcastle and Kempton before finishing runner-up in a couple of Graded events, including the Dovecote Novices' Hurdle at Kempton. Seventh in the Supreme Novices' Hurdle at Cheltenham, he may not be the easiest horse to place off his mark but he has had a good long break, which he needed. We will be looking towards the decent handicap hurdles for him.

## FIDUX (FR) 4 b g Fine Grain (JPN) – Folle Tempete (FR)

Ex-French, he won at Catterick and Kempton before finishing third in the Adonis Hurdle at the latter track in February. I thought he was on a high enough mark after his run in the Fred Winter but he ran well last time at Sandown on the final day of the season finishing third. He could be one for the four year old hurdle at Chepstow (14th October).

## FORGETTHESMALLTALK (IRE) 5 b g Flemensfirth (USA) – Mylane Du Charmil (FR)

We bought him at the Cheltenham November Sale having won an Irish point-to-point. He showed promise in three runs, including when narrowly beaten at Ludlow on his hurdles debut. He has done particularly well during the summer and will continue in two mile six to three miles novice hurdles.

### GIBRALFARO (IRE) 5 b g Dalakhani (IRE) – Ronda
I think we are going to send him novice chasing. He is not an easy horse to work out because he ran well against his own age group but then appeared to struggle in open handicaps. Placed at Chepstow and Newbury last season, two and a half miles seems to suit him.

### GIVEAWAY GLANCE 4 br f Passing Glance – Giving
She had a good first season over hurdles winning two and finishing second at Warwick. A winner on the Flat at Leicester since, we gave her a break after that. She will have another run or two on the Flat before going handicap hurdling.

### GOOD MAN PAT (IRE) 4 b g Gold Well – Basically Supreme (IRE)
A twelve lengths winner of an Irish point for Denis Murphy, we purchased him at the Doncaster May Sale. He is only 16hh, which I think kept his price down, but we did a bit of work with him when he first arrived and I was very pleased with him. He is one for novice hurdles.

### HAREFIELD (IRE) 4 b g Doyen (IRE) – Bobbi's Venture (IRE)
A fine big horse who finished second on his debut at Exeter in February. He then ran well in the sales bumper at Newbury the following month even though I think he was past his best by that stage of the season. I am hoping he will develop into a decent novice hurdler.

### HEREWEGO HEREWEGO (IRE) 6 b g Kalanisi (IRE) – Downtown Train (IRE)
Back in work having missed the whole of last season, he isn't the easiest to train but he has shown he has plenty of ability finishing fourth and second in his two runs over hurdles at Newbury. A horse with a good pedigree, he is a half-brother to Puffin Billy. He will either continue in novice events or go handicapping having been given a mark of 127.

### HIDDEN CARGO (IRE) 5 b g Stowaway – All Heart
He has always worked like a good horse at home but was still quite weak last year and I hope he will improve this time around. Third in a bumper at Newbury on his debut, he was placed a couple of times over hurdles but wasn't quite finishing off his races. I am hoping that was due to immaturity. Still a novice, we also have the option of running him in handicaps.

### INNER DRIVE (IRE) 9 b g Heron Island (IRE) – Hingis (IRE)
Restricted to only one run last season, he ran very well to finish second over two miles. The trip was too sharp and we intended running him again but the ground dried up. I have always liked him.

### JUST IN TIME 3 b g Excelebration (IRE) – Flying Finish (FR)
Ran an encouraging race at Leicester on the Flat on his reappearance in August. He appeared to be struggling at one stage but the penny dropped and he stayed on well to finish second. The ground that day would have been soft enough for him, too. He confirmed the promise with victory in another twelve furlongs handicap at Goodwood less than three weeks later. Following a few more races on the Flat, he is likely to go juvenile hurdling.

### KEEP IN LINE (GER) 5 b g Soldier Hollow – Kastila (GER)
Started well over hurdles winning at Huntingdon and Bangor, he also ran respectably in Graded events at Cheltenham in November and Ascot the following month. However, by the spring he had been on the go for a long time and has benefited from a summer break. Two and a half miles handicap hurdles will be his target, although he doesn't want it too soft.

### KOZIER (GER) 3 ch g Muhtathir – Kasumi (GER)
Gelded during the winter, he was a running on fifth at Wolverhampton on his reappearance in July. We then stepped him up to two miles at Goodwood the following month and he was beaten a short head. He will have another run on the Flat before going juvenile hurdling. He loves his jumping and wants some ease in the ground.

**LABEL DES OBEAUX (FR) 6 b g Saddler Maker (IRE) – La Bessiere (FR)**

Took well to chasing winning three times, culminating in a very good performance at Ayr's Scottish National meeting. Raised six pounds since, he is rated 154 and is likely to be aimed at the Ladbrokes Gold Cup (formerly the Hennessy Gold Cup) at Newbury (2nd December) following one run beforehand. For some reason, he doesn't seem to like Cheltenham and has twice finished distressed there. He appears to handle any ground.

**MELODY OF SCOTLAND (FR) 3 b f Youmzain (IRE) – This Melody (FR)**

She arrived in August having won over hurdles in France in May. Owned by J.P.McManus, she looks a quality filly who will be going juvenile hurdling. Her first main target will be the Listed juvenile fillies' hurdle at Aintree (9th December).

**MIA'S STORM (IRE) 7 b m September Storm (GER) – Letitia's Gain (IRE)**

A four times winner over hurdles last season, she was very good on her final start at Haydock in May. I was concerned about the rain beforehand but she was impressive winning by eight lengths. The step up in trip seemed to suit her, too. A winning pointer, she will go novice chasing and be aimed at mares' only events.

**MIDNIGHT MAESTRO 5 b g Midnight Legend – Calamintha**

He looks well having strengthened up over the summer and I feel there is still plenty of mileage in his rating. A dual winner over hurdles at Warwick and Stratford, his last run came in a series final at Haydock but he made a bad mistake and Barry (Geraghty) pulled him because he thought he may have injured himself. Thankfully, he was fine. We haven't decided whether to remain over hurdles or go novice chasing. Yet to race beyond two miles, he will stay further if necessary.

**MIDNIGHT TOUR 7 b m Midnight Legend – Uppermost**

Previously trained by David Loder, she looked good when arriving and was an easy winner at Hereford on her first run for us. However, we rather lost her during the winter but she really bounced back in the spring and I was very pleased with her progress. Sixth at the Festival in the David Nicholson Mares' Hurdle, she then rounded off the season by winning a Listed mares' event at Cheltenham in April by half a dozen lengths. We are going to aim her at the valuable Graded mares' hurdles over two and a half miles plus.

**MINELLA CHARMER (IRE) 6 b g King's Theatre (IRE) – Kim Hong (IRE)**

He is a decent horse but was unlucky last season falling at the fourth last on his chasing debut at Wetherby when still going well. He then jumped badly to his left at Exeter so we decided to switch him back to hurdles. Unfortunately, he then fell again at Newbury when still very much in contention at the penultimate flight. We will therefore keep him over hurdles for the time being but he will go chasing again at some stage.

**PADDY BOSS (IRE) 5 ch g Gamut (IRE) – Algadora (FR)**

I have always liked him and it was no surprise when he made a winning debut in a bumper at Warwick in the spring. He took a bit of time to hit top gear but was well on top at the line and it took Wayne (Hutchinson) a while to pull him afterwards, which is always a good sign. Bought by Max McNeill since, he may have another run in a bumper, otherwise we will send him straight over hurdles. He will start off over two miles.

**PAGEBURG (FR) 3 b g Sageburg (IRE) – Peace of Oasis (FR)**

Successful in his only race on the Flat in France at Marseille in April, I don't know a lot about him yet but the plan is to send him juvenile hurdling.

**PASSING CALL 4 b f Passing Glance – Call Me A Legend**
She is a big strong filly out of a useful mare we trained. Placed in two of her three bumpers, she has summered well and will go for mares' only novice hurdles.

**PEGGIES VENTURE 6 b m Presenting – Peggies Run**
A maiden over hurdles, she was runner-up in a Listed mares' bumper at Huntingdon in December. I am sure we still haven't seen the best of her.

**PERFECT HARMONY (IRE) 5 b g Definite Article – Brandam Supreme (IRE)**
Unlucky not to win his only Irish point when falling at the last, we bought him at the Cheltenham November Sale. He won a bumper on his Rules debut at Newbury before running respectably in the Cheltenham Festival championship bumper. A lovely horse who will go novice hurdling over two and a half miles plus.

**POTTERMAN 4 b g Sulamani (IRE) – Polly Potter**
He looked good when winning on his debut in a bumper at Huntingdon in late May. Mind you, I would have been upset if he hadn't won because he had done plenty of work beforehand and I have always liked him. A horse who doesn't carry a lot of condition, he could run in another bumper before going jumping. He shows plenty of speed at home and possesses a big engine.

**RIVER FROST 5 b g Silver Frost (IRE) – River Test**
Enjoyed a good season over hurdles winning at Plumpton and Kempton twice. I thought he ran well in the Coral Cup, too, finishing ninth. Yet to decide whether he continues over hurdles or jumps fences, he is suited by two and a half miles.

**SABRE SQUADRON (IRE) 4 b g Lope De Vega (IRE) – Caravan of Dreams (IRE)**
Yet to run for us, he won over a mile on the Flat at Leicester last year for Peter Chapple-Hyam and remains lightly raced. He hasn't been with us for long and we haven't schooled him yet. The plan is to send him jumping though after a few runs on the Flat.

**SCEAU ROYAL (FR) 5 b g Doctor Dino (FR) – Sandside (FR)**
Had a good season winning at Cheltenham and the Elite Hurdle at Wincanton. Third in the Kingwell Hurdle behind Yanworth at the latter track, he will go novice chasing and could be exciting over fences. Two miles is his trip and I have been pleased with him during the summer.

**SECOND TIME AROUND 5 b g Midnight Legend – Silk Rope (IRE)**
He is a big laid back horse at home so it was a surprise when he raced so keenly on his debut at Southwell and didn't get home. It was so out of character compared to what he is like at home. Fourth next time at Huntingdon, he then won at Market Rasen and was suited by the strong early gallop because he was able to settle much better. Last season was all about educating him and he will go novice hurdling in the Autumn.

**SEGO SUCCESS (IRE) 9 b g Beneficial – The West Road (IRE)**
Without a win last season, I thought he was unlucky at Kempton because he looked like winning until coming down at the third last. He appeared to have his rivals in trouble at the time. I always felt he was a soft ground horse but I don't think that's necessarily the case. The handicapper has given him a chance and he will continue in staying handicap chases.

**SIMPLY A LEGEND 8 b g Midnight Legend – Disco Danehill (IRE)**
Absent last season due to a leg injury, he is back in work and will go novice chasing. A three times winner over hurdles, he is suited by two and a half miles.

### SIR ANTHONY BROWNE 5 ch g Black Sam Bellamy (IRE) – Shayaza

He had an issue with his wind and therefore underwent a tie-back operation hence he didn't reappear until February. Twice a winner at Wincanton and Newbury, he then finished third at Ayr's Scottish National meeting but the handicapper raised him twelve pounds. That will make life tougher but he will be aimed at handicap hurdles over two and a half miles.

### SMAD PLACE (FR) 10 gr g Smadoun (FR) – Bienna Star (FR)

He has been a fantastic horse for us over the years and owes us nothing. The old boy is in great form at home and the intention is to start him off in the Charlie Hall Chase at Wetherby (4th November).

### SULA ISLAND 3 ch f Sulamani (IRE) – Cosmea

A half-sister to Cosmeapolitan and William Hunter, she is likely to go juvenile hurdling. She ran promisingly on her debut on the Flat at Lingfield but didn't handle the ground next time at Windsor, plus she stumbled on the bend.

### TALKISCHEAP (IRE) 5 b g Getaway (GER) – Carrigmoorna Oak (IRE)

Unbeaten in three Irish points before we bought him at Cheltenham in November, he was progressive last season. Placed in two bumpers, he then won two out of two over hurdles at Fontwell and Warwick. Both those victories came in May so he remains a novice for this season. The handicapper hasn't taken any chances giving him a mark of 133, but he is a likeable horse who is capable of winning more races. I think he wants two and a half miles plus.

### TARA VIEW 6 b m Kayf Tara – Temptation (FR)

She had a very good season winning a bumper at Bangor before scoring three times over hurdles at Ludlow. She then stayed on well under top weight in the mares' final at Newbury in the spring finishing fourth. We will start her off in mares' Graded hurdles and I wouldn't mind stepping her up to three miles at some stage. If that doesn't work out, we have the option of sending her novice chasing.

### THE DEVILS DROP (IRE) 4 b g Court Cave (IRE) – Concernforkillen (IRE)

Acquired at the Cheltenham April Sale, he finished runner-up in his only Irish point-to-point and is a likeable sort. Athletic, we did a bit of work with him when he arrived and I was pleased with him. He will go novice hurdling.

### THE UNIT (IRE) 6 b g Gold Well – Sovana (FR)

Very progressive last year, he is a horse we have always liked but it has taken him a long time to learn to relax. A winner over hurdles at Doncaster and Taunton twice, he was also third in Grade 1 company at Aintree on his final start. He will go novice chasing over two and a half miles.

### TILLYTHETANK (IRE) 4 b f Stowaway – All Heart

A full-sister to Hidden Cargo, I liked her at the Cheltenham summer sale and she showed a lot of promise in her two starts in Irish points. We did a bit of work with her and she has put on plenty of condition during the summer and looks well. Mares' only novice hurdles will be her aim.

### VOIE DANS VOIE (FR) 4 br g Coastal Path – Peggy Pierji (FR)

Purchased at the Cheltenham March Sale, he was placed in both his point-to-points in Ireland for Harry Kelly. He looks a good prospect and will go novice hurdling this season.

### WHO DARES WINS (IRE) 5 b g Jeremy (USA) – Savignano

He has had a great year under both codes winning the Gerry Feilden Hurdle at Newbury and finishing third in the Coral Cup at Cheltenham. Switched to the Flat, he was fourth in the Chester Cup and third in the Ascot Stakes at the Royal meeting during the summer. He never lets us down and I am convinced there is a big race in him. The Cesarewitch at Newmarket (14th October) is his first target before he goes back over jumps. He stays two and a half miles very well.

### WILDE BLUE YONDER (IRE) 8 b g Oscar (IRE) – Blue Gallery (IRE)
Off the track since the spring of last year, he is back and we will aim him at a handicap hurdle and then decide whether to send him chasing. He was a very useful novice hurdler a few years ago finishing fifth in the Supreme Novices' Hurdle at the Festival.

### WILLIAM H BONNEY 6 b g Midnight Legend – Calamintha
He is another who I feel is capable of winning a big handicap. A winner at Cheltenham's Trials meeting in January, I then ran him in the *Betfair* Hurdle at Newbury but I think that took the edge off him. Even though he ran well in the Swinton Hurdle at Haydock on his final start, he wasn't at his best. I think his mark is OK and he will continue to contest the good two mile handicap hurdles.

### WILLOUGHBY HEDGE 10 b g King's Theatre (IRE) – Mini Mandy
He was on the transfer list in the spring but he then won at Haydock and has earned another season. His main target is the Becher Chase at Aintree (9th December) with one run beforehand.

### WINTER ESCAPE (IRE) 6 b g Robin Des Pres (FR) – Saddleeruppat (IRE)
I think he is a very good horse but was never right last season. Sick after his run in the Greatwood Hurdle in November, he returned in the spring and ran a tremendous race in the County Hurdle at the Festival finishing fifth. That run may have left its mark when he went to Ayr for the Scottish Champion Hurdle because he was below par there. There is a possibility he will stay over hurdles and I think he prefers better ground because he is such a good actioned horse.

### WISHING AND HOPING (IRE) 7 b g Beneficial – Desperately Hoping (IRE)
Things never really happened for him over fences so we switched him back to hurdles in the second half of the season. He ran well at Kempton finishing third behind River Frost and will continue over hurdles for the time being. Still lightly raced, he lacks match practice and should improve. Two and a half to two miles six looks ideal.

### YANWORTH 7 ch g Norse Dancer (IRE) – Yota (FR)
He looks great and we are looking forward to schooling him over fences with a view to going chasing this winter. A winner of four of his five races last season, I was delighted with him at Aintree winning the Grade 1 Liverpool Hurdle over three miles. It was the first time he had tackled the trip but he saw it out very well. We will start him off over two and a half miles over fences and he is obviously an exciting prospect.

---

**TRAINER'S HORSE TO FOLLOW: POTTERMAN**

---

# Tom LACEY
**Stables: Cottage Field Stables Ltd., Sapness Farm, Woolhope, Herefordshire.**
**2016/2017: 21 Winners / 102 Runners 21% Prize-Money £107,655**
**www.cottagefield.co.uk**

### BRANDON HILL (IRE) 9 b g Beneficial – Annesbanker (IRE)
A yard favourite who won twice at Warwick and Newbury last season. He jumps well and likes soft ground and hopefully will win another handicap or two off his mark. Three miles is his trip.

### COLT LIGHTNING (IRE) 4 b g Flemensfirth (USA) – Shannon Theatre (IRE)
Runner-up in his only point-to-point at Dingley in late May, he found the ground quick enough and came back with sore shins. A typical Flemensfirth, he wants soft ground and will go straight over hurdles over two and a half miles.

## EQUUS AMADEUS (IRE) 4 b g Beat Hollow – Charade (IRE)

A lovely big horse who appreciates better ground. Third on his first two starts in bumpers, he won nicely at Exeter last time. We will start him off in a maiden hurdle on decent ground. Ultimately, he will stay three miles even though he isn't slow. However, he still needs to learn to settle and will be campaigned over shorter trips. A good jumper, he was schooled over fences before he raced.

## FLASHING GLANCE 4 b g Passing Glance – Don And Gerry (IRE)

With hindsight, I shouldn't have run him at Ayr in the spring. He tends to pull hard so we held him up in order to get him settled but the leaders got first run on him. He eventually finished fifth but I thought he ran better than the bare result suggests. Fifth in a Listed bumper at Cheltenham on New Year's Day before he joined us, he was disappointing on his hurdles debut at Bangor in early September. He didn't jump very well and Richard (Johnson) said he was hanging. I think he wants decent ground.

## HATTAAB 4 b g Intikhab (USA) – Sundus (USA)

A well bred horse who we bought at the Doncaster January Sales having finished runner-up in a bumper at Musselburgh. However, he was very jarred up when he arrived so we let him down almost immediately. Following his break, he has been in pre training and is plenty forward enough now. He is moving well and, while his schooling hasn't been the most fluent, he will go novice hurdling over two miles in the Autumn.

## JESTER JET 7 br m Overbury (IRE) – Hendre Hotshot

She was progressive in the spring winning three times at Wetherby, Ludlow and Perth before finishing third at Aintree. Sean Bowen rode a very good race on the winner that day but our filly still ran well. She is a lovely filly who has improved twenty four pounds. Suited by two and a half miles plus, she stays well and will jump a fence, too. All three of her wins were gained on good ground but she will cope with good to soft.

## KATESON 4 b g Black Sam Bellamy (IRE) – Silver Kate (IRE)

A very nice unraced four year old out of Silver Kate, he is one to watch out for in a bumper during the Autumn. I like him.

## KIMBERLITE CANDY (IRE) 5 b g Flemensfirth (USA) – Mandys Native (IRE)

He looks very well following his summer holiday at Martinstown in Ireland. Anything he achieved over hurdles was a bonus. He won at Ascot and Newcastle last season. A winning pointer, he has always loved jumping and his schooling has been very good. He will stay three miles eventually but I'd imagine we will start him off over fences over shorter.

## MARY ELEANOR 5 b m Midnight Legend – Lady Rebecca

She is Lady Rebecca's last foal and I thought she was unlucky not to win a bumper last season. Narrowly beaten on her debut at Huntingdon, she then finished third at Newbury and then ran back too soon at Bangor on her most recent start. I would expect her to go over hurdles now and she will win races. She will be suited by two and a half miles.

## POLYDORA (IRE) 5 b g Milan – Mandysway (IRE)

A half-brother to dual Grade 2 winner Roberto Goldback, I think he is an extremely good horse. I was very disappointed with his two runs in bumpers last season at Market Rasen and Newbury but he suffered with major feet problems and he has been hard to keep sound. We have done some remedial work on his feet and, if he can deliver on the track what he has shown at home, he could be very good. It is possible he will have another run in a bumper but is more likely to go hurdling.

### SIR EGBERT 4 b g Kayf Tara – Little Miss Flora

Ran well on his debut in a bumper at Warwick finishing third but then found the ground too quick at Exeter next time. A big raw horse, he needs to strengthen up and, with that in mind, we will keep him to shorter distances until he does. He jumps well at home and wants soft/heavy ground.

### SUPER SID (IRE) 5 b g Westerner – Super Sammy

Runner-up in an Irish point for Eric McNamara, he was subsequently bought at the Cheltenham November Sales. Third in a bumper at Ffos Las in April, I was very pleased with the run especially as the ground was quicker than ideal. He will want a trip over hurdles.

### SWORD OF FATE (IRE) 4 b g Beneficial – Beann Ard (IRE)

A very nice horse who raced twice in point-to-points finishing third at Larkhill on his second start. A typical Beneficial, I don't think he was strong enough in his points, hence he wasn't getting home. A ten lengths winner of a bumper at Exeter in late April, he won well. Inclined to be a bit free, he will start off over two miles over hurdles and appears to appreciate better ground. He will stay further in time once he has strengthened up and learned to race.

### THE BIG BITE (IRE) 4 b g Scorpion (IRE) – Thanks Noel (IRE)

From a good family, he was an impressive winner of an all-weather bumper at Lingfield in March. I suppose his victory was a bit of a surprise because we didn't really know what to expect beforehand. Noel Fehily rode him and was very taken by him. We intended running him in the championship bumper at Aintree but he was balloted out. He still has a lot to learn and lacks experience but he is a promising young horse who has the speed for two miles.

### VADO FORTE (FR) 4 b g Walk In The Park (IRE) – Gloire (FR)

Very impressive at home, I love him. I was expecting him to run well on his debut at Kempton last spring but he was disappointing. However, he came back very sore through his back having torn muscles. He has had three months box rest and is back in work now. Handling him mentally will be a trickier job than training him and we will keep him to two miles because it will help him settle.

### Unnamed 5 b g Kayf Tara – Marello

A homebred half-brother to Midnight Monty, who we trained last season, he is from a very good family. He is a horse I like a lot and he will start off in a bumper in the Autumn. Proper jumping ground will suit him.

*Below are three promising young horses Tom sold during the spring/summer and are worth looking out for this winter.*

### BLACKBOW (IRE) 4 b g Stowaway – Rinnce Moll (IRE)

Sold to **Willie MULLINS** for £150,000 at the Aintree April Sale.

"He was an impressive winner of his only point-to-point at Maisemore Park in March. A lovely horse who found his work easy, he stays well."

### SKY PIRATE 4 b g Midnight Legend – Dancingwithbubbles

Sold to Lady Bamford for £150,000 at the Cheltenham March Sale, he has joined **Jonjo O'NEILL**. "I thought he was very good. He hosed up in his only point-to-point at Larkhill in February. There is nothing flash about him but he is a grinder who keeps finding. He has every attribute to be a very good horse."

**SPACE SAFARI (FR) 4 b g Kapgarde (FR) – Prodiga (FR)**

A sixteen lengths winner of his second point-to-point at Dingley in May (2m 4f), he was subsequently bought privately by Perthshire based trainer **Lucy NORMILE**.

"He has got gears and I think he will be perfect for racing in the North."

> **TRAINER'S HORSE TO FOLLOW: Unnamed 5yo by Kayf Tara - Marello**

# Olly MURPHY
### Stables: Warren Chase Stables, Wilmcote, Stratford Upon Avon.
### www.ollymurphyracing.com

**BALLINSLEA BRIDGE (IRE) 5 b g Pierre – Feelin' Looser (IRE)**

We purchased him at the Cheltenham Sale in June and he was a twelve lengths winner of his final Irish point. He looks a sharp type and the sort to come to hand quickly. Not short of speed, he will run in a bumper in the Autumn and then go hurdling over two miles.

**CAPTIVA ISLAND (IRE) 4 b g Scorpion (IRE) – Sapphire Eile**

Placed in two of his three bumpers at Uttoxeter and Worcester during the spring/summer when trained by Gordon (Elliott), his work at home has always been very good. We will send him hurdling over two and a half miles and I will be disappointed if he doesn't win plenty of races.

**CRAIGMOR (IRE) 5 b g Craigsteel – Twilight Princess (IRE)**

He was a fifteen lengths winner of an Irish point on his last run for Stuart Crawford in April. A horse with a good attitude, I think he will be suited by some cut in the ground and we will aim him at a bumper before going over hurdles.

**FRESH NEW DAWN (IRE) 5 ch g Flemensfirth (USA) – Star Shuil (IRE)**

Another we bought at the Cheltenham June Sale, he finished second in his only Irish point-to-point for Jim Dreaper in the spring. He looks a staying type who will be start off in a soft ground bumper in the Autumn before going hurdling.

**KAHALEESI 5 b m Shirocco (GER) – Maiden Voyage**

Yet to run for us, she is a nice mare who has disappointed over hurdles so far. However, her bumper form was OK and I would like to think she will win races off her mark. She wants soft ground.

**KNIGHT COMMANDER 4 br g Sir Percy – Jardin**

Twice a winner at Newton Abbot and Uttoxeter within the space of five days in July, I think he will be one of those horses who will be suited by a better race with a lesser weight. He has been winning over two miles but I would expect him to stay two and a half and he also looks capable of winning on the Flat.

**MIZEN MASTER (IRE) 4 b g Captain Rio – Nilassiba**

He won first time out for us at Stratford before finishing second at Bangor, where his jumping was novicey and he found the trip too sharp. Stepped up in trip, he returned to winning form at Market Rasen over two and a half miles before finishing a close second at Cartmel in late August. Suited by two and a quarter miles plus, he is no star but I think he will continue to improve.

### MON PORT (IRE) 5 b g Scorpion (IRE) – Sounds Charming (IRE)
An exciting prospect who was in training with Ben De Haan last season but is now owned by Terry Warner. He had some very good form in bumpers finishing a neck second behind Dans Le Vent (sixth in the Cheltenham Festival bumper) at Ludlow before winning by fifty five lengths at Warwick last time. We will start him off in a maiden hurdle over two or two and a half miles.

### MULLAGHBOY (IRE) 6 b g Beneficial – Mellowthemoonlight (IRE)
Previously trained by Stuart Crawford, we bought him cheaply at the Doncaster May Sales. He is lightly raced and goes nicely at home, although we haven't done any fast work with him yet. I think he will do a job for us over hurdles and then fences eventually.

### RIO QUINTO (FR) 4 b g Loup Breton (IRE) – Seal of Cause (IRE)
A gorgeous horse and very much one to look forward to. Placed in both his Irish points for Donnchadh Doyle, we bought him at the Cheltenham June Sale and he looks an above average sort. His form has worked out well and we are hoping he will develop into a Saturday horse. Not a big robust horse, he looks as though he will be a two or two and a half mile horse over jumps but we will start him off in a bumper in the Autumn. It is early days but he certainly doesn't strike me as a slow staying type.

### ROYAL PLAZA (IRE) 6 b g King's Theatre (IRE) – Friendly Craic (IRE)
Another new recruit, he was a winner over hurdles for Alan King last season and ran consistently over fences. Still a novice over fences, he is rated 120 and we will look for a suitable novices' handicap over two or two and a half miles. We have operated on his wind since arriving, which will hopefully help him and bring about some improvement.

### SKILLED 6 b g Mastercraftsman (IRE) – Treacle (USA)
A horse I know well having been previously trained by Gordon (Elliott). I have been pleased with the way he has taken to fences winning at Stratford and Southwell during the summer and he will provide plenty of fun for his owners and win more races in his grade. Two and a half miles on nice ground are his optimum conditions.

### TUNNEL CREEK 5 b g Tobougg (IRE) – Free Offer
A well bred horse, he was trained in Ireland by Tommy Cooper and looks to be on a nice mark. Versatile in terms of ground conditions, he seems to be suited by two or two and a half miles.

### WISHFULL DREAMING 6 ch g Alflora (IRE) – Poussetiere Deux (FR)
A full brother to Wishfull Thinking, Mr and Mrs Whateley have kindly sent him to me. A Listed bumper winner at Cheltenham a few years ago, he won over hurdles at Chepstow last season but has never quite fulfilled his potential. However, if we can get him back to the sort of form he showed in bumpers then he could be an interesting horse over fences. The plan is to send him novice chasing in the Autumn.

---

**TRAINER'S HORSE TO FOLLOW: RIO QUINTO**

# Paul NICHOLLS

**Stables: Manor Farm Stables, Ditcheat, Somerset.**
**2016/2017: 171 Winners / 673 Runners 25% Prize-Money £2,529,250**
**www.paulnichollsracing.com**

### ADRIEN DU PONT (FR) 5 b g Califet (FR) – Santariyka (FR)
A Grade 1 winning juvenile hurdler a couple of seasons ago, last year was always going to be a tough one but he finished third in the champion four year old hurdle at Auteuil in November. He will go novice chasing over two and a half miles plus and that is what he was bought for.

### ALCALA (FR) 7 gr g Turgeon (USA) – Pail Mel (FR)
He has been in awesome form during the spring/summer winning six times over fences, including the Listed Summer Plate at Market Rasen in July. I think the Turgeon's want a bit of time and they seem to appreciate better ground. He will continue until the ground changes and then come back in the spring.

### AMOUR DE NUIT (IRE) 5 b g Azamour (IRE) – Umthoulah (IRE)
Bought out of Sir Mark Prescott's yard last October, he has won twice over hurdles at Taunton and Newton Abbot and remains a novice until the 1st November. With that in mind, we are going to aim him at the Grade 2 Persian War Novice Hurdle at Chepstow (15th October) before going handicapping.

### ANTARTICA DE THAIX (FR) 7 gr m Dom Alco (FR) – Nouca De Thaix (FR)
She had a very good season over fences winning three times, including a Listed mares' chase at Huntingdon. Over the top by the time she ran at Cheltenham on her final start, I am not sure the track suited her anyway. She will continue to contest the good mares' chases.

### AS DE MEE (FR) 7 b g Kapgarde (FR) – Koeur De Mee (FR)
He won the Grand Sefton over the National fences at Aintree last season and, in all likelihood, he will go back there for the same race (9th December) and we will probably give him an entry in the Grand National itself later on.

### ATAGUISEAMIX (FR) 4 b g Al Namix (FR) – Olafane (FR)
We bought him after he had finished second in his only Irish point in the spring for Denis Murphy. Only four, he will probably have a run in a bumper before going hurdling.

### BINGE DRINKER (IRE) 8 b g Spadoun (FR) – Our Honey (IRE)
A new horse to the yard, he had some very good form for Rebecca Curtis winning four times over hurdles and, on his only start over fences, he beat Might Bite by four lengths at Ffos Las last November. Absent since, he will be in action from Christmas onwards and is an interesting horse.

### BLACK CORTON (FR) 6 br g Laverock (IRE) – Pour Le Meilleur (FR)
He keeps improving winning three times over hurdles last season and has already won three over fences during the summer. We have stepped him up in trip and he stays well. Another who likes decent ground, he will have a winter break before coming back in the spring. In the meantime, we will aim him at some of the better novice races in the Autumn.

### BOUVREUIL (FR) 6 b g Saddler Maker (IRE) – Madame Lys (FR)
Ran some good races in defeat last season, including at the Festival where he was placed for the third consecutive year. Rated 145, he will continue in the good two and a half mile handicaps, although I think he will stay three.

### BRELAN D'AS (FR) 6 b g Crillon (FR) – Las De La Croix (FR)
A winner over hurdles in France, he has only raced twice for us. He won a handicap comfortably at Wincanton in November but then missed the remainder of the season. Rated 144, he will go novice chasing.

### BRIO CONTI (FR) 6 gr g Dom Alco (FR) – Cadoulie Wood (FR)
Progressive over hurdles last season, he appreciated the step up to two and a half miles winning at Doncaster and a valuable handicap at Kempton in March. Fifth in Grade 1 company at Aintree last time, he goes chasing and is a very nice horse. We will start him off over two and a half but he will stay three miles in time.

### BUBBLE O'CLOCK (IRE) 4 ch g Robin Des Champs (FR) – Flaithiuil (FR)
A very nice unraced four year old who pleased us in his work during the spring. He will start in a bumper and is one to watch out for.

### CAPELAND (FR) 5 b g Poliglote – Neiland (FR)
He won over hurdles at Newton Abbot last Autumn and was unlucky not to win more. Still lightly raced, we will give him another run in handicap or two before deciding whether to send him chasing.

### CAPITAINE (FR) 5 gr g Montmartre (FR) – Patte De Velour (FR)
A Grade 2 winner over hurdles at Ascot in December, he then finished runner-up in the Grade 1 Tolworth Hurdle at Sandown. Switched to fences in May, he won well on his chasing debut at Newton Abbot and is an exciting prospect. He appreciated the better ground in the spring.

### CAPTAIN CATTISTOCK 4 b g Black Sam Bellamy (IRE) – Pearl Buttons
He won his only point-to-point for Jack Barber last season and will run in a bumper before going novice hurdling.

### CASH AGAIN (FR) 5 br g Great Pretender (IRE) – Jeu De Lune (FR)
A French bumper winner, he finished second in a bumper at Newbury on his first run for us a couple of seasons ago but hasn't been at his best over hurdles so far. Well held in the EBF Final at Sandown last time, he is capable of better.

### CASKO D'AIRY (FR) 5 b g Voix Du Nord (FR) – Quaska D'Airy (FR)
Yet to run for us, he won a bumper and then finished runner-up on his hurdles debut at Auteuil for Guy Cherel before we bought him. Absent last season, he is a very nice horse who will go novice hurdling. I like him a lot.

### CEREAL KILLER (FR) 5 b g Buck's Boum (FR) – Dombrelle (FR)
He is a promising young horse who won both his point-to-points for Jack Barber. Another who is likely to have a run in a bumper before going jumping.

### CHAMERON (FR) 4 b g Laveron – Chamanka (FR)
Despite winning twice over hurdles at Auteuil for Guy Cherel last season, he was big and backward when arriving so we decided to give him some time to develop. He looks a very nice prospect for the future. There is a possibility we will aim him at the champion four year old hurdle at Auteuil in November. Otherwise, we may send him novice chasing.

## CHIEF CRAFTSMAN 3 b c Mastercraftsman (IRE) – Eurolink Raindance (IRE)
A maiden on the Flat for Luca Cumani, he was placed three times over ten and twelve furlongs and is rated 77. Mr and Mrs Cotton have sent him to me to go juvenile hurdling.

## CHOIX DES ARMES (FR) 5 b g Saint Des Saints (FR) – Kicka
Seventh in a bumper at Ascot last November, he was still very backward so we decided to give him the rest of the season off. He can only improve and will go novice hurdling.

## CLAN DES OBEAUX (FR) 5 b g Kapgarde (FR) – Nausicaa Des Obeaux (FR)
His chasing career started well with an impressive victory at Newbury's Hennessy meeting in a Grade 2 novice event followed by a narrow defeat in the Dipper Chase at Cheltenham on New Year's Day. However, he seemed to lose his confidence and started jumping to his right. We have operated on his wind during the summer and we may give him a run over hurdles before aiming him at Graduation chases.

## CLIFFS OF DOVER 4 b g Canford Cliffs (IRE) – Basanti (USA)
He was a revelation over hurdles last season winning six of his seven starts, including a Listed juvenile at Wetherby and a Grade 2 at Doncaster. Unfortunately, he incurred an injury after the latter victory and missed the remainder of the season. He came back into work on the 1st September and the plan is to give him a run on the Flat before aiming him at the Christmas Hurdle at Kempton on Boxing Day. He likes good ground.

## COASTAL TIEP (FR) 5 b g Coastal Path – Jaltiepy (FR)
A bumper winner at Chepstow last Autumn, he also won on his hurdles debut at Kempton and was placed at the same track later in the season. He is a winning pointer and will come into his own over fences this time around.

## COILLTE LASS (IRE) 6 b m Beneficial – Black Mariah (IRE)
Another ex-pointer, she won her first three races over hurdles for us, including a Listed mares' event at Taunton in December. We may give her one more run over hurdles before going down the mares' novice chase route.

## CONNETABLE (FR) 5 b g Saint Des Saints (FR) – Montbresia (FR)
Despite winning on his chasing debut at Wincanton, he proved a bit disappointing last season. I think he will benefit from stepping up in trip and going back over hurdles this year and could develop into a Pertemps contender.

## COPAIN DE CLASSE (FR) 5 b g Enrique – Toque Rouge (FR)
Rated 132 over hurdles, he won at Chepstow and Wincanton. I think he is a very nice horse who will go novice chasing and I will be disappointed if he doesn't win more races this year.

## COUP DE PINCEAU (FR) 5 b g Buck's Boum (FR) – Castagnette III (FR)
A dual bumper winner, including at Ascot in the Autumn, he ran well on his hurdles debut when finishing second at Kempton in November. Absent since, he was still backward last year hence we didn't run him again. He will continue in novice hurdles.

## CYRNAME (FR) 5 b g Nickname (FR) – Narquille (FR)
A big backward horse who won over hurdles in France. He had a couple of runs at Ascot last season but was very free. The plan is to send him novice chasing and I think he will improve over fences.

## DAN McGRUE (IRE) 5 b g Dansant – Aahsaypasty (IRE)
He won a bumper in Ireland before joining Jack Barber, for whom he won all three of his point-to-points last season. We may run him in a bumper before going novice hurdling.

### DARLING MALTAIX (FR) 4 b g Voix Du Nord (FR) – Rosalie Malta (FR)
A lovely horse who won a bumper for Guy Cherel in France. Still backward last season, we decided to give him time and leave him as a novice for this year.

### DENSFIRTH (IRE) 4 b g Flemensfirth (USA) – Denwoman (IRE)
He is a nice big unraced horse who is related to Denman. We will start him off in a bumper.

### DIAMOND GUY (FR) 4 b g Konig Turf (GER) – Unique Chance (FR)
An easy winner of a four runner bumper at Wincanton in the spring, he is a nice horse who I like. We will send him straight over hurdles starting off over two miles.

### DIEGO DU CHARMIL (FR) 5 b g Ballingarry (IRE) – Daramour (FR)
He won two competitive handicap hurdles, including the Listed Scottish County Hurdle at Musselburgh. A former Cheltenham Festival winner, he will go novice chasing over two miles and appreciates decent ground.

### DOLOS (FR) 4 b g Kapgarde (FR) – Redowa (FR)
A dual winner at Chepstow, we may start him off in the four year old hurdle at the same track in October (14th). He could then go novice chasing.

### DR RHYTHM (IRE) 4 b g Kalanisi (IRE) – Muscova Rose (IRE)
He was a very easy winner of his only point-to-point for Jack Barber last season. A promising type, he is only four and will therefore have a run in a bumper before going hurdling.

### DYNAMITE DOLLARS (FR) 4 b g Buck's Boum (FR) – Macadoun (FR)
Ran in three bumpers, including when finishing third in a Listed event at Cheltenham on New Year's Day. Sixth at Newbury last time, he was still backward and can only improve. He is a nice horse who will stay two and a half miles over hurdles.

### EL BANDIT (IRE) 6 b g Milan – Bonnie Parker (IRE)
A very nice horse who won six times over hurdles, including the Grade 2 Persian War Novices' Hurdle at Chepstow. He also won impressively on his chasing debut at Warwick in May and is an exciting prospect for novice chasing. Three miles on good ground is ideal, although he is quick enough over two miles five or two miles six.

### EMERGING TALENT (IRE) 8 b g Golan (IRE) – Elviria (IRE)
Missed the whole of last season, but is back now and will go novice chasing. A three times winner over hurdles the previous year, he stays two and a half miles well.

### FRODON (FR) 5 b g Nickname (FR) – Miss Country (FR)
He enjoyed a great season over fences winning six times, including the Grade 2 Rising Stars Novice Chase at Wincanton and the Pendil Novice Chase at Kempton, plus a valuable handicap at Cheltenham in December. Two and a half miles suits him and his first target is an intermediate chase at Newton Abbot (13th October) and then we will make a plan for the rest of the season.

### GET OUT THE GATE (IRE) 4 b g Mahler – Chartani (IRE)
A six lengths winner of his only Irish point-to-point in May, he will have a run in a bumper before going novice hurdling.

### GIBBES BAY (FR) 5 gr g Al Namix (FR) – Nouvelle Donne (FR)
Rated 114 over hurdles, he is on a good mark if he can get his jumping together. Third last time at Kempton, he won a bumper at Ayr the previous season and is a horse with plenty of ability. We will aim him at a novices' handicap hurdle.

## GIVE ME A COPPER (IRE) 7 ch g Presenting – Copper Supreme (IRE)

He is a very nice horse who I like a lot. A winner of two of his three races over hurdles, including at Ayr last time, he is quick enough for two and a half miles but stays three as well. His only defeat came in the River Don Novices' Hurdle at Doncaster when he wasn't right. A winning Irish pointer, he should make an exciting novice chaser.

## GRAND SANCY (FR) 3 b g Diamond Boy (FR) – La Courtille (FR)

A nice unraced three year old, the intention is to send him juvenile hurdling.

## HIGH SECRET (IRE) 6 b g High Chaparral (IRE) – Secret Question (USA)

He won a couple of times over hurdles at Taunton and finished fourth in a Grade 1 at Aintree. Switched to the Flat during the summer, he was runner-up at Goodwood and wasn't disgraced at Royal Ascot. Rated 141 over jumps, he will be aimed at the good handicaps hurdles on decent ground.

## IBIS DU RHEU (FR) 6 b g Blue Bresil (FR) – Dona Du Rheu (FR)

A former Cheltenham Festival winner, he didn't manage to win over fences last season but ran well in defeat against some smart novices, including Thistlecrack, Popples Bay and Royal Vacation. He was unlucky to keep bumping into such good opposition. He will continue in staying novice chases.

## IF YOU SAY RUN (IRE) 5 b m Mahler – De Lissa (IRE)

A lovely mare who won her only Irish point before we bought her at the Cheltenham December Sale. A thirteen lengths winner of a mares' bumper at Chepstow in the spring, she will be aimed at mares' only novice hurdles.

## JESSBER'S DREAM (IRE) 7 b m Milan – Maddy's Supreme (IRE)

Despite finishing second in a Listed mares' hurdle at Warwick in February, she was disappointing overall last season. However, she had a few issues with her breathing and we have therefore operated on her wind which will hopefully make a difference. She will go novice chasing.

## KAPCORSE (FR) 4 b g Kapgarde (FR) – Angesse (FR)

He finished fourth on his only start over hurdles at Auteuil last Autumn. Bought by J.P.McManus since, he is an interesting prospect for novice hurdles.

## LE MERCUREY (FR) 7 b g Nickname (FR) – Feroe (FR)

Suited by small fields, he finished second behind Native River in the Grade 2 Denman Chase at Newbury and also filled the same position behind the ill-fated Many Clouds in a Listed chase at Aintree. We will aim him at conditions chases, including the same race at Liverpool in December (9th), which is now a Grade 2.

## LE PREZIEN (FR) 6 br g Blue Bresil (FR) – Abu Dhabi (FR)

Despite proving a bit disappointing in the spring, he had a good first season over fences winning twice, including a Grade 2 novice chase at Cheltenham in November. Effective over two and two and a half miles, he is likely to be given an entry in the Betvictor Gold Cup at Cheltenham (18th November).

## MAGOO (IRE) 5 gr g Martaline – Noche (IRE)

A half-brother to Sam Winner, he missed last season but is back in work. A winner on the Flat and over hurdles in France, he may go straight over fences.

## MALAYA (FR) 3 b f Martaline – Clarte D'Or (FR)

An exciting prospect who won two of her three races over hurdles in France. A three lengths winner of a Listed hurdle at Auteuil last time, she will go juvenile hurdling.

### MARRACUDJA (FR) 6 b g Martaline – Memorial (FR)

Twice a winner over fences at Newton Abbot and Cheltenham last Autumn, he isn't the easiest to get right but has plenty of ability. Suited by fast ground, he will be running in two mile handicap chases.

### MODUS 7 ch g Motivator – Alessandra

I am looking forward to sending him novice chasing. Runner-up in the Greatwood Hurdle at Cheltenham, he was suited by the step up in trip in the Lanzarote Hurdle at Kempton winning in good style. Not disgraced in the Coral Cup at the Festival under a big weight, he is an exciting prospect for fences.

### MONSIEUR CO (FR) 4 b g Turgeon (USA) – Cayras Style (FR)

A winner over hurdles and fences in France, he has only raced twice for us winning at Wincanton before disappointing at Warwick. Still backward, we gave him a long break after his last run and I think he will benefit from better ground this year being by Turgeon. We will send him chasing and make the most of his four year old allowance in handicaps.

### MONT DES AVALOIRS (FR) 4 b g Blue Bresil (FR) – Abu Dhabi (FR)

A full-brother to Le Prezien, he is a lovely horse who I like. Runner-up in a bumper at Chepstow in the spring, he may have another run in a bumper before going novice hurdling.

### MOVEWITHTHETIMES (IRE) 6 ch g Presenting – Dare To Venture (IRE)

Another lovely horse who had a good season over hurdles winning twice and finishing second in the *Betfair* Hurdle at Newbury. He was due to run in the Supreme Novices' Hurdle but an injury ruled him out. He is OK now but we haven't decided whether he will have another run over hurdles or go straight over fences. Two miles suits him, although he will stay further.

### MR MIX (FR) 6 gr g Al Namix (FR) – Royale Surabaya (FR)

A winner over fences at Worcester in May, he is a novice for this season. He has benefited from stepping up in distance and is the sort to win a good long distance chase one day.

### OLD GUARD 6 b g Notnowcato – Dolma (FR)

We have operated on his wind during the summer and hopefully that will make a difference. Successful in one of his two chases last season, we will probably mix and match between hurdles and fences this season. We will have a look at some of the Graduation chases for him, too.

### OVERLAND FLYER (IRE) 6 b g Westerner – Love Train (IRE)

A dual winning pointer with Jack Barber, he won by twenty two lengths on his first run for us in a three mile maiden hurdle at Taunton in January. He then injured himself when disappointing at Musselburgh next time. A real stayer, he will go novice chasing.

### PEAK TO PEAK (IRE) 5 br g Authorized (IRE) – Bayourida (USA)

A three times winner over hurdles including at Plumpton and Chepstow during the spring, he will be aimed at the Silver Trophy at Chepstow (14th October) and then continue in two and a half miles handicap hurdles.

### PERSIAN DELIGHT 7 b g Lucarno (USA) – Persian Walk (FR)

Having missed the previous season due to injury, he returned last year and, following two placed efforts, he won over hurdles at Wincanton in February. A seven year old, he will go novice chasing.

**PETER THE MAYO MAN (IRE) 7 ch g Dylan Thomas (IRE) – Mommkin**
A useful hurdler for Neil Mulholland last season, he won three times and was third in the Grade 2 Dovecote Novices' Hurdle at Kempton. The Million In Mind partnership bought him at the Doncaster May Sales and the plan is to send him novice chasing.

**POLITOLOGUE (FR) 6 gr g Poliglote – Scarlet Row (FR)**
A high-class novice chaser last season, he won three times including a Grade 2 at Ascot and held every chance when falling at the last in the Grade 1 Maghull Novices' Chase at Aintree. Although he stays two and a half miles, I think two miles may prove to be his optimum trip being ridden positively. He spent the summer with his owners and, provided he is ready in time, we may aim him at the Haldon Gold Cup at Exeter (7th November).

**POSH TRISH (IRE) 4 b f Stowaway – Moscow Demon (IRE)**
An easy winner of her only Irish point-to-point for Shark Hanlon, we bought her at the Cheltenham March Sale. She looks a soft ground mare who will probably have a run in a bumper and then go hurdling.

**PRESENT MAN (IRE) 7 b g Presenting – Glen's Gale (IRE)**
A Grade 2 winner at Doncaster over three miles, he enjoyed a very good season over fences winning four times overall and is now rated 142. Still a novice over hurdles, we may give him a run over hurdles before aiming him at the Badger Ales Chase at Wincanton (11th November).

**PTIT ZIG (FR) 8 b g Great Pretender (IRE) – Red Rym (FR)**
Rated 158 over hurdles and 157 over fences, he isn't the easiest horse to place. He ran some good races in defeat over hurdles last season though including when third in a Grade 1 at Auteuil in November. Runner-up at Sandown on the final day of the season, he may go back over fences.

**RIDGEWAY FLYER 6 b g Tobougg (IRE) – Running For Annie**
A bumper and dual winner over hurdles for Harry Fry, he joined us during the summer. Rated 130 over hurdles, he will go novice chasing and appears to be effective over two and two and a half miles.

**RISK AND ROLL (FR) 3 b g No Risk At All (FR) – Rolie De Vindecy (FR)**
A new recruit from France, he is a nice horse who finished fourth in a Listed hurdle at Auteuil in April on his only start. He will go juvenile hurdling.

**ROMAIN DE SENAM (FR) 5 b g Saint Des Saints (FR) – Salvatrixe (FR)**
He is a nice horse who won over fences at Leicester before running well at Aintree and Ayr in the spring. Runner-up at the latter venue over two miles, we will step him up in trip and aim him at something like the Betvictor Gold Cup at Cheltenham (18th November).

**SAMETEGAL (FR) 8 b g Saint Des Saints (FR) – Loya Lescribaa (FR)**
Absent last season, he is back and will be running in the good two and a half miles handicap chases. He has only had a handful of races over fences and hasn't raced since winning the Grade 3 Greatwood Gold Cup at Newbury in March 2016.

**SAO (FR) 3 b g Great Pretender (IRE) – Miss Country (FR)**
A half-brother to Frodon, he is another French recruit who won over hurdles at Compiegne in May for Guillaume Macaire. He is an interesting prospect for juvenile hurdles.

### SAN BENEDETO (FR) 6 ch g Layman (USA) – Cinco Baidy (FR)
He had a fantastic season over fences winning six times, culminating in victory in the Grade 1 Maghull Novices' Chase at Aintree on Grand National day. Benefitting from dropping back to two miles and racing on decent ground, he will start in the Haldon Gold Cup at Exeter (7th November) and then go to Ascot for a £100,000 two mile chase (25th November).

### SAPHIR DU RHEU (FR) 8 gr g Al Namix (FR) – Dona Du Rheu (FR)
Ran a cracker in the Cheltenham Gold Cup finishing fifth, having won at Kelso on his previous start. Unfortunately, he injured himself when falling in the Grand National and therefore won't be running until after Christmas. His main target is the Gold Cup once again.

### SECRET INVESTOR 5 b g Kayf Tara – Silver Charmer
A very nice horse who won his only point-to-point in Ireland before we purchased him. He needed his first run for us at Ascot in November but still ran promisingly finishing second. Keen that day, he will continue in two and a half mile novice hurdles. I like him a lot.

### SILSOL (GER) 8 b g Soldier Hollow – Silveria (GER)
A better hurdler than chaser, he won the Grade 2 West Yorkshire Hurdle at Wetherby but then suffered an injury and missed the rest of the campaign. Back in work, he will go back to Wetherby for the same race (4th November).

### SOME MAN (IRE) 4 b g Beat Hollow – Miss Denman (IRE)
He is a very nice four year old who we bought at the Aintree Grand National sale in April. A half-brother to Polly Peachum, he was a five lengths winner of his only Irish point the previous month. Only four, he will have a run in a bumper and then go novice hurdling.

### THE DELLERCHECKOUT (IRE) 4 b g Getaway (GER) – Loreley (IRE)
From the family of Granville Again and Morley Street, he won his only point-to-point in Ireland in March and we purchased him on behalf of John Hales later the same month at the Cheltenham Sale. He is another who will probably start off in a bumper.

### TOMMY HALLINAN (IRE) 3 b g Intense Focus (USA) – Bowstring (IRE)
A very consistent horse on the Flat in Ireland trained by Willie McCreery. Placed in his first four races on soft and heavy ground, he won over ten furlongs at Cork on fast ground in May and was bought soon afterwards. A horse with plenty of size, he will go juvenile hurdling.

### TOMMY SILVER (FR) 5 b g Silver Cross (FR) – Sainte Mante (FR)
Had a good season winning twice, including the Sussex Champion Hurdle at Plumpton, before running creditably in the Scottish Champion Hurdle. He will go novice chasing over two miles on decent ground.

### TOPOFTHEGAME (IRE) 5 b g Flemensfirth (USA) – Derry Vale (IRE)
A big horse who won his only Irish point-to-point, we purposely looked after him last season because his future lies over fences. A winner over hurdles at Ascot in December, he was narrowly beaten at the same track on his final run. He is a very nice prospect for novice chases over two and a half miles plus.

### TOUCH KICK (IRE) 6 b g Presenting – Bay Pearl (FR)
A winner over hurdles at Taunton, he remains a novice until the end of October. We may therefore give him another run over hurdles before going novice chasing. That will be his job.

### VICENTE (FR) 8 b g Dom Alco (FR) – Ireland (FR)
Unfortunately, he fell at the first in the Grand National but gained ample compensation a fortnight later when winning the Scottish National for the second consecutive year. He has always been a better horse in the spring when racing on good ground and we will be aiming him at the good handicaps, culminating in the Grand National once again.

### WARRIOR'S TALE 8 b g Midnight Legend – Samadara (FR)
A three times winner over fences and rated 143, he won a couple of handicaps at Newbury in the spring. He is a nice horse who will be running in two and a half mile handicap chases on decent ground.

### WESTERN HONOUR (IRE) 5 b g Westerner – Cailins Honour (IRE)
Bought at the Cheltenham Sale in March on behalf of the Thompsons, he won his only Irish point-to-point for Stuart Crawford earlier the same month. He looks a nice horse to run in a bumper before going hurdling.

### WINNINGTRY (IRE) 6 br g Flemensfirth (USA) – Jeruflo (IRE)
Benefited from stepping up in trip in the spring winning over two and a half miles at Wincanton and then over three miles at Ayr's Scottish National meeting. Rated 130 over hurdles, he will go novice chasing.

### WORTHY FARM (IRE) 4 b g Beneficial – Muckle Flugga (IRE)
A half-brother to Dan Skelton's Mister Miyagi, he is a very nice young horse who won his only point-to-point by a long way for Jack Barber. He is another who will make his Rules debut in a bumper.

### ZUBAYR (IRE) 5 b g Authorized (IRE) – Zaziyra (IRE)
Beaten a short head in the Scottish Champion Hurdle at Ayr, he has been running very well on the Flat during the summer winning at Kempton and finishing a nose second at Haydock. He will go back over hurdles and I think two and a half miles on good ground is ideal.

The following are set to go **HUNTER CHASING**:
**CAID DU BERLAIS, VIRAK, VIVALDI COLLONGES, WONDERFUL CHARM.**

---

**TRAINER'S HORSE TO FOLLOW: POLITOLOGUE**

---

# Ben PAULING
Stables: Bourton Hill Farm, Bourton-On-The-Water, Gloucestershire.
2016/2017: 32 Winners / 199 Runners 16% Prize-Money £294,864
www.benpaulingracing.com

### A HARE BREATH (IRE) 9 b g Alkaadhem – Lady Willmurt (IRE)
He has undergone an operation on his back after we found he was suffering from a kissing spine. He wasn't jumping as well as he can. I have been pleased with him since the operation and he looks fantastic. Despite winning over fences at Bangor last season, I think he is more of a hurdler so we are going to keep him over timber. Fourth in the Greatwood Hurdle at Cheltenham (19th November) last season, he was hampered late on and would have finished even closer with a clear run. Only a couple of pounds higher now, he is a year older but I think it is worth having another crack at the race. He deserves to win a big race and, even though he is a nine year old, there are very few miles on the clock. The *Betfair* Hurdle at Newbury in February is another possible target later on.

### ALPINE SECRET (IRE) 5 br g Stowaway – Squaw Valley (IRE)

Backward mentally, I am hoping he is well handicapped off a mark of 103. He was in the process of running well on his latest outing at Warwick when nearly carried out at the third last. An out and out chaser in the making, he will continue over hurdles for the time being though.

### ALWAYS LION (IRE) 7 b g Let The Lion Roar – Addie's Choice (IRE)

A lovely horse who returned from a lengthy spell on the sidelines to win on his chasing debut at Market Rasen in May. He only just does enough in his races and therefore will hopefully stay ahead of the handicapper. Two and a half miles on a stiff track is OK but he stays three miles as well. Raised five pounds for his win last time, he remains on a fair mark.

### BALLY GILBERT (IRE) 6 ch g Stowaway – Reedsbuck (FR)

I thought a lot of him as a bumper horse chasing home Mount Mews at Market Rasen one day. However, he flattered to deceive over hurdles last season. He made his hurdles debut at Cheltenham in November but came back badly jarred up. There is no doubt he is a horse with ability and I thought he would win on his final run at Newbury in March. Halfway down the backstraight though, Nico (De Boinville) said he made a noise so we have operated on his wind since. A relentless galloper, he will go over fences and we will start him off in a novices' handicap chase over two and a half or three miles. A very good jumper, if he can get in a rhythm over fences I think he will do well.

### BARLEY HILL (IRE) 4 ch g Stowaway – Saysi (IRE)

A nice unraced horse, he is a proper chasing type for the future. Physically, he has done well and shown a bit of promise in his work at home. We will start him off in a bumper before going over hurdles.

### BARTERS HILL (IRE) 7 b g Kalanisi (IRE) – Circle The Wagons (IRE)

He is in very good form at home and I am really pleased with him at the moment. When we turned him out for the summer, he had some swelling around his hock. However, we have hopefully sorted that out and he has been moving well since. He is spending plenty of time on the water treadmill and then he will be ridden out. He appears to be very happy within himself and I am more confident that he will be racing around Christmas time or just after than I was previously. He will only run when he is ready though and we certainly won't rush him because he owes us nothing. The plan would be to revert to hurdling because I feel he is still a well handicapped horse.

### BOREHAM BILL (IRE) 5 b g Tikkanen (USA) – Crimond (IRE)

A horse I hold in high regard, he overcame greenness to win on his debut at Market Rasen. We then ran him in the Listed bumper at Cheltenham in November and he battled all the way to the line before finishing second. A very enthusiastic horse, he ran flat next time though in another Listed contest at Ascot. Following that run, he went weak and, while he ran OK at Huntingdon in the spring, he wasn't at his best. He is a brilliant jumper and we will send him novice hurdling over two and a half miles. David Bass believes he wants nice ground and, all being well, he will be in action by late October/early November.

### CANGODEMAYO 5 b m Lucarno (USA) – Cadoutene (FR)

By an unfashionable sire, she won her only Irish point-to-point before we bought her at the Cheltenham February Sale. We like her a lot and toyed with the idea of running her in a bumper at the Punchestown Festival. We decided to give her a break instead but she has shown enough to suggest she can win a mares' bumper. She could be the nicest mare I have trained.

## CARLOS DU FRUITIER (FR) 5 b g Diableneyev (USA) – Odyssee Madrik (FR)

Placed in an Irish point, we didn't really know what we had got when he had his first run for us in a bumper at Warwick. He won well though and then finished runner-up at Newcastle conceding a stone to the winner. We ran him in the championship bumper at Aintree and, while he ran respectably, my horses weren't right at the time. An athletic horse, I view him as a 130s/140s horse for novice hurdles this season. Two and a half miles is likely to be his trip, although it wouldn't surprise me if he won over two miles before we step him up in distance. He isn't slow.

## CAVERNOUS (IRE) 4 br g Court Cave (IRE) – Willoughby Sue (IRE)

An unraced full-brother to Willoughby Court, he is a horse I like a lot. He didn't race last season having gone weak but his work has pleased us and I would fully expect him to win a bumper. Indeed, I think he could be Aintree bumper class. He does have a few of his brother's traits, including being slightly nervous.

## COEUR PENSIF (FR) 5 br g Laveron – Lady Easter (FR)

We purchased him at the Doncaster May Sales having finished runner-up in his only Irish point. French bred, I think he has been on the go since being a two year old but is a nice type with a touch of class. He jumps well, handles soft ground and is likely to want two and a half to three miles over hurdles.

## CREEP DESBOIS (FR) 5 b g Great Pretender (IRE) – Brigade Mondaine (FR)

He didn't enjoy the smoothest of campaigns last term. Despite running well on his reappearance at Newbury, he wasn't at peak fitness and was then in the process of running a big race at Wetherby when stumbling on landing at the third last. He flew home to finish fourth having lost valuable ground. A good winner at Doncaster in February, we were aiming him at the EBF Final at Sandown the following month but he got cast in his box ten days before the race, which was frustrating to say the least. He then missed the cut at Aintree before ending his season by finishing third at Kempton in April. It was too sharp for him though. A horse I like, he wants to win and I think he will do well in novice handicap chases this season. However, he will have another run over hurdles beforehand. He will stay three miles.

## CYRIUS MORIVIERE (FR) 7 b g Vendangeur (IRE) – Sagesse Moriviere (FR)

Endured a frustrating season over fences but he has plenty of ability. He was in the process of running well against Might Bite on his chasing debut at Doncaster when falling and then he was unfortunate not to win at the same track in January when the saddle slipped two out. I didn't want to lose his novice status at the end of the season so we decided to let him take his chance in the Grade 1 novice chase at Aintree and give his owners a day out. The key to him is getting into a rhythm over fences. If he can do that, then he will be hard to beat. He is more than capable of winning races over two and two and a half miles.

## DELIRE D'ESTRUVAL (FR) 4 b g Youmzain (IRE) – Question D'Estruval (FR)

I am delighted to be training for Simon Munir and Isaac Souede. Only a four year old, he is a nice horse who has been placed over hurdles and fences in France. Runner-up in a chase at Auteuil in early April, the form looks good and, while he isn't the biggest, he jumps well and has produced some smart pieces of work since arriving. I think trips around two and a quarter and two and a half miles will bring out the best in him.

## DRUMACOO (IRE) 8 b g Oscar (IRE) – My Native (IRE)

A fragile horse but one with a lot of ability. We considered running him in the Hennessy last season but decided it was too tough a task first time out. We did, however, run him at Newbury in a Graduation chase the following month but he fell at the third and hasn't raced since. We sent him back to Ireland for the spring/summer but he is back now and I still think he can win a nice staying handicap. I envisage him winning one of those decent Saturday races at Sandown during the winter. The key to him though is soft ground.

## EQUUS SECRETUS (IRE) 5 b g Brian Boru – Bodega Bay (IRE)

I like him. He won his only English point-to-point before we bought him at the Cheltenham April Sale. I think he could be useful and above average for an English pointer. He must be one of the strongest horses I have ever trained. A good jumper, he strikes me as the sort who will travel well in his novice hurdles this season.

## GOWITHTHEFLOW (IRE) 4 b g Westerner – Maryiver (IRE)

Successful in his point-to-point for Denis Murphy in Ireland, we acquired him at the Cheltenham Sale in June and he arrived with a big reputation. I think the fact he won on quick ground put quite a lot of people off at the sale but he appears to have everything. Both Nico (De Boinville) and David (Bass) have ridden him at home and like him a lot. I will be surprised if he doesn't win a bumper.

## HERO'S CREEK (IRE) 4 br g Kalanisi (IRE) – Iktitafs Sister (IRE)

One of our nicest unraced bumper horses, he would have run last season but he slipped on the ice and cracked his hip. A great big rangy chasing type, he is naturally talented and floats along the ground. When he returns, I think he will take high rank.

## HIDDEN GLEN (IRE) 4 ch g Stowaway – Gleanntan (IRE)

Another very nice unraced bumper horse who has shown plenty at home. He moves well and has the air of a very good horse. He was nearly ready to run in the spring but we gave him more time and he should be in action during the Autumn.

## HIGH BRIDGE 6 b g Monsun (GER) – Ameerat

He is in good order and I think he is another for the Greatwood Hurdle at Cheltenham (19th November). He had a fantastic season prior to the Cheltenham Festival winning three times at Newbury (twice) and Catterick. We then ran him in the Supreme Novices' Hurdle and I thought he would finish in the first three. However, I gave Alex (Ferguson) the wrong instructions and he saw too much daylight throughout. He still ran creditably finishing ninth. Rated 141, he remains on a workable mark and the *Betfair* Hurdle at Newbury is another likely target in the second half of the season. A big strong horse who travels well, the flat track at Newbury suits him well.

## JALEO (GER) 5 ch g New Approach (IRE) – Jambalaya (GER)

A winner on his first start for us at Lingfield in December, he suffered two nasty falls later in the season and they left their mark. We ran him in the County Hurdle at the Festival but he got worked up beforehand and then fell at the final flight. Despite the fact he is Flat bred, I think he will jump fences one day. In the meantime, he remains nicely handicapped over hurdles with two and a half miles being his trip.

## KILDISART (IRE) 5 br g Dubai Destination (USA) – Princess Mairead (IRE)

Runner-up in an Irish point, he is a nice horse who has only raced once for us. Second in a bumper at Bangor in December, he wasn't 100% afterwards so we gave him the rest of the season off and an early summer break. Capable of winning a bumper, he jumps well and will be suited by two and a half miles over hurdles.

## LE BREUIL (FR) 5 ch g Anzillero (GER) – Slew Dancer

I think the world of him and I've never hidden the regard in which I hold him. He wasn't fully tuned up when beaten on his reappearance in a bumper at Bangor but then won easily over hurdles at Sedgefield in November. Returning in March, he looked very good when winning at Newbury beating Benatar (subsequently fourth behind Finian's Oscar in a Grade 1 at Aintree) by nine lengths. We then took him to Aintree but I would put a line through that performance because our horses weren't right at the time, plus he was sick afterwards. I think he is out of the top drawer. The plan is to stay over hurdles because I believe we have got unfinished business and we will target him at a decent handicap off his mark of 139. I think he will be a Graded horse by mid season.

### LINENHALL (IRE) 5 ch g Stowaway – Option (IRE)
We have always thought a lot of him but things never really fell into place last season. Placed in two of his four bumpers, he jumps well and Nico (De Boinville) likes him. I think he will do well over hurdles and, while he will start off over two and a half miles, he will stay three.

### MARKOV (IRE) 7 b g Morozov (USA) – Willoughby Sue (IRE)
A half-brother to Willoughby Court, I think he is well handicapped. Still a maiden over hurdles, he was unlucky not to win at Doncaster in March when hitting the front too soon. Over the top by the end of the season, he will go over fences and be aimed at novice handicap chases. I like him.

### MARTEN (FR) 5 b g Martaline – Commande Blue (FR)
We like him a lot and he won a bumper at Warwick on his second run benefiting from a patient ride. He then took his chance in a Listed bumper at Newbury in February but hated the ground. Given a good break since, he is a very big horse who should be useful over hurdles this season. Two and a half miles ought to be to his liking.

### MONK'S VIEW 4 bl g Multiplex – Evelith Abbey (IRE)
Unraced, he is a very smart horse who really fills the eye. Measuring 16.2hh, his homework has been very good and, if reproducing that on the track, he could be our best bumper horse.

### NESTOR PARK (FR) 4 b g Walk In The Park (IRE) – Cila (FR)
Another nice unraced bumper horse for this season, he was too weak to run in the spring. A lovely honest type, he has a huge stride and I think he will be suited by soft ground.

### NOBUTTABOY (IRE) 6 b g Darsi (FR) – Buckalong (IRE)
An able horse, he won over hurdles at Southwell last season but we realised he wants a break of around five weeks between his races. With that in mind, he will only have four or five races this term. Another who will go novice handicap chasing, he handles soft ground and has plenty of scope.

### PERFECT PIRATE 5 b g Black Sam Bellamy (IRE) – Supreme Gem (IRE)
He is a lovely horse who won on his hurdles debut at Towcester before finishing second under a penalty in bad ground at Kelso. I would forget his final run at Uttoxeter because the ground was like glue. He wants two and a half miles and we are going to send him over fences. He has grown since last season and is another with plenty of scope.

### RED INDIAN 5 b g Sulamani (IRE) – Rafiya
Endured something of a stop start season last year. He won at Ffos Las in December but was then very sick afterwards. Runner-up at Kelso on his next start, he was sick again and didn't return until mid May. Only beaten half a length at Warwick, I think he will make a decent handicap hurdler this season. Two miles in testing conditions is fine but he stays two and a half on better ground.

### SILVER HOLLOW 5 gr g Beat Hollow – Onemix
He wasn't himself on his debut at Exeter and returned with a snotty nose. A laid back individual, I like him and he will go straight over hurdles.

### TEL'ART (FR) 3 b g Montmartre (FR) – Textuelle (FR)
Unraced, he came in during the summer and looks a sharp horse. It wouldn't surprise me if he was running in junior bumpers before Christmas.

### TENNEWROW (IRE) 5 b m Stowaway – Silent Supreme (IRE)
Bought at the Doncaster May Sales, she won the second of her two Irish points. She goes nicely at home and will be aimed at mares' only novice hurdles over two and a half to three miles.

### TWO SWALLOWS 7 b m Kayf Tara – One Gulp
I was delighted with her because she had a great season three of her five races and never finishing out of the first two. She has a fabulous attitude and really tries in her races. A mare with a lot of heart, she is only tiny but she jumps well and we are going to send her novice chasing.

### WAY BACK THEN (IRE) 6 b g Robin Des Champs (FR) – Ashwell Lady (IRE)
He could be useful over hurdles this season. An ex-Irish pointer, he won a decent bumper at Ludlow in November on his first run for us. However, he came back with a hairline fracture of his knee and missed the remainder of the campaign. He has been with Henrietta Knight during the summer and she has been pleased with him. The plan is to send him straight over hurdles.

### WHIN PARK 5 b g Great Pretender (IRE) – Pocahontas (FR)
He goes well at home and there is no doubt he has ability but has failed to reproduce it on the track so far. He will benefit from stepping up to two and a half miles and could be well handicapped if translating his homework to the racecourse.

### WILLOUGHBY COURT (IRE) 6 br g Court Cave (IRE) – Willoughby Sue (IRE)
Has summered brilliantly, I couldn't be happier with him and he is becoming more sensible every year. We were obviously delighted with him last season winning three times, culminating in victory in the Neptune Investments Novices' Hurdle at the Cheltenham Festival. It was my first Festival winner, he proved how good he is and his victory there showed he handles any ground because it was on the quick side of good that day. As regards this season, we have two options. I have always considered him a chaser in the making and that is the most likely route we will take. We will start schooling him over fences and I have a feeling he will be electric. The other possibility is staying over hurdles and seeing if he is good enough to develop into a Stayers' Hurdle contender, although I am keen to keep him to shorter distances for the time being. In all likelihood, he will start off over fences at somewhere like Bangor or Huntingdon in late October/ early November (2m 4f) and we will go from there. Something like the Dipper Novices' Chase at Cheltenham on New Year's Day is an obvious mid season target but, if we decided to step him up to three miles, then the Kauto Star Novices' Chase at Kempton on Boxing Day comes into the equation. Either way, he is a very exciting prospect.

### WORLD PREMIER (FR) 4 gr g Montmartre (FR) – Kelbelange (FR)
Despite being green, he looked very good when making a winning debut in a bumper at Warwick. His victory wasn't a surprise because he had produced some nice work at home beforehand. He has been sold to stay in the yard and now belongs to J.P.McManus, which I am delighted about. It is great for the yard to have an owner of his stature. We will discuss plans whether he has another run in a bumper but I would have thought he is more likely to go novice hurdling over two and a half miles. I think he could be very useful.

---

**TRAINER'S HORSE TO FOLLOW: BOREHAM BILL**

**TRAINER'S TOP 4 UNRACED BUMPERS HORSES (Alphabetical order):**
**CAVERNOUS, HERO'S CREEK, HIDDEN GLEN & MONK'S VIEW**

# David PIPE

**Stables: Pond House, Nicholashayne, Wellington, Somerset.**
**2016/2017: 59 Winners / 487 Runners 12% Prize-Money £778,983**
**www.davidpipe.com**

### ALDRIN (FR) 4 b g New Approach (IRE) – Trip To The Moon
Owned by ValueRacingClub.co.uk, he was bought at the Goffs January Sale at Doncaster having run twice on the Flat for Godolphin. He has always shown a lot of speed at home since arriving and, having raced keenly on his hurdling debut at Uttoxeter in June, he benefited from a more patient ride at Bangor next time winning easily. We decided to drop him in and he quickened up well. Only fifth next time in a handicap at Newton Abbot, he made a noise and will have surgery on his wind at some stage. He still has a bit to learn jumping wise but hopefully he will provide his owners with plenty of fun both over hurdles and on the Flat. I think he is a top of the ground horse, who will have a winter break.

### AURILLAC (FR) 7 gr g Martaline – Ombrelle (FR)
A new arrival, we haven't done a lot with him yet but he is a lovely stamp of a horse. I have always followed his career because his part owner Derrick Mossop had Soll in training with us and he had some good form over fences last season without winning. Placed on four occasions at the likes of Chepstow, Ascot and Newbury, he lost his way a bit thereafter and remains a novice.

### BIDOUREY (FR) 6 b g Voix Du Nord (FR) – Love Wisky (FR)
He is a lovely horse but unfortunately he has had his issues and hasn't raced since the end of 2015. All being well, he will be back in action during the second half of the season and we still have high hopes for him. Thankfully, he still has time on his side. I would imagine he will stay over hurdles.

### CHAMPERS ON ICE (IRE) 7 gr g Robin Des Champs (FR) – Miss Nova
He is in good form at home and, while he has always been a very laid back horse, he was even more so last season. Despite winning on his chasing debut at Uttoxeter and running a good race behind American at Warwick, which is strong form, he is not a natural over fences. He made too many mistakes in the four miler at the Festival and returned with a nasty cut so we left him off for the rest of the campaign. I would expect him to continue over fences though and we are hoping for better this year. He stays well with something like the Welsh National at Chepstow (27th December) a logical target.

### DAKLONDIKE (IRE) 5 b g Gold Well – Strong Irish (IRE)
Related to Great Endeavour, he is a bit quirky similar to him. He won over hurdles at Lingfield but didn't progress on his next two outings. Hopefully, he will be more relaxed this year and will get back on track. A winning Irish pointer, there is every chance he will go chasing over two and a half miles plus.

### DELFACE (FR) 4 b g Della Francesca (USA) – Septieme Face (USA)
A winner over hurdles in Ireland for Liz Doyle, we bought him in the spring and he has only raced once for us. Successful at Ffos Las in late May, it wasn't the strongest of races but it was a good performance nevertheless making all the running. A novice until the end of October, we have given him a good break since and I am sure he will stay further this time around. He handles soft ground and his mark looks fair.

### DELIRANT (FR) 4 b g Khalkevi (IRE) – Kusea (FR)

An exciting prospect who showed a good level of form in France winning both his starts in APQS Flat races, including a Grade 1 event at Saint-Cloud in November. He was in training with us last season and, while he worked nicely, he was still on the weak side so we decided to give him time. He has arrived back from his summer holiday looking stronger and we are looking forward to running over hurdles, starting over two miles.

### DOCTOR HARPER (IRE) 9 b g Presenting – Supreme Dreamer (IRE)

Narrowly beaten at Cheltenham on New Year's Day, he is probably in the grip of the handicapper. Despite the fact he is by Presenting, soft ground seems to suit him well and he is capable of picking up a decent long distance handicap chase.

### DUC DE BEAUCHENE (FR) 4 b g Saddler Maker (IRE) – Quatia D'Angron (FR)

Suited by soft ground, he will be campaigned in staying novice hurdles. I was pleased with his first run in a bumper at Ffos Las finishing a close second but then the ground had dried out too much at Wetherby next time and we shouldn't have run him. He has summered well and is hopefully a decent prospect.

### EAMON AN CNOIC (IRE) 6 b g Westerner – Nutmeg Tune (IRE)

He did well last season winning twice showing plenty of speed to score at Fakenham and Haydock. Tom (Scudamore) felt he didn't get home over two miles seven in a Pertemps qualifier at Exeter on his final start. I would imagine we will try him over longer distances again at some stage but he is likely to start off over shorter trips and there is every chance he will go chasing.

### EUR GONE WEST (IRE) 4 b g Westerner – Floating Euro (IRE)

Ran well in his only Irish point for Colin Bowe finishing third before we bought him at the Cheltenham June Sale. A well built horse, I think he will be suited by cut in the ground and we will probably start him off in a bumper. I like him.

### FRIDAY NIGHT LIGHT (FR) 4 b g Air Chief Marshal (IRE) – Peninsula (FR)

Previously trained in France by Elie Lellouche, we bought him at the Arqana Sale last November. A winner over a mile and a half on the Flat, he has yet to run for us but he goes nicely at home and we decided to keep him as a novice for this season. We haven't sold him yet but he jumps well and has the speed for two miles.

### GREAT TEMPO (FR) 4 b g Great Pretender (IRE) – Prima Note (FR)

He won a three runner maiden hurdle at Hexham on his first run for us but didn't build on it and was disappointing in his subsequent starts. We have given him a long break which will hopefully sweeten him up because I didn't think he was giving 100%. Only four, he will continue in handicap hurdles.

### ILOVEMINTS 5 b m Kayf Tara – La Harde (FR)

She is a nice mare who ValueRacingClub.co.uk bought at the Doncaster May Sale. She ran in four mares' bumpers for Warren Greatrex winning on her debut at Bangor and finishing third last time at Taunton. We will be aiming her at mares' novice hurdles and, while she will start off over two miles, there is no reason why she won't stay further. She has raced largely on sharp, fast tracks and may benefit from running on more galloping ones this year.

### IRISH PRINCE (IRE) 4 br g Presenting – Court Leader (IRE)

A half-brother to Paloma Blue, who finished runner-up in the championship bumper at Punchestown last spring for Henry De Bromhead, he is a nice unraced horse. Still weak last year, he wasn't a great grubber but has strengthened up and will run in a bumper in the Autumn.

**IT'S OBVIOUS 5 gr g Tobougg (IRE) – Hiho Silver Lining**
Forced to miss last season due to an injury, he was runner-up in an Irish point before we bought him. Back in now, he looks well and it is a case of hopefully making up for lost time. There is every chance he will have a run in a bumper before going hurdling.

**JUST MIDAS (IRE) 4 b g Shantou (USA) – Desert Grail (IRE)**
Another nice unraced horse by a good sire, I have been pleased with him. He has strengthened up during the summer having been weak last year hence he didn't run. He is another who will run in a bumper.

**KEATING (IRE) 5 b g King's Theatre (IRE) – Tus Nua (IRE)**
Bought out of Philip Hobbs' yard at the Doncaster May Sales, he was placed a couple of times over hurdles. He had his first run for us at Newton Abbot in August and I thought he ran well finishing fourth. We then stepped him up in trip at Worcester a fortnight later and he was still leading when losing his rider at the last. I don't think he is going to want the ground too soft.

**KING'S SOCKS (FR) 5 b g King's Best (USA) – Alexandrina (GER)**
He had some very good form in France winning over hurdles and fences and was runner-up in a Grade 1 hurdle last year. Unfortunately, he suffered a tendon injury last Autumn and therefore missed the whole of last season. All being well, he will be running in the second half of this season and we will aim him at decent races.

**LA VATICANE (FR) 8 gr m Turgeon (USA) – Taking Off (FR)**
A winner of a three mile handicap chase at Doncaster last season, she will follow a similar programme and we will look towards some of the mares' chases. Versatile in terms of trip, she isn't always the easiest to predict but she is very capable on her day and I am sure she will win more races.

**MAX DO BRAZIL (FR) 5 b g Blue Bresil (FR) – Lili Valley (FR)**
Listed placed over hurdles in France, he was very disappointing in three runs for us. We liked him at home but he never reproduced it on the track. I think he wants soft ground and two and a half miles is possibly his trip but he needs to show more this season.

**MISS TYNTE (IRE) 5 b m Mahler – Top Quality**
A nice mare who I like, but she was held up with niggling problems last year. She ran well for a long way in a bumper at Carlisle but didn't finish off her race and we haven't run her since. We may give her another run in a bumper before aiming her at mares' novice hurdles.

**MOON RACER (IRE) 8 b g Saffron Walden (FR) – Angel's Folly**
Unfortunately, he suffered with colic during the summer and underwent surgery. Thankfully, they didn't have to take anything out but plans are on hold. He won't be running until the end of the season, if at all this year, but it would be nice if we could get him back for Cheltenham in March. He will be staying over hurdles whenever he does return.

**MR BIG SHOT (IRE) 6 br g Flemensfirth (USA) – Une Etoile (IRE)**
A very big horse, he has done nothing wrong throughout his career winning all three of his races, including twice over hurdles. Workmanlike in victory at Wetherby on his reappearance, he was impressive next time at Carlisle even though he probably didn't beat much. Yet to race beyond two miles, he will get further and is only just starting to fill into his frame. For a big horse, he is very agile but he has been backward mentally and everything is still a game to him. When he won his bumper first time out at Uttoxeter, the penny only dropped with a couple of furlongs to run. I think a step up to two and a half miles will suit him.

### ORCHARD THIEVES (IRE) 5 b g Ask – Ballycleary (IRE)

Runner-up in his only Irish point-to-point before we purchased him at the Cheltenham Festival Sale last year, he was close to running for us before going wrong and therefore missed the whole season. Back in work now, we were pleased with what he did last year before his injury. We had planned to start him in a bumper last season but he is a year older now so we may send him straight over hurdles.

### POKER PLAY (FR) 4 ch g Martaline – Becquarette (FR)

He won over hurdles in France and we bought him at the Cheltenham December Sale. It is never ideal acquiring a horse halfway through the season but I thought he ran a decent race at Kempton in January on a track which wouldn't have suited him. I think he wants soft ground and conditions had dried out too much by the time he ran in the Fred Winter at Cheltenham in March. Only four, he will develop into a lovely chaser one day because that is what he was bought for. In the meantime, he will run in handicap hurdles and should benefit from a step up in trip.

### RAMSES DE TEILLEE (FR) 5 gr g Martaline – Princesse D'Orton (FR)

A winning pointer, he is a nice horse who I have always liked. Placed over hurdles at Taunton and Doncaster, I thought he ran well in the EBF Final at Sandown because it was a rough race and he didn't get the clearest of passages. Still a novice, we have the option of going handicapping as well. Two and a half miles suits him.

### RATHLIN ROSE (IRE) 9 b g Bonbon Rose (FR) – A Plus Ma Puce (FR)

He enjoyed a fantastic season winning the Royal Artillery Gold Cup and Grand Military Cup under Guy Disney at Sandown. Pulled up last time at Haydock, he came back with a nasty cut but that has healed since. A strong stayer who likes soft ground, he will be running in the decent long distance chases.

### SHAAMA GRISE (FR) 5 gr m Montmartre (FR) – Shaama Rose (FR)

She had a good season over hurdles but also a frustrating one. A winner at Chepstow, she finished runner-up in her other three races and ran her heart out every time. Raised in the handicap, as a result, she has a very good attitude. In all likelihood, she will go novice chasing in mares' only events. She jumps well, likes soft ground and I think she will stay three miles eventually. Only five, she has strengthened since last year and is a nice mare who should do well over fences.

### SKINFLINT (IRE) 5 b g Scorpion (IRE) – Gales Hill (IRE)

Another ex-Irish pointer who was close to a run last season, but he suffered an injury and we therefore pulled up stumps and left him off. He has returned to work and may run in a bumper before going hurdling.

### STARCHITECT (IRE) 6 b g Sea The Stars (IRE) – Humilis (IRE)

He is a good horse but I don't think the handicapper has been too kind to him over fences. A winner at Ayr, he ran two decent races at the major Festivals in the spring finishing fifth at Cheltenham and third at Aintree. Despite that, I think three miles one may have stretched him at Aintree, although he could have been feeling the effects of his run at Cheltenham three weeks earlier. He had certainly had enough for the season by the time he ran at Cheltenham again in April. Given a break since, he is a class horse who will hopefully be mixing it in the top two and a half mile handicaps.

### TAJ BADALANDABAD (IRE) 7 ch g Shantou (USA) – Last Chance Lady (IRE)

Missed last season but is back now and hopefully he will provide his owner with more fun having won two bumpers and four times over hurdles. We haven't discussed any plans, but he is likely to go over fences. He likes soft ground and stays well and ought to make a nice chaser.

### TIGGER TWO (IRE) 5 b g Getaway (GER) – Anne Hathaway (IRE)
A nice unraced horse who was in training last year but was still weak. He is light framed and doesn't carry much condition but I like him and we may run him in a bumper in the Autumn.

### TIMEFORBEN (IRE) 5 ch m Beneficial – Shokalocka Baby (IRE)
She won her only point-to-point in Ireland in November and we bought her the following month at the Cheltenham Sale. She wasn't the healthiest when she arrived so we decided to leave her off and give her time. We will look for a mares' bumper before going hurdling.

### UN TEMPS POUR TOUT (IRE) 8 b g Robin Des Champs (FR) – Rougedespoir (FR)
He came up trumps once again winning the Ultima Handicap Chase at the Cheltenham Festival for the second consecutive year. He has been a fantastic horse for his connections and we have found he is a better horse during the second half of the season. There is every chance he will have an entry in the Grand National and we will probably mix and match between hurdles and fences in the meantime.

### VANITEUX (FR) 8 br g Voix Du Nord (FR) – Expoville (FR)
Purchased at the Doncaster May Sale, he had a very good level of form for Nicky Henderson, including two Listed chase wins at Kempton and Ayr last season. Officially rated 158 over fences and 150 over hurdles, he won't necessarily be the easiest horse to win with but I think he will earn plenty of prize-money contesting good races. Suited by two and two and a half miles, we can mix and match between hurdles and fences, which will give us plenty of options.

### VIEUX LION ROUGE (FR) 8 ch g Sabiango (GER) – Indecise (FR)
He had a great season winning the Becher Chase at Aintree and Grand National Trial at Haydock. Sixth in the Grand National in April, he got a bit closer than the previous year but once again didn't quite see out of the trip. I am sure his owners would love to have another crack at the race and I must say he looks the best he has ever done following his summer break. He seems to jump the National fences better than park fences and I would think he will head back to Aintree for the Becher Chase (9th December) once again in the meantime.

### WARTHOG (FR) 5 gr g Martaline – Shekira (FR)
A ten lengths winner of an Irish point for Denis Murphy, he had two runs for us in bumpers during the spring. A good second at Chepstow, he ran well for a long way next time at Punchestown but didn't quite see the race out. An old fashioned chasing type, he wants soft ground and there is a possibility he will go straight over fences. He jumped very well when winning his point gaining ground at nearly every fence. I like him.

---

**TRAINER'S HORSE TO FOLLOW: MR BIG SHOT**

---

# Colin TIZZARD
**Stables: Spurles Farm, Milborne Port, Sherborne, Dorset.**
**2016/2017: 57 Winners / 405 Runners 14% Prize-Money £2,041,055**
www.colintizzard.co.uk

### ALARY (FR) 7 ch g Dream Well (FR) – Cate Bleue (FR)
He had some high-class form in France being placed twice at Grade 1 level. However, he took time to acclimatise having arrived towards the end of last year. Despite that, I thought he ran well in the Ryanair Chase at Cheltenham. I have been pleased with him during the summer because he has really filled out. The plan is to give him one run and then the Ladbrokes Gold Cup (formerly the Hennessy Gold Cup) at Newbury (2nd December). Even though he is quick enough to run over shorter trips, we will be campaigning him over three miles plus for the time being.

### BALLY LONGFORD (IRE) 9 b g Gold Well – Stay On Line (IRE)

Restricted to only three races last season due to a stress fracture, he was placed twice at Cheltenham over trips ranging from two miles to three and a quarter. All being well, he will be in action at Cheltenham's first meeting (27th/28th October) and I think he is better suited by longer distances. His mark looks OK.

### BANG ON FRANKIE (IRE) 5 br g Kalanisi (IRE) – Shuil Abbey (IRE)

A lovely horse who surprised me when running so well on his debut in a Listed bumper at Ascot finishing third. His next run at Newbury was adequate but he is a big horse who can only improve. There is a possibility he will have another run in a bumper before going hurdling. Trips around two or two and a half miles will suit him because he has plenty of speed.

### CUE CARD 11 b g King's Theatre (IRE) – Wicked Crack (IRE)

He looks immaculate following his summer break and is running around like a three year old. I think he is every bit as good as he was and enjoyed another a great season winning two Grade 1s, including the *Betfair* Chase at Haydock for a third time. He will follow the same route starting off in the Charlie Hall Chase at Wetherby (4th November), the *Betfair* Chase again (25th November) and then the King George. Depending on how he performs, I would imagine he will then contest the Ascot Chase again, which he won last season, and a decision will be made whether he tackles the Gold Cup or Ryanair Chase at Cheltenham in March.

### DARLAC (FR) 4 b g Lucarno (USA) – Pail Mel (FR)

Bought at the Cheltenham June Sale, he was unlucky not to win the second of his two Irish points when making a mistake at the last fence and being headed on the run-in. I haven't sold him yet but he is a lovely horse who looks the business. Only four, he will run in a bumper before going hurdling.

### ELEGANT ESCAPE (IRE) 5 b g Dubai Destination (USA) – Graineuaile (IRE)

A gorgeous horse, he is a lovely big chaser in the making and that will be his job this season. I was very pleased with him last year winning twice over hurdles at Chepstow and Ascot. Fourth in the Grade 1 Challow Hurdle at Newbury, he ran well at the Festival, too, finishing seventh in the Albert Bartlett Novices' Hurdle. A former pointer, he has everything to make a very nice chaser. We will probably start him off over two and half miles but he is a stayer who will come into his own over three.

### FINIAN'S OSCAR (IRE) 5 b g Oscar (IRE) – Trinity Alley (IRE)

An exciting horse, he is back cantering and we are going to send him novice chasing. A dual Grade 1 winner over hurdles last season at Sandown and Aintree, he was headed on the line at Punchestown but ran another very good race. I don't view him as a Champion Hurdle horse or a Stayers' Hurdle one either so we are keen to send him over fences. Two and a half miles suits him well and there is no doubt he is very classy. A winning Irish pointer, he jumps well at home and is a gorgeous horse. He is the sort every trainer would love to have.

### FOX NORTON (FR) 7 b g Lando (GER) – Natt Musik (FR)

He had a tremendous season winning three times, including the Grade 1 Melling Chase at Aintree and Champion Chase at Punchestown. He very nearly won the Queen Mother Champion Chase at Cheltenham, too, failing by a head to catch the winner Special Tiara. I am sure he will stay three miles but Alan Potts is keen to keep him and Sizing John apart. We will therefore start him off over two miles with the Shloer Chase at Cheltenham (19th November), a race he won last year, likely to be his first target followed by the Tingle Creek at Sandown (9th December). Obviously, circumstances could change and I am sure we will give him an entry in the King George just in case something happens in the meantime. He looks very well following his summer holiday.

## GOLDEN SUNRISE (IRE) 4 ch g Stowaway – Fairy Dawn (IRE)

Only four, he is a beautiful young horse. Fourth on his debut in a bumper at Fontwell in February, he may have at least one more run in a bumper before going novice hurdling. He is a lovely big horse and hopefully one for the future.

## KALARIKA (IRE) 4 br f Kalanisi (IRE) – Katariya (IRE)

A nice big mare, she ran very well first time out in a bumper at Newbury but had a hard race. Third next time at Chepstow, she could have another run in a mares' bumper before going hurdling.

## KILBRICKEN STORM (IRE) 6 b g Oscar (IRE) – Kilbricken Leader (IRE)

We bought him at the Doncaster May Sales having won the third of his three Irish points. A six year old by Oscar, he looks a nice horse who will run over hurdles to begin with and then we will decide whether to send him chasing in the New Year.

## KINGS WALK (IRE) 6 b g King's Theatre (IRE) – Shuil Sionnach (IRE)

He will go chasing and is one we have always liked. A winner over hurdles at Plumpton, he finished third at Sandown in a competitive handicap on the final day of the season. We have been waiting for him to show his true ability because he works well at home. Rated 120, we will aim him at a novices' handicap chase and go from there. Yet to race beyond two and a half miles, he looks a stayer and will get three miles.

## LOSTINTRANSLATION (IRE) 5 b g Flemensfirth (IRE) – Falika (FR)

Fourth in his only Irish point last year, he has yet to run for us but ought to be out in October. We were going to run him in the spring but the ground was too firm. He may start in a bumper before going hurdling.

## MICK THONIC (FR) 7 gr g Maresca Sorrento (FR) – Mick Madona (FR)

A winner over fences at Cheltenham in April, he remains a novice until the end of October. With that in mind, he will go back to Cheltenham for their first meeting (27th/28th October). We have operated on his wind since his last run and I think he will improve. He stays two and a half miles but is rapid over his fences and is probably at his best over the minimum trip.

## MOLINEAUX (IRE) 6 b g King's Theatre (IRE) – Steel Grey Lady (IRE)

A full brother to Grade 1 winning hurdler Voler La Vedette, I think he is one to watch out for. Placed in his two races over hurdles at Wincanton and Taunton, he has taken time to come to himself but looks very well at the moment. We turned him out after his final run and kept him as a novice for this season. I have always liked him.

## NATIVE RIVER (IRE) 7 ch g Indian River (FR) – Native Mo (IRE)

Had a very successful season winning the Hennessy, Welsh National and Denman Chases. Even though he ran very well in the Cheltenham Gold Cup finishing third, he wasn't quite right after the race and came back stiff. He endured hard races each time he ran last season and they may have taken their toll by the time the Festival came around. The race we want to win is the Gold Cup so he probably won't run until Christmas time, possibly over hurdles, before going back to Newbury for the Denman Chase in February and then Cheltenham. The Grand National may also be on his agenda. He is always very good on his second and third runs of the season and we want him at his best in the spring.

## PINGSHOU (IRE) 7 b g Definite Article – Quest of Passion (FR)

A remarkable horse who arrived from Ireland last season with a health warning. He was reportedly a bleeder when trained over there but he has shown no signs of it since coming over and he ended the campaign with a Grade 1 win at Aintree and running a cracker at the Punchestown Festival. We are therefore going to train him as a Champion Hurdle horse. If it doesn't work out, then we will send him chasing in the New Year. The Fighting Fifth at Newcastle (2nd December) is a possible target. He is a huge big tanking horse who achieved a lot in a short space of time last season.

## QUITE BY CHANCE 8 b g Midnight Legend – Hop Fair

A winner at Ascot last Autumn, he also ran some good races in defeat, including at Cheltenham in December, and earned over £60,000 in prize-money. However, I suspect the handicapper has got him at the moment but he will follow a similar path and start off again at Ascot (4th November) in the same race he won last year.

## ROBINSFIRTH (IRE) 8 b g Flemensfirth (USA) – Phardester (IRE)

Not the easiest to train, but he is a very good horse on his day. A winner over fences at Exeter, he then cracked his pelvis at Chepstow and missed the rest of the season. I would like to give him one run and then aim him at the Ladbrokes Gold Cup (formerly the Hennessy) at Newbury (2nd December). If we can get a clear run with him, he is capable of winning a big race because he possesses a hell of an engine. A huge horse, it is amazing he managed to win a bumper first time out as a four year old.

## ROYAL VACATION (IRE) 7 b g King's Theatre (IRE) – Summer Break (IRE)

Despite disappointing on his final two runs, he had a very good season over fences winning three times, including the Grade 1 Kauto Star Novice Chase at Kempton on Boxing Day. He suffered with sore shins and also his wind later on, so he has undergone surgery on the latter since his last run. Hopefully that will make a difference and he has summered well. He is another who could be aimed at the Ladbrokes Gold Cup (Hennessy) at Newbury (2nd December).

## SHANAHAN'S TURN (IRE) 9 b g Indian Danehill (IRE) – Chanson Indienne (FR)

A fine looking horse who won the Galway Plate a couple of years ago when trained in Ireland. He hasn't run for us yet having suffered a stress fracture last season, but he is OK now and we know from his form he is a decent horse. We haven't made any plans but hopefully he will do well for us over fences this season.

## SILVERHOW (IRE) 6 br g Yeats (IRE) – Monte Solaro (IRE)

A half-brother to Altior, we bought him at the Doncaster May Sales and, having raced five times after Christmas last season, winning twice at Sandown and Cheltenham, he looks ideal for his new syndicate. He isn't the biggest but the plan is to send him chasing and I hope he will provide his owners with a lot of fun.

## SIZING CODELCO (IRE) 8 b g Flemensfirth (USA) – La Zingarella (IRE)

He came good in the spring winning by thirteen lengths at Aintree before following up at Punchestown. We tried him in blinkers at the Cheltenham Festival but they didn't work and then left them off at Aintree and he looked a different horse. However, it won't be easy for him now off a mark of 160. We are going to have to pitch him to the big races though with Wetherby and Haydock possibilities. The Ladbrokes Gold Cup at Newbury and Welsh National are other races we will consider. If he went close at Newbury off a mark of 160 then he isn't far off being a Gold Cup horse. Robbie Power thought he improved for the better ground at Aintree.

## SIZING GRANITE (IRE) 9 br g Milan – Hazel's Tisrara (IRE)

Another horse who was going nowhere until the spring. We operated on his wind and he produced a very good performance to win over two and a half miles at Punchestown from Viconte Du Noyer. Raised eleven pounds to 157, he looks bloody well following his summer break – a big black horse who was a Grade 1 winner a couple of years ago. I don't think he is a two miler nowadays and we will be looking towards the top handicaps and conditions chases for him over two and a half miles, although he may stay three.

## SIZING TARA (IRE) 4 b g Kayf Tara – As Was

A lovely unraced horse owned by Alan Potts, he didn't quite make it to the racecourse last spring. He looks well now though and is very strong and is one for bumpers in the Autumn.

## SIZING TENNESSEE (IRE) 9 ch g Robin Des Champs (FR) – Jolivia (FR)

Still a novice over fences, he ran some good races in defeat last season including twice at Cheltenham. He wasn't beaten far but I don't think he was at his very best and I was keen to keep him for another season. He has been around for a while but I think he will be ideal for those early season novice chases and is capable of winning a nice race.

## SLATE HOUSE (IRE) 5 b g Presenting – Bay Pearl (FR)

A beautiful creature who we purchased at the Cheltenham March Sale. A ten lengths winner of an Irish point for Ian Ferguson, he is a big horse who has only raced twice in his life. It is everyone's dream to have a horse like him because he appears to have everything. He was ready to run in April but the ground was too firm so we put him away for the summer. Back cantering, he will probably have a run in a bumper before going novice hurdling.

## STORM HOME (IRE) 5 br g King's Theatre (IRE) – Miss Mayberry (IRE)

Bought at the Cheltenham November Sale, he fell in his only point-to-point when still leading at the last (the unbeaten bumper horse Getabird won the race). Unfortunately, he did the splits at the same time and must have injured himself because he was never quite right last year hence he never raced for us. He is back cantering now and, while he has to stand training, he is potentially very nice. A good looking horse, his form is rock solid and is hopefully one to look forward to.

## TEMPESTATEFLORESCO 9 b g Storming Home – Empress Dagmar

Arrived last year as a three times winning pointer, I thought we would be doing well to win a race with him. He has proved a revelation though winning four times, including the Summer Cup at Uttoxeter in July. Raised nine pounds since to a mark of 146, he is another I may consider for the Ladbrokes Gold Cup (Hennessy) at Newbury in early December. In the meantime, he may have another run over hurdles having finished second in a novice event at Newton Abbot in September. Even though he has been winning on good or faster ground, I don't think it is paramount for him because he also ran well in slower conditions at Chepstow last winter.

## THE BROTHERS (IRE) 4 b g Flemensfirth (USA) – Laboc

A well bred unraced four year old, we have got a lot of young horses who will start off in bumpers and he is one of them. Still weak last year, he was in training during the spring but the ground was too quick. I think he is a nice horse.

## THEATRE GUIDE (IRE) 10 b g King's Theatre (IRE) – Erintante (IRE)

He had another good season winning at Cheltenham in December and then finishing third in the Betbright Chase at Kempton and Bet365 Gold Cup at Sandown. Only beaten half a length at Sandown, he was making a noise during his races though so we have operated on his wind once again. He has had his soft palate done in the past. I am hoping this will be his season and there is every chance he will run in the Ladbrokes Gold Cup (Hennessy Gold Cup) for the fourth time. There is also a possibility he will develop into a Grand National horse, although his owner isn't keen on the idea.

### THISTLECRACK 9 b g Kayf Tara – Ardstown

He is one of the best horses I have seen, producing a brilliant performance to win the King George at Kempton on only his fourth run over fences. Narrowly beaten in the Cotswold Chase at Cheltenham by Many Clouds, we found some heat in his leg about ten days afterwards, which suggests it must have happened during the race. It was only a minor tear on his tendon but enough to stop and he has been fired since. Back in work, the plan is to either give him one run or a racecourse gallop before he attempts to defend his crown in the King George. That run beforehand could be over hurdles.

### ULTRAGOLD (FR) 9 b g Kapgarde (FR) – Hot D'Or (FR)

Another horse who had a productive season winning twice, including the Topham Chase. We had been running him over shorter trips but he was a winner over two miles six at Auteuil before joining us so we decided to step him back up in distance at Aintree. We are going to aim him at the Becher Chase (9th December) and, if he ran well, then he will be targeted at the Grand National.

### VALHALLA (IRE) 7 b g Scorpion (IRE) – Fox Theatre (IRE)

A winner over hurdles at Taunton in the spring, we tried him once over fences at Newbury but he didn't run that well. However, a few of ours weren't at their best at the time so we are going to give him another go and send him novice chasing. He is rated five pounds lower over fences compared to his hurdles mark. I think he could do alright in small field novice events.

### VICONTE DU NOYER (FR) 8 gr g Martaline – Zouk Wood (USA)

Looked very good when he won first time out for us in a valuable staying chase at Cheltenham in November and he also ran well on his final start when runner-up behind Sizing Granite over two and a half miles at Punchestown. We tried him over the National fences in the Becher Chase in between but I don't think he was quite right. He looks brilliant at the moment and will be aimed at the nice handicap chases over two and a half to three miles plus.

### VISION DES FLOS (FR) 4 b g Balko (FR) – Marie Royale (FR)

A beautiful horse who was bought at the Punchestown Sale in April having won the Goffs Land Rover bumper two days earlier. Well related, we rode him out for a week after he arrived and we have been very pleased with him during the summer. I would think he will go straight over hurdles and is a lovely horse for the future.

### WEST APPROACH 7 b g Westerner – Ardstown

Despite only winning once over hurdles, he achieved a very high rating (157). Placed three times at Cheltenham, including in the Grade 2 Cleeve Hurdle in January, I was guilty of over facing him because I am sure he would have won three or four races at the smaller tracks. Disappointing in his final two races at Cheltenham and Aintree, he will go novice chasing and hopefully we can get a couple of wins into him before stepping up in class. He is a very robust horse who stays three miles but has the speed for shorter trips.

### WHITE MOON (GER) 5 gr g Sholokhov (IRE) – Westalin (GER)

A wide margin winner of his final Irish point in May, the runner-up has won by eighteen lengths since. He is a gorgeous big horse who will go novice hurdling. I think he is a lovely horse.

# BROMLEY'S BEST BUYS

 **Anthony Bromley**, along with David Minton and Tessie Greatrex, represent the Highflyer Bloodstock's buying team and the latest 2016/2017 N.H. season was a record-breaking one for them with their purchases winning an astonishing 84 Graded or Listed races in the U.K., Ireland and France. They had 6 Cheltenham Festival winners and a further 7 at Aintree/Punchestown with the likes of **ALTIOR, BUVEUR D'AIR, MIGHT BITE, WILLOUGHBY COURT** and **YANWORTH** flying the flag for them in the very top races. In France, 3 of the 4 Grade 1 events of 2017 have fallen to Anthony's purchases for Simon Munir and Isaac Souede, headed up by the French Champion Hurdle winner, L'Ami Serge.

*Bromley's Best Buys* produced **40 winners** in last year's *One Jump Ahead* at a strike-rate of **27%**. For the EIGHTEENTH consecutive year, Anthony Bromley has kindly put together a list of names he has bought in France and Ireland, who are set to make an impact in their new surroundings in the UK this winter.

### ARTICLE FIFTY (IRE) 4 b g Doyen (IRE) – Annie Go (IRE)
**Trainer: Warren GREATREX**
A good-looking, tall four year old who was originally bought as a three year old store by David Minton for Philip Rowley, with a view to point-to-pointing in the UK and selling him on if he showed ability. This he did in no uncertain terms, quickening up well to comfortably win his sole English point at Chaddesley Corbett in early May. He was subsequently bought by Tessie for her husband Warren and he should have the pace for a bumper first as his point was over two and a half miles.

### CANELO (IRE) 4 ch g Mahler - Nobody's Darling (IRE)
**Trainer: Alan KING**
This scopey, deep-girthed chestnut is the Million In Mind horse at Barbury Castle for this season. He also originated from the English point-to-point ranks and ran an eye-catching second in a two and a half miles maiden at Maisemore behind a Tom Lacey-hotpot called Blackbow. The latter was subsequently sold at the Aintree Sale for £150,000 to join Willie Mullins, whilst we got this chap for £26,000 at the Cheltenham April Sale. He was only beaten one and a half lengths, so I hope he proves to be good value for the Partnership.

### CHOSEN PATH (IRE) 4 b g Well Chosen - Karsulu (IRE)
**Trainer: Alan KING**
This attractive gelding ran a promising third in one of the hot early Irish four year old point-to-points in February behind Sunset Showdown and Gigginstown's Master Of Tara who himself won impressively subsequently. I thought he represented decent value at £60,000 when selling as Lot 3 in the Cheltenham Festival Sale and I purchased him on behalf of the McNeill Family, for whom I have previously bought the likes of Grumeti, Mille Chief and Walkon.

### CLASH OF D TITANS 4 b g Gold Well - Give Us A Look (IRE)
**Trainer: Warren GREATREX**
Warren won with his first horse for Million In Mind last season (Boagrius) and this fellow will be his second one for the Partnership. He made a very promising debut when second in his four year old maiden point behind a more experienced stablemate called Heroesandvillains (£140,000 at the same sale, to join Noel Meade) and he was in front of subsequent easy winners Moonshine Bay (£120,000 to join Jessica Harrington) and Everybody's Talkin (£65,000 and now with Nigel Twiston-Davies). He looks a real galloping type who may be able to win a bumper around a staying track but it should be over jumps where he should be seen to best effect.

**CRACKING DESTINY (IRE) 4 b g Dubai Destination (USA) - Cracking Gale (IRE)**
**Trainer: Nicky HENDERSON**

Nicky (Henderson) had a great season last time for owners Mike Grech and Stuart Parkin with recruits we found from the point-to-point ranks (River Wylde, Claimantakinforgan, Lough Derg Spirit, Constantine Bay, etc.) and this smashing sort was one of three new purchases from the sales this spring for Nicky to train for them. He was impressive when winning in a really good time the Sunday before the Cheltenham Festival Sale and I hopeful he will prove above average in novice hurdles this time.

**DESIRABLE COURT (IRE) 4 b f Court Cave (IRE) - Desirable Rhythm (IRE)**
**Trainer: Alan KING**

This is a lovely mare who was purchased on behalf of Simon Munir and Isaac Souede at the Cheltenham May Sale after demolishing a field of four year old maiden fillies on her Irish point-to-point debut (12th May). I am a fan of her sire and think she is one to watch out for against her own sex this season. She appeared to have some gears in her point so she may start off in a bumper.

**DESIREMOI D'AUTHIE (FR) 4 b g Cachet Noir (USA) - Toietmoi D'Authie (FR)**
**Trainer: Alan KING**

This four year old AQPS-bred won his only French "bumper" in March in good style in the Provinces and I purchased him for Jared Sullivan shortly after. The race was probably nothing special (although the 5th, 6th and 10th have all managed to win subsequently) but it was the manner in which he did it which impressed me. I would have thought he will go straight into two mile National Hunt novice hurdles.

**GOOD MAN PAT (IRE) 4 b g Gold Well - Basically Supreme (IRE)**
**Trainer: Alan KING**

This is a really bonny horse whom Alan King and I liked at the Goffs UK May Sales at Doncaster soon after he had spread-eagled a field of four year old Irish pointers and we bought him for one of Alan's stalwart owners, David Sewell. He was very impressive that day and had a legitimate excuse for his debut when losing a shoe and having to be pulled up. I am rather excited to see how he progresses this winter.

**GOWITHTHEFLOW (IRE) 4 b g Westerner – Maryriver (IRE)**
**Trainer: Ben PAULING**

His year-older half-brother is the decent prospect Lough Derg Farmer and the same Irish handler, Denis Murphy, sold us this fellow this time around. He looked a sharper type in his point than his elder sibling and narrowly beat a more experienced four year old called Darlac. Both the first two horses struck Tessie and Ben as interesting types and, whilst they were underbidder for the latter, they did manage to secure this good-moving son of Westerner who comes from the family of Celtic Shot.

**INDIAN HAWK (IRE) 5 b g Westerner - Yorkshire Girl (IRE)**
**Trainer: Nicky HENDERSON**

This is another athletic son of Westerner who won his point-to-point but this was achieved in the U.K. for Nicky Tinkler when pulverising the opposition by forty lengths at Tabley in Cheshire in mid-May. His rider rode without irons for the first half of the contest as he had been virtually unseated at the first fence and, although he probably beat little, the performance was exceptionally eye-catching. He comes from the good dual-purpose Aga Khan family of Behera, Banasan and Behrajan and was bought at the May Sales at Doncaster.

**KUPATANA (IRE) 4 b f Westerner - Kildea Cailin (IRE)**
**Trainer: Nicky HENDERSON**
Another new recruit to the Grech and Parkin string, this mare absolutely bolted up in her only Irish four year old mares' maiden point-to-point making all. She looked a really smart prospect that day and posted a good time in the process. I harbour big hopes for her this season.

**LOVEHERANDLEAVEHER (IRE) 5 b m Winged Love (IRE) - Rowdy Exit (IRE)**
**Trainer: Nicky Henderson**
Tessie Greatrex purchased this rangy mare at the re-arranged Cheltenham February Sale after winning her mares' maiden point-to-point in effortless fashion at the end of January. The second and third from that race have both won subsequently and she appears to have enough pace to allow her to go for a mares' bumper first.

**MONBEG ZENA (IRE) 5 ch m Flemensfirth (USA) -Mandys Gold (IRE)**
**Trainer: Nicky HENDERSON**
A really big flashy full sister to the useful but ill-fated Sizing Gold, this mare came to one of the first Irish point-to-points of the season with a big reputation and, despite taking a while for the penny to drop, she ended up winning very decisively in soft/heavy ground. The fourth and sixth both won subsequently and the second, Kygo, was a distance clear when falling two out on her only subsequent start. This mare looks an above-average sort and was bought for Jared Sullivan, for Nicky Henderson to train.

**MR WHIPPED (IRE) 4 br g Beneficial – Dyrick Daybreak (IRE)**
**Trainer: Nicky HENDERSON**
The third of three new recruits for Mike Grech and Stuart Parkin to join Nicky Henderson, this well-related son of Beneficial looked a really useful prospect when gamely holding off the Gordon Elliott-trained Flawless Escape in his only four year old point-to-point at Lingstown in mid-March. The third horse, Heroesandvillains, franked the form by winning subsequently and was sold at the new Cheltenham Sale to Noel Meade and I would be surprised if this horse does not win his fair share of races this season.

**NEWTIDE (IRE) 4 br g Getaway (GER) – C'est Fantastique (IRE)**
**Trainer: Kim BAILEY**
David Minton bought this son of the up-and-coming sire Getaway at the Punchestown Sale on behalf of Lord and Lady Dulverton and he has joined Kim Bailey. He made an eye-catching debut in his only four year old point-to-point, staying on really well into second place at Oldcastle for Irish trainer Colin Bowe, behind Onefortheroadtom, who made £100,000 at the Cheltenham April Sale when purchased by J.P. McManus.

**ON THE BLIND SIDE (IRE) 5 b g Stowaway - Such A Set Up (IRE)**
**Trainer: Nicky HENDERSON**
Tessie Greatrex purchased this good-looking five year old at the Cheltenham February Sale on behalf of Alan Spence, after winning his only Irish point-to-point in mid-January in soft ground. He clocked an impressive time that day, readily despatching the seventeen runner field, which produced five subsequent winners. An exciting prospect, he is a horse who will more than likely go straight over jumps I would think rather than the bumper route first.

**ORTENZIA (IRE) 3 b f Lawman (FR) – Ondoyante (IRE)**
**Trainer: Charlie LONGSDON**
The cheapest purchase in this list at €9,000, she looked a clever buy by Tessie and Charlie at the Arqana July Sale, being catalogued in the breeding section rather than the racing one. An update to the catalogue page was that she had won a ten furlongs handicap at Strasbourg on 30th May and she was rated in the seventies. Runner-up on her hurdles debut at Worcester in late August, she should pay her way in juvenile hurdles.

## OVERWORKDUNDERPAID (IRE) 4 b g Getaway (GER) - Another Whiparound (IRE)
## Trainer: Charlie Longsdon
An extremely good-looking son of Getaway, Tessie bought him to join Charlie Longsdon after he had won his four year old maiden point on his third career start. A gutsy, game, staying sort who jumps well, I see him perhaps coming into his own only once he gets over fences but he acts on proper soft ground so he can win over hurdles first this winter.

## PACIFIC DE BAUNE (FR) 4 gr g Al Namix (FR) - Perle De Baune (FR)
## Trainer: Nicky HENDERSON
This tall grey looked like he had plenty of improvement to come when we bought him in April off Pat Doyle, who has previously sold me subsequent Grade 1 winners Tataniano and Royal Boy. This son of one of my favourite sires, Al Namix, raced with the choke out a bit in his only Irish point-to-point, eventually finishing three lengths second in soft ground over three miles. The feeling is that he will appreciate shorter trips and I rather hope he could make up into a useful novice hurdler at up to two and a half miles this season.

## PECULIAR PLACES (IRE) 5 b g Presenting - Blu Louisiana (IRE)
## Trainer: Warren GREATREX
A smashing stamp of horse by Presenting, Tessie and Warren bought him for one of the Highclere Partnerships at the Cheltenham May Sale. He had run a lovely debut race in a Market Rasen bumper at the end of April leading throughout until just getting caught near the line by Settie Hill, who David Minton had bought for Nicky Henderson to train a week earlier at the Doncaster Sales. Highflyer clearly took a strong view on this bumper and a good plus about this particular horse is his pedigree for the longer term, being a three parts brother to the top-class Dunguib.

## PETER THE MAYO MAN (IRE) 7 ch g Dylan Thomas (IRE) - Mommkin
## Trainer: Paul NICHOLLS
A great big horse, he had a good novice hurdle season last time around with Neil Mulholland, winning three times and finishing with a rating of 137. He was also placed in a couple of smart two mile hurdles behind some horses I know well in River Wylde and Lough Derg Spirit at Kempton and Musselburgh respectively in February and it appeared to be a step too high for him when upped to Grade 1 company at the Punchestown Festival on his last outing. We are hoping he can make into a decent two mile novice chaser for the Million In Mind Partnership but, if that does not quite work out, there are plenty of valuable two mile handicap hurdles for him to have a go at.

## ROYAL RENDEZVOUS (IRE) 5 b g King's Theatre (IRE) – Novacella (FR)
## Trainer: Willie MULLINS
David Minton bought this grand looking five year old at the Aintree Sale for a new owner to the racing game and, following a summer's break in Ireland, he has joined Willie Mullins. He showed plenty of talent but was a bit unlucky in his first two Irish points, looking likely to beat subsequent bumper winner De Rasher Counter when falling on his second run, but he then made no mistake when cruising to victory on soft ground at Castletown in early April. He looks an above average recruit.

## SETTIE HILL (USA) 4 b g Cape Blanco (IRE) - Claire Soleil (USA)
## Trainer: Nicky HENDERSON
This big half-brother to the top-class Flat performer Toast Of New York, won his only bumper by a neck from the previously mentioned Peculiar Places at Market Rasen at the end of April. David Minton bought him on behalf of Michael Buckley and Lord Vestey to join Nicky Henderson. He was backed as if defeat was out of the question in his bumper and, although the ground was officially good, it rode a lot softer than that as it had rained a lot that day, which augurs well for a winter campaign over hurdles.

## SOME MAN (IRE) 4 b g Beat Hollow - Miss Denman (IRE)
**Trainer: Paul NICHOLLS**

This rangy four year old was bought for the Grech and Parkin duo and was sent to Paul Nicholls, which was fitting given that he is out of a full sister to Grade 1 winners Denman and Silverburn, whom Paul trained. Donnchadh Doyle of Monbeg Stables trained him and he also sold Claimantakinforgan to the same owners last year. The horse went to the races with a big reputation and, after an effortless five lengths win in his four year old point, he came to the sales with an even bigger one. Given the strength of the market this spring, I was pleased to secure him for the price we did and it would not surprise me if he turns out to be one of the best of the Irish pointers we bought this year.

## SOMMERVIEU (FR) 3 gr g Rajsaman (FR) - Simple Solution (USA)
**Trainer: Charlie LONGSDON**

This tough maiden three year old ran five times over hurdles this spring/summer for Francois Cottin, placing on four occasions, prior to going to the Arqana July Sale only two days after running third in a winners' hurdle race at Clairefontaine. He has since been gelded and given a short break but should be out in the early autumn. He is an accomplished jumper who should do well over here and could well be a battle hardened sort for a race like the Fred Winter next spring.

## THE BOTTOM BAR (IRE) 5 br g Stowaway - Serenade Leader (IRE)
**Trainer: Nicky HENDERSON**

A grand big unfurnished five year old who is very typical of his sire, he proved to be rather raw and weak early last season for his previous trainer, Paul Webber, but apparently started to flourish in the late spring. He managed to get a run into him just before the Doncaster May Sale and did everything right bar win, as he got caught near the line in a Market Rasen bumper won by a well-regarded youngster of Alan King's called Second Time Around. He is still a horse who may need another year to strengthen up fully to his frame and is probably more of a two season project.

## THE BUTCHER SAID (IRE) 4 b g Robin Des Champs (FR) - Georgina Valleya (IRE)
**Trainer: Warren GREATREX**

Warren and Tessie have bought a number of exciting form horses at the sales this spring and none more than this four-year-old who was only a narrowly beaten second of twenty three in the four year old only bumper at the Punchestown Festival on his only career start. He was purchased outside the ring after his reserve had not been reached inside it and, with the third and fourth placed horses of Joseph O'Brien's both winning bumpers impressively since, the form looks rock solid.

## THE VOCALIST 5 b m Recharge (IRE) - Ivy Edith
**Trainer: Nicky HENDERSON**

The Million In Mind Partnership have had a good success rate from the Crawford Brothers in Northern Ireland with recent scorers The Organist, Toberdowney and Got The Nac all originating from their academy. This year we purchased this athletic mare from them after she had won her mares' bumper impressively at Carlisle in mid April by eleven lengths. She had earlier in the season finished a creditable second at Kelso and, with the fourth placed filly Illwalktheline going on to win her next two bumpers, the form looks OK, too. I imagine she may go straight over hurdles, unless Nicky is tempted by the Listed mares' bumper at the Cheltenham November meeting.

**TILLYTHETANK (IRE) 4 b f Stowaway - All Heart**
**Trainer: Alan KING**
This is a really interesting mare who I thought was a good-value purchase (£30,000) at the Cheltenham May Sale. She is a flashy individual who at the sales looked rather in need of a summer's break, having just run a cracking second of fifteen in a strong-looking four year old mares' maiden point at Bartlemy on her second outing. She was only two lengths behind a really nice filly called Ifyoucatchmenow who made £100,000 to join Willie Mullins at the same sale and, in her debut point Tillythetank had also been a promising third to Princess Roxy, who had realised £115,000 at the previous Cheltenham sale. This half-sister to Alan's Hidden Cargo could be the type to start off in a mares' bumper, although jumping will surely be her forte.

**VOIE DANS VOIE (FR) 4 br g Coastal Path - Peggy Pierji (FR)**
**Trainer: Alan KING**
A very well-related French-bred four year old, he was bought near the end of the Cheltenham Festival Sale, having been placed in two smart early season four year old maiden point-to-points in Ireland. He stayed on resolutely each time in soft/heavy ground behind Bitingthebullet (£170,000 to join Evan Williams) and Getareason (£140,000 to join Willie Mullins) at Punchestown and also when runner-up to the well-regarded Gigginstown owned Master Of Tara at Lemonfield. He has plenty of scope and I can see him doing even better over a fence down the line, but he should be up to winning novice hurdles in the meantime.

**WE HAVE A DREAM (FR) 3 b g Martaline - Sweet Dance (FR)**
**Trainer: Nicky HENDERSON**
A medium-sized attractive youngster, he showed progressive form in three juvenile hurdles in his native France, finishing fourth twice on his last two outings. His latest effort was his best when he was staying on really well to the line to be only three lengths behind the J.P. McManus owned Demopolis. He is by Martaline who has been a lucky sire for this horse's owners, Simon Munir and Isaac Souede, with the likes of the two current top French four year old chasers Edward d'Argent and Srelighonn, as well as their Aintree regular Ucello Conti, all being by him.

**NOVICES**
For the novice chase division this season, I am particularly excited about the likes of **YANWORTH, WHOLESTONE** and **SCEAU ROYAL** going over the bigger obstacles as well as the less exposed pair **FIXE LE KAP** and **TOPOFTHEGAME**. There are a number of exciting horses in the Grech and Parkin string (like **RIVER WYLDE, LOUGH DERG SPIRIT, LOUGH DERG FARMER, CONSTANTINE BAY** and **STOWAWAY MAGIC**) who could all make really useful novice chasers this time but I imagine at least a couple of these will be held back a year over hurdles but those decisions have not yet been made.

Of last season's bumper horses, I am hoping that Tessie's purchase **WESTERN RYDER** can take high order in the novice hurdle division, along with Mike Grech and Stuart Parkin's **CLAIMANTAKINFORGAN**.

---

**HIGHFLYER BLOODSTOCK'S HORSE TO FOLLOW: FIXE LE KAP**

---

For all the latest news and how to get involved in the
**Million In Mind** partnership, please visit

**www.millioninmind.co.uk**

# ENGLISH POINTERS

When it comes to the English pointing scene, there are few better judges than my *Racing UK* colleague **Jonathan Neesom**. The *Talking Trainers* section of *One Jump Ahead* contains a number of horses who plied their trade 'between the flags' on this side of the Irish Sea last winter and are set to race under Rules for the first time this season. Therefore I have consulted Jonathan regarding many of them and he has kindly offered his thoughts on their prospects for the weeks and months ahead.

**CAPTAIN CATTISTOCK** (Paul Nicholls): "Won a two and a half miles maiden at Trebudannon (favoured track for Barber maidens, deep in Cornwall - they won two more races there at the May meeting with similar types). Described as "good bodied" and beat a horse who had run well before."

**CEREAL KILLER** (Paul Nicholls): "A five year old, he won at Cotley and Stafford Cross in April, both in easy style. Described as "lengthy" and interesting that they gave him two runs (beat three rivals in the second)."

**DAN MCGRUE** (Paul Nicholls): "Another five year old, he won an Irish bumper in the summer of 2016. Three out of three in British points, his first was a Restricted at Buckfastleigh against thirteen rivals and his other two wins were doddles. More exposed than others but I like his profile."

**PRESENT IN COURT** (Gordon Elliott): "Won at Bangor in March. The third and fourth won subsequently but were both, along with the runner-up, beaten in lots of races as well, which is a pity because the time of the race is good. Owner has had lots of decent horses in his time. Subsequently bought for £65,000 by Pearl Bloodstock, he has joined Gordon Elliott."

"Another from Jack Barber's yard, **ROBIN WATERS**, was an impressive winner of his only start in a good time. He is described as having stringhalt, however."

"I saw a horse called **SANTINI** win on his debut at Didmarton in March. He had spent some time with Nicky Henderson, prior to going back to Ed Walker (aka Polly Gundry). The race was run at a crawl but he won impressively. He was subsequently sold to Dan Skelton for £150,000."

**SKY PIRATE** (Jonjo O'Neill): "Won his only start at Larkhill in February by three lengths easily (25 lengths back to the third). Runner-up won next time and the favourite, who finished a disappointing fifth, won twice later on. Time only just slower than rest of card and I always take Larkhill form (up to the end of February) seriously. I did like what I could see."

**SPACE SAFARI** (Lucy Normile): "Pulled up on debut in February (Evens, no apparent reason). Was lobbing along in front at Dingley (12 ran) when he hit the ditch (four out) and ran off the course. Rejoined about twenty lengths behind and sliced through the field in about three furlongs to win by sixteen lengths. It was the only two and a half miles race on the card but the time looks good (making comparisons with other meetings held there). He clearly has an engine and could be very interesting."

# FRENCH REVOLUTION

This feature nominates some potentially exciting recruits from France who have yet to race in either Britain or Ireland. Largely unknown, some of them will hopefully develop into household names in years to come. In last year's edition, there were **23 winners** at a strike-rate of **25%** including unbeaten juvenile hurdler and triple Grade 1 winner **DEFI DU SEUIL** (7 from 7 – including the Triumph Hurdle), **BAPAUME, DINARIA DES OBEAUX, MONTALBANO** and **MELON**. I have categorised the horses by either trainer or owner.

## WILLIE MULLINS
## Owner: RICH & SUSANNAH RICCI

### ANTEY (GER) 4 b g Lord of England (GER) – Achinora
Bought for €130,000 at the Arqana Sale in November last year, the former Laurent Viel trained gelding raced twice on the Flat in France winning on his debut at Les Sables-d'Olonne (1m 5f : Good/Soft) by a head in July. The four year old then finished third at Lyon (1m 3f : Soft) in early November (10 days before the sale). Given time to mature since, he could be a force in two mile novice hurdles.

### BURROWS SAINT (FR) 4 b g Saint Des Saints (FR) – La Bombonera (FR)
Described as a stunning looking four year old by his connections, the former Guillaume Macaire trained gelding is eligible for both novice hurdles and novice chases. Runner-up over timber at Compiegne (2m 1f – four lengths behind subsequent Fred Winter Juvenile Hurdle winner Flying Tiger) and Bordeaux, he had four runs over hurdles before switching to fences last November. Fourth on his chasing bow at Auteuil (2m 1f), he was then five lengths runner-up over the same course and distance the following month. A step up to two and a half miles may suit and he is an exciting prospect whichever route he heads down this winter.

### DEAL D'ESTRUVAL (FR) 4 b g Balko (FR) – Option D'Estruval (FR)
Despite racing three times over hurdles during the spring earlier this year, the four year old is described as still being backward and a real chaser in the making. From the same source as Burrows Saint, namely Guillaume Macaire, he finished fourth and third on his first two races at Lyon (2m & 2m 2f). Only beaten half a length at Fontainebleau (2m 1f : Very Soft) last time in mid April, the Balko gelding was acquired in June. His experience will stand him in good stead.

### EPICURIS 5 b g Rail Link – Argumentative
Purchased for 140,000gns at the Newmarket Horses In Training Sale last October, the former Criquette Head-Maarek trained gelding didn't always look the most straightforward but there is no doubt he was a high-class horse as a two and three year old. A two and a half lengths winner of the Group 1 Criterium de Saint-Cloud (1m 2f : Heavy) as a juvenile, he finished fifth behind Golden Horn in the Epsom Derby the following summer. A three times winner on the Flat, he could be a very smart hurdler if he takes to jumping. There is a question mark though.

### KESSELRING 4 ch c New Approach (IRE) – Anna Oleanda (IRE)
A half-brother to Group 3 Horris Hill Stakes winner Piping Rock, the son of New Approach was a six lengths winner at Goodwood (1m 2f : Soft) in June 2016 and runner-up over twelve furlongs at Ascot (Good/Firm) the following month. Rated 78 on the Flat for Richard Hannon, he handles most types of ground and is one for two miles maiden/novice hurdles.

**SHARJAH (FR) 4 b g Doctor Dino (FR) – Saaryeh**
Trained by Henri-Francois Devin, the gelded son of Doctor Dino raced eight times on the Flat in France winning over a mile and a half on the all-weather at Deauville in July last year. Runner-up on three other occasions, he hasn't raced since finishing third at Saint-Cloud (1m 4f : Good) in September 2016 before being bought a couple of months later.

# Others with Mullins

**BREAKEN (FR) 3 b g Sunday Break (JPN) – Kendoretta (FR)**
Showed very little in three starts on the Flat last year before being transferred to Patricia Butel with a view to going hurdling. A half-brother to the aforementioned and new stablemate Salsaretta, he made an immediate impact over obstacles when a length and three quarters runner-up behind Chikito Du Berlais in a conditions hurdle at Auteuil (2m 1f : Very Soft) in June. He could be a smart juvenile hurdler for Mullins.

**CHELKAR (FR) 4 b g Azamour (IRE) – Cherryxma (FR)**
A potentially exciting prospect who cost €160,000 at the Arqana Sale last November. The four year old was previously owned by the Aga Khan and trained by Jean-Claude Rouget. Successful in three of his five races on the Flat, he gained two wins at Chantilly (1m 1f : AW) and La Teste Buch (1m 2f : Good – only run on turf). Although soft ground is an unknown, he looks a speedy type with two mile novice hurdles on his agenda.

**CONCERTISTA (FR) 3 ch f Nathaniel (IRE) – Zagzig**
Acquired for €75,000 at the Arqana Sale in July, the Nathaniel filly was bought on behalf of Simon Munir and Isaac Suede. She won one of her six races on the Flat for Christophe Ferland taking a ten furlongs handicap at La Teste Buch (Good) in May. Placed at Fontainebleau (1m 2f) and Nantes (1m 4f), she was fourth on her final start at Saint-Cloud four days before her sale. By the same sire as the brilliant four times Group 1 and dual Classic winning filly Enable, she is one for juvenile hurdles.

**DEFY DE MEE (FR) 4 b g Country Reel (USA) – Koeur De Mee (FR)**
He is a half-brother to Paul Nicholls' EBF Final and Grand Sefton Chase winner As De Mee. Previously handled by Jerry Planque in France, the four year old showed progressive form in bumpers. Runner-up at Lion-D'Angers (1m 3f) in May, he then won by three parts of a length at Senonnes (1m 3f : Soft) in June. Sold to Mullins for €190,000 the following month, he is another interesting prospect for novice hurdles.

**DUC DES GENIEVRES (FR) 4 gr g Buck's Boum (FR) – Lobelie (FR)**
An unbeaten four year old, he made a winning start to his hurdling career at Moulins (Very Soft) in May. Trained by Eric Vagne, he was purchased during the summer and will go novice hurdling.

**HARRIE (FR) 5 br g Le Havre (IRE) – Honorable Love**
Trained across the English Channel by Laurent Viel, he was a length and a half runner-up on his hurdles debut at Fontainebleau (Heavy) in November. The winner has scored again at Auteuil and this Le Havre gelding was snapped up by Ireland's champion trainer a few days after the race. The five year old is owned by Supreme Horse Racing Club.

**PAKORA (FR) 4 gr f Gentlewave (IRE) – Panthesilea (FR)**
A well bred filly by Gentlewave, she was trained in France by Philippe Sogorb and won two of her eight races on the Flat. A winner at Chantilly (1m 1f : AW) on her racecourse debut last year, she was a length scorer at Vichy (1m 4f : Good/Soft) in July 2016. Runner-up twice in Listed company at Toulouse (1m 2f & 1m 4f), she was purchased in September last year and has been allowed to mature and settle into her new surroundings.

### REAL STEEL (FR) 4 b g Loup Breton (IRE) – Kalimina (FR)
Another from the Viel stable, who has been a very good source of talent for Mullins, the four year old raced three times on the Flat last year. His best effort came at Angers when finishing second in October. Seventh and fifth on his other two outings, he showed improved form when sent hurdling. Beaten a nose at Fontainebleau (Very Soft) in March, he was purchased the following month and will take some beating in a maiden hurdle.

### SAGLAWY (FR) 3 b c Youmzain (IRE) – Spasha
Bloodstock agent Harold Kirk bought him for €52,000 at the Arqana Sale in July. A half-brother to a five furlongs Listed winner, the son of Youmzain won one of his eight races on the Flat for Nicolas Clement. A winning juvenile at Lyon last year, he was Listed placed at Fontainebleau (1m 1f : Very Soft) and finished fifth in a couple of Group 3 events at Chantilly.

### STORMY IRELAND (FR) 3 b f Motivator – Like A Storm (IRE)
Trained on the Flat by Eric Libaud, the Motivator filly finished fourth and second over ten furlongs last year. Transferred to Dominique Bressou to go jumping, she finished a neck second in a debutants conditions hurdle at Auteuil (1m 7f : Very Soft) behind the Robert Waley-Cohen owned Santa Adelia (won again since and Listed placed) in March. Sent off a warm favourite for another conditions hurdle at Compiegne (2m : Very Soft) in early May, she was once again narrowly denied failing by a short neck behind Artemidor (finished fourth and fifth since in Listed and Graded hurdles at Auteuil). Bought later the same month on behalf of **Sullivan Bloodstock Limited**, she is an interesting prospect for juvenile hurdles.

### STRATUM 4 b g Dansili – Lunar Phase (IRE)
John Gosden trained Nichols Canyon and Thomas Hobson before being bought by the Mullins team. The Closutton outfit paid 160,000gns for another Clarehaven Stables inmate last October at the Horses In Training Sale in this son of Dansili. Rated 92, he was thoroughly consistent winning his maiden by eight lengths at Windsor (1m 2f : Good/Firm) and being placed in six of his other seven starts. Runner-up on heavy ground, he stayed a mile and a half and looks a cracking prospect for two mile novice hurdles. He has been gelded since joining his new yard.

# VENETIA WILLIAMS

### CHAMBARD (FR) 5 b g Gris De Gris (IRE) – Regina Park (FR)
From the family of the 1999 Welsh National winner Edmond, he may prove a good buy at €40,000 having been acquired at the Arqana Sale last November. Successful in three of his seven bumper races, the Gris De Gris gelding never finished out of the first four for Alain Couetil. A winner at Argentan (1m 4f : Good), Lion-D'Angers (1m 3f : Good) and Saint-Cloud (1m 4f : Good), the last of those came in a Grade 1 APQS bumper in September 2016. Proven on easy ground, too, he has yet to race beyond a mile and six and is likely to start off in a two mile maiden/novice hurdle.

### COMMODORE (FR) 5 gr g Fragrant Mix (IRE) – Morvandelle (FR)
Bought by agent Guy Petit for €77,000 last November on behalf of owner Mrs Robert Watson, the five year old is a really interesting prospect who has only raced three times. Handled by Augustin Adeline de Boisbrunet, he was a length and a half second behind Corlay (joined Jonjo O'Neill since) on his hurdles debut at Auteuil (2m 1f : Very Soft) in September 2016 before switching to fences. The Fragrant Mix gelding won by two and a half lengths on his chasing bow at Lignieres (2m 5f : Good) the following month before finishing fourth of ten at Auteuil (Very Soft) over the same trip eight days before he was sold. Still a novice over hurdles, he handles any ground and could be a useful recruit.

**DESQUE DE L'ISLE (FR) 4 b g Special Kaldoun (IRE) – Naiade De L'Isle (FR)**
As discussed, Emmanuel Clayeux has been a very good source for British and Irish National Hunt trainers over the years, including Triumph Hurdle winner Defi Du Seuil, and this four year old could be a good addition to the UK scene this winter. Purchased for €60,000 at the Arqana November Sale, the Special Kaldoun gelding had two runs in APQS bumpers finishing fifth and fourth at Moulins and Cluny over twelve furlongs in August and September respectively last year. However, he showed improved form once sent jumping filling the runners-up berth on his hurdles debut at Lyon (2m 1f) only half a length behind San Pedro De Senam (fourth in a Listed hurdle at Auteuil since) with four and a half lengths back to the third. His new owner is the Hon Lady Heber-Percy.

**SAINT CALVADOS (FR) 4 b g Saint Des Saints (FR) – Lamorrese (FR)**
This ex-Sebastien Culin trained four year old looks a most exciting recruit for the Herefordshire yard and owner Andrew Brooks. A winner of three of his four races over hurdles, he was a two lengths scorer on his debut at Fontainebleau (2m 2f : Heavy) in November before following up by eight lengths at Cagnes-Sur-Mer (2m 2f : Soft) over Christmas. The Saint Des Saints gelding then beat subsequent Grade 3 chase winner Dica De Thaix by two and a half lengths in a conditions hurdle at Auteuil (2m 2f : Very Soft) in late March earlier this year. Despite losing his unbeaten record when only sixth in the Grade 2 Prix Amadou at the same track (2m 3f) a month later, he looks a high-class horse who promises to be even better over fences. It is hoped novice chasing is on his agenda.

**SHALAKAR (FR) 4 b g Cape Cross (IRE) – Shalanaya (IRE)**
Another acquisition from the Arqana November Sale (€50,000) last year, the Aga Khan owned and bred four year old raced six times on the Flat when trained by Mikel Delzangles in 2016. Unraced as a juvenile, he was a neck winner on his racecourse debut at Fontainebleau (1m 3f : Soft) in May and was sent off evens favourite when capturing a conditions event at Chantilly (1m 7f : Good) less than two months later. Well held in three subsequent Listed races, the son of Cape Cross has been gelded since joining his new stable and given plenty of time to mature. He ought to stay two and a half miles over timber.

# GIGGINSTOWN HOUSE STUD

**AZUA EMERY (FR) 3 b f Califet (FR) – Take Emery (FR)**
By a good sire, she finished a length and a half runner-up on her only start on the Flat in a fillies' event at Saumur (2m – Left Handed) in April. The winner, Muhtatop has subsequently finished second and fifth over hurdles and the third (Espoir De L'Oasis, who is owned by Simon Munir and Isaac Souede) was runner-up next time. Bought by Gigginstown in early July, she will go three year old hurdling for **Gordon Elliott**. Califet has already produced some smart juveniles including Analifet and Clarcam for the same owners and Grade 1 winner Adrien Du Pont.

**DIS DONC (FR) 4 b g Kingsalsa (USA) – Skarina (FR)**
Bought at the Cheltenham December Sale by Mags O'Toole for £125,000, the Kingsalsa gelding had three races in French bumpers for Alain Couetil winning twice. A short neck runner-up on his debut at Les Sables-d'Olonne (1m 5f) behind the subsequent 131 rated hurdler Domperignon Du Lys, he then beat the highly regarded Duca De Thaix by two lengths at Chateaubriant (1m 5f : Soft). His final start came in a Grade 3 event at Nantes (1m 4f : Very Soft) and the four year old ran out a neck winner with Didero Vallis (won over hurdles for Willie Mullins at Downpatrick in August) back in third. He will go novice hurdling over two miles for **Noel Meade**.

### DUCA DE THAIX (FR) 4 b g Voix Du Nord (FR) – Nouca De Thaix (FR)

A half-brother to Paul Nicholls' Listed chase winner Antartica De Thaix, he joined **Gordon Elliott** before Christmas last year but has yet to run for his new connections (held an entry in the Triumph Hurdle). The Voix Du Nord gelding raced in three French bumpers finishing second behind the aforementioned Dis Donc before winning by five lengths at Fontainebleau (1m 5f : Good/Soft) in October. Trained by Guy Cherel, the four year old then turned his attentions to jumping and was a neck winner from Dame De Compagnie in a debutants event at Auteuil (2m 2f : Very Soft) with the pair ten lengths clear of Dreamcatching (won three times since for Paul Nicholls). No longer eligible for novice events, he is likely to be aimed at conditions hurdles with his long-term future lying over fences. He is an exciting prospect who arrived from France with a big reputation.

### MITCHOUKA (FR) 3 b g Creachadoir (IRE) – Minnaloushe (FR)

Another for juvenile hurdles this winter, the Creachadoir gelding had three different trainers on the Flat in France. Successful in three of his eight races, he gained wins at Fontainebleau (1m : Very Soft) and Marseille (7f : Good) last year and was a five lengths winner at Compiegne (1m : Very Heavy) in March. Third in a Listed event at Saint-Cloud (1m : Soft) on his final outing eleven days later, he never raced beyond a mile on the level and looks a speedy sort. His sire's best jumper to date is Grade 1 winner Footpad.

### VENGEFUL (FR) 4 b g Zoffany (IRE) – Miss Bex (IRE)

Previously owned by Qatar Racing and trained by Mikel Delzangles, he is another four year old who joined **Gordon Elliott** last winter but hasn't seen a racecourse in Ireland yet. Acquired for €135,000 at the Arc Sale last October, he raced five times on the Flat and showed improved form when stepped up to middle distances as a three year old. Runner-up three times over eleven and twelve furlongs (Good and Heavy ground), he was a ten lengths winner on his final start at Le Croise-Laroche (1m 4f : Good/Soft) in September. Expect him to make his jumping debut in a two mile maiden hurdle.

# J.P. McMANUS

### DEMON D'AUNOU (FR) 4 b g Martaline – Jimagine II (FR)

A full-brother to Noel Meade's Coquine D'Aunou, he had two runs in French bumpers. Beaten around four lengths on his debut at Argentan (2m 1f : Very Soft) in early October, the Louis Baudron trained gelding then chased home the aforementioned Dostal Phil (bought since for €295,000) at Deauville (1m 4f : Good) eighteen days later. He was then snapped up by the McManus team at Cheltenham's November sale for £130,000 and is now in training with **Jonjo O'Neill**. A smashing prospect for novice hurdles.

### DEMOPOLIS (FR) 3 b g Poliglote – Princess Demut (GER)

As discussed, **Philip Hobbs'** reward for doing such a splendid job with the unbeaten Defi Du Seuil is being sent two exciting recruits from France who will sport the famous green and gold silks. They include this unbeaten Poliglote gelding. Under the care of Guy Cherel, he was a neck winner of the Prix Rocking Chair, a conditions hurdle at Auteuil (1m 7f : Soft) in late May. The runner-up Shark Du Berlais had the benefit of experience having finished fourth and third at the same venue beforehand and the third (Enfant Du Pays) had been runner-up on his debut at Angers. Philip Hobbs has already captured the Triumph Hurdle three times and the Minehead team may have a live contender for the 2018 renewal.

**ESPOIR D'ALLEN (FR) 3 b g Voix Du Nord (FR) – Quadanse (FR)**
Handled by Mlle Anne-Sophie Pacault, he was owned by Walter Connors and the Voix Du Nord gelding was a half length winner from Etat De Grace (won since) in an APQS bumper at Lignieres (1m 4f) in April. Bought later the same month and now in training with **Gavin Cromwell**, he will go juvenile hurdling and could be above average. The same owner/trainer combination enjoyed dual Grade 1 success in 2016 with another juvenile hurdler Jer's Girl.

**MELODY OF SCOTLAND (FR) b f Youmzain – This Melody**
An exciting three year old filly who has joined **Alan King**, she was bought privately out of Guillaume Macaire's yard during the summer. Three and a half lengths runner-up at Fontainebleau (2m : Very Soft) in April, she was an easy six lengths winner next time at Bordeaux (2m : Soft) the following month under Bertrand Lestrade. According to her new trainer, a Listed fillies' juvenile hurdle at Aintree (9th December) may be her first port of call.

Finally, keep an eye out for the following:
**CHANTE NEIGE (FR) 3 b f Martaline – Russian Taiga (FR)**
A filly with scope but reportedly quite hot, the daughter of Martaline didn't race on the Flat or in any bumpers and was sent straight over hurdles by Guillaume Macaire. Ridden by Kevin Nabet, she contested the Prix Auricula, a conditions hurdle for debutants at Auteuil (1m 7f : Very Soft) in late March. Beaten five and a quarter lengths by stablemate Santa Adelia (won next time and finished second in a Listed hurdle at the same track) in third, the form looks solid with the fourth winning next time before finishing third in a Grade 3 hurdle. She was purchased a month later and could be very useful juvenile hurdler, if going the right way temperament wise.

**CHEF D'EQUIPE (FR) 5 b g Presenting – Millesimee (FR)**
A half-brother to the ill-fated Irish chaser Un Beau Matin, the five year old was bought by Bloodstock agent Guy Petit on behalf of owner **David Maxwell** for €130,000 at the Arqana Summer Sale with a view to him riding the gelding this season. The ex-French gelding has joined **Philip Hobbs**, who also trains hunter chasers Mendip Express and Persian Snow for the same patron. A maiden over hurdles, he finished runner-up on three occasions but improved once switched to fences earlier this year. Second at both Angers (2m 3f) and Lyon (2m 1f), the Presenting gelding then stepped up to two and three quarter miles at Auteuil (Very Soft) in June and beat Chao Chao by two and a half lengths. Unexposed over fences, he will be aimed at handicap chases to start with, according to his new trainer, but has the option of running in hunter chases later on.

**DAME DE COMPAGNIE (FR) 4 b f Lucarno (USA) – Programmee (FR)**
The Lucarno filly was trained in France by Adrien Lacombe and she was a four lengths winner of a bumper at La Roche Sur Yon (1m 4f) on her debut in April last year. Third and second in similar contests at Vichy and Craon, she then turned her attentions to hurdling and ran a race full of promise at Auteuil (2m 2f : Very Soft) in mid October. Contesting a sixteen runner debutants hurdle, she was beaten a neck by the aforementioned Duca De Thaix with ten lengths back to the third. Purchased at the end of the same month, she ought to be a real force in mares' only novice hurdles at least this winter.

# IRISH POINTERS

Irish point expert **Declan Phelan** has once again compiled his list of horses which caught his eye 'between the flags' last winter. Last year's article produced **27 winners at a strike rate of 24%.** They featured promising youngsters **BLACK OP, CAUSE TOUJOURS, ELEGANT ESCAPE (10/1 & 8/1), ESPOIR DE TEILLEE (10/1), LOUGH DERG SPIRIT,** the ill-fated **NEON WOLF (Grade 2 winner)** and **REIGNING SUPREME.**

### ACTIVE FORCE (IRE) 4 b g Oscar (IRE) – Terracotta Queen (IRE)
**Trainer: Noel MEADE**　　　　　　　　　　　**Form Figures: 1**
Successful on his only start at Courtown (Left Handed) (Yielding/Soft): anchored at the rear for most of the race, then made a decisive move approaching the third last (first of three fences up homestraight): in a matter of strides he closed up to lead, and with others departing in the closing stages, he kept on gamely to record a victory in a decent time. The performance hinted he had a change of gear and, whilst not necessarily top notch, he should pay his way for new connections as a 115-135 track racer. Bought by Gigginstown for a steep £165,000 at Cheltenham Sales in April, he should be competitive in bumpers, though unlikely to figure as a Cheltenham novice hurdle prospect this season.

### BREWIN'UPASTORM (IRE) 4 b g Milan – Daraheen Diamond (IRE)
**Trainer: Dan SKELTON**　　　　　　　　　　**Form Figures: 1**
The Easter maiden for the four year olds at Quakerstown (**L**) (Good/Yielding) has in the past decade built up quite a reputation as a source of potential stars: Champagne Fever and Bacardys previous winners. Consequently, many trainers are now targeting the race, with the expectation that talent arising from this event will make a premium price. The 2017 renewal was very competitive, attracting a field of fourteen: many were still in contention heading to the third last. Brewin'Upastorm was given a squeeze approaching the second last and in an instant he opened up a lead of five lengths and jumping the last fence neatly, powered away to win by eight lengths. He was one of a handful of pointers to inject pace at a critical juncture in a race this past season and that trait would promote him as an above average sort. He also clocked a commendable time in comparison to previous renewals. He is a rather plain looking individual, though the engine under his bonnet should ensure winning a bumper is a formality, and he may become quite a tasty performer in middle distance novice hurdles and become a player for races such as the Neptune Hurdle: he looks banker material to land at least Grade 3 or better contests over hurdles and fences. His dam has already produced a number of winners including Kimberlite King (failed to fulfil his initial potential due to physical problems). Dan Skelton has done well with other graduates from the Timmy Hyde academy in Tipperary and he clearly had confidence in this latest Hyde product as he bid £250,000 to add the gelding to his string via the Cheltenham April Sale.

### CASTLEBROOK (IRE) 4 b g Oscar (IRE) – Monty's Sister (IRE)
**Trainer: Jimmy MANGAN**　　　　　　　　　**Form Figures: 12**
A towering four year old who turned the heads of many judges when running his rivals ragged in an early four year old maiden in February. Racing on his hometrack for landowner Jimmy Mangan, jockey Eoin O'Brien elected to kick him out in front at Tallow (**L**) (Soft) and this bay gelding produced a very impressive display of crisp clean jumping as he simply pulverised the opposition to post a taking victorious effort. Mangan had purchased this horse as a foal for £10,000 because his dam was related to the past Mangan star Monty's Pass, and following this success, in a deal brokered by jockey Davy Russell, the trainer accepted an offer in excess of £300,000 with the proviso the horse remain in the yard from Alan Potts. With the money banked the pressure was off the handler and it was decided to test the horse in the point to point confined bumper at Gowran (Soft/Heavy) in March. Four year olds rarely contest this race

against their elders and that age group have had no success in the race: that trend continued as Castlebrook ran a gallant second to the older and stronger six year old Ministerforsport. Ridden that day by Patrick Mullins, said jockey was very complimentary about Castlebrook in defeat. Based with a yard more noted for handicappers than graded material, I would expect this horse to be carefully minded next term as a hurdler, with a maiden hurdle and possibly a minor winners event the target as further down the line the aspirations of team Mangan may be to work the horse towards becoming a Grand National style chaser. He enjoyed soft conditions in his two starts to date and given his size he may always be the type who will prefer some cushion underfoot.

## CHOOSEYOURWEAPON (IRE) 4 b g Flemensfirth (USA) – Definite Love (IRE)
**Trainer: Evan WILLIAMS**                          **Form Figures: 1**
Impressed with both his application and attitude when scoring on his debut at Inch (Right-Handed) (Good) in April: he jumped to the front at the fifth last and, whilst surviving a peck on landing at the third last, at that same moment he was tackled by his rivals. To his credit he quickly regained his rhythm, eyeballed his dangers and, upon landing over the final fence, stretched away to put six lengths daylight between himself and the remainder. He struck me as a horse willing to battle, always a key asset in the locker of decent chasers. A stiff well run three mile race will play to his stamina strengths. Another product from the Monbeg/Doyle team, they had paid £30,000 for him previously, and by dent of this victory they made a significant profit as Evan Williams bid a price of £210,000 to secure his services. Said Welsh trainer has forked out plenty of money in recent years on ex-Irish pointers and it could be argued has fallen short on subsequent track returns: in 2017 Williams has again been actively recruiting from Ireland and from his haul this tough white faced bay son of Flemensfirth could prove to be the smartest acquisition.

## COLREEVY (IRE) 4 b f Flemensfirth (USA) – Poetics Girl (IRE)
**Trainer: Willie MULLINS**                          **Form Figures: F**
A fine stamp of a mare, and one of my favourite of her sex in the four year old age category. She was in the care of Pat Doyle for her only point outing at Lemonfield (L) (Heavy) in March. She was very comfortable in her movement on the testing terrain, almost floating: held up, she sat ten lengths off the leaders four out. Inching closer, she gave Posh Trish a six lengths lead turning for home: inside the last two furlongs racing towards the final jump, she had closed right up only to fall at the last without jockey Barry O'Neill applying any pressure. I would hold the firm view that she would certainly have landed the race but for that untimely exit. If kept by new handler Mullins within the mares' division for bumpers and hurdles she could prove to be a very high class racehorse: winning a bumper is a near certainty and she can achieve graded wins over hurdles. Impossible to say if she will be versatile groundwise, though her body language through this point race recommends she may be effective from two miles to three miles in terms of trip. Her half-brother Runfordave (140 rated) placed third at the 2017 Cheltenham Festival and Colreevy has the talent to match such a rating.

## COOL GETAWAY (IRE) 5 b g Getaway (GER) – Coolnacarriga (IRE)
**Trainer: Gordon ELLIOTT**                          **Form Figures: 1**
Captured the headlines as he made a price of £305,000 at the Cheltenham Sales in December. He had landed a decent punt on his debut the previous month at Tattersalls Farm (R) (Soft) when victorious on his debut. Saddled that day by the Stuart Crawford yard, and backed from 6/1 to 6/4, always moving with poise, he hit the front at the second last and injecting pace was drawing clear when clouting the last fence: surviving the blunder, he kept on to beat King Of Kilmeague by three lengths. The form has been franked, with the 3rd, 5th and 8th all winning maiden points. This is a strong and muscular bay gelding by an increasingly popular emerging jumps sire. His dam won a bumper and she has produced one other winner: I note that dam and said other winner were best at the start of their track career and did not really progress:

further down his pedigree page, I note his grand-dam produced the 2014 Irish Grand National winner Shutthefrontdoor. Family history emits mixed messages. Now owned by Gigginstown, I assume there must have been a problem as he received no entries (in bumpers etc) during the spring time. He is likely to become a high end handicapper (130+) or Grade 2 or 3, hurdler/chaser. At £300,000 odd you nearly expect to have a natural Grade 1 animal, I think he has more than a bit to prove to get to that level. Being such a big unit, it may be the case that he will prefer more degree of ease in the ground: tripwise, I fancy he will be as comfortable functioning at two and a half miles as three miles.

### COPPER GONE WEST (IRE) 4 b f Westerner – Copper Dusht (IRE)
**Trainer: Tim VAUGHAN**            **Form Figures: 1**

Posted both a smart win and decent time when dominating her opponents en route to a ten lengths victory at Inch (**R**) (Good) in April. She was launched to challenge at the third last and found herself left in the lead when the pacesetter fell. From then to the finish she steadily drew clear. The "Copper" family are long associated with the Coffeys from Carrigtwohill and the dam of this youngster is a half-sister to multiple track winners Presenting Copper and Give Me A Copper. In fact Presenting Copper won the identical point at Inch in 2006 before moving to Philip Hobbs and enjoying a six race winning track career. Tim Vaughan dug deep into his purse strings in paying £100,000 to purchase this racy mare and she can certainly land some bounty for the Welsh handler over hurdles and fences, though I would imagine she may fall shy of becoming top notch.

### CRACKING DESTINY (IRE) 4 b g Dubai Destination (USA) – Cracking Gale (IRE)
**Trainer: Nicky HENDERSON**            **Form Figures: 1**

Defied an alarming pre-race market drift as he made all to win on debut at Horse And Jockey (**L**) (Yielding/Soft) in March. He was quite business-like throughout, popping his fences and he had the measure of his nearest pursuers when they fell independently in the closing stages, allowing him to win by a very wide margin from only one other finisher. It may well have been a modest collection contesting that race. This bay gelding then fetched £100,000 at Cheltenham March sales and he may have his work cut out to justify that price level. His sire struggles to throw up high class jumpers and there is little to excite on the damline side of this horse's pedigree.

### DEFI BLEU (FR) 4 b g Saddler Maker (IRE) – Glycine Bleue (FR)
**Trainer: Gordon ELLIOTT**            **Form Figures: 2**

Made the headlines initially at the 2016 Tattersalls Derby Sale as Willie Mullins at the time in unison with Gigginstown paid £255,000 for him as a three year old store. His first test as a racehorse saw him lose no honour in defeat as he split a couple of above average rivals when a four lengths second at Oldtown (**R**) (Yielding). He contented with the ill-fated Flemenshill at the second last and failed to quicken with that rival in the closing stages of this two and a half mile point. With the winner and third (Palmers Hill) commanding deep six figure sales prices, the general view is that the form is trustworthy. Defi Bleu is a well put together four year old and a half-brother to the consistent 140+ chaser Upsilon Bleu: most of the family are happiest racing between two miles and two and a half miles, and it will be worth noting if the same pans out with this fellow.

### DJARKEVI (FR) 4 b g Khalkevi (IRE) – Onvavoir (FR)
**Trainer: Charlie LONGSDON**            **Form Figures: 21**

French bred from the family of Grand National winner Pineau De Re: performed with distinction when second on his debut at Ballysteen (**L**) (Good), and only two weeks later illustrated his toughness and ability to handle a quick turnaround as he picked up best from a well clustered field to win his maiden at Grennan (**R**) (Good/Firm) in May: to date he has run on two speed biased courses and on relatively fast ground. The signs are that he will be at his optimum on good ground possibly at two and a quarter to two miles six: I think Longsdon, who bought him for £68,000 at Doncaster Spring sales, can place him to win races and this gelding may be a midweek horse capable of rising to a mark of 120.

## FLAWLESS ESCAPE 4 gr g Sagamix (FR) – Sainte Kadette (FR)
**Trainer: Gordon ELLIOTT**      **Form Figures: 2**

A tall, to date, unfurnished grey gelding: he travelled to Lingstown (**R**) (Soft) for his sole start in March and gave a fine account of himself. A little inconvenienced by the tight turning track, he was prominent for most of the race: when Mr Whipped launched his bid and quickened into a four lengths clear between the last two fences, Flawless Escape was initially caught flat footed. Once pressurised, he suddenly found second wind and narrowed the gap on the winner to one length by the winning post. Peering through his French pedigree, which includes Yala Enki, I note a predominance of soft/heavy ground favouring kin. He will win races in testing conditions and, given his stature, I think he will prefer galloping tracks as opposed to tight circuits.

## GALLAHERS CROSS (IRE) 5 b g Getaway (GER) – Raheen Lady (IRE)
**Trainer: Peter FAHEY**      **Form Figures: 1**

Rumoured to be talented, this five year old made a sparkling debut at Punchestown (**R**) (s) in February: always coasting along, he soon settled the race after the third last as he spreadeagled the field and won in a respectable time. In victory, this bay gelding with a white face and notably long ears, was supplying then trainer Sandra Hughes with one of her final winners before she retired from the training ranks: some insiders reported Gallahers Cross to be the best of the young talent in the yard. He was entered at one of the sales, though failed to make an appearance as connections decided to retain him. Like a number of the now ex-Hughes horses, he will be handled by progressive handler Fahey. Pedigree-wise he hails from an old stock jumping line, containing many winners though no stars. I like the way he cruised through that race at Punchestown and, if he develops in a positive fashion, he may easily become a graded performer over hurdles/fences, and is one I recommend you to keep on your side this coming winter.

## GLOBAL CITIZEN (IRE) 5 b g Alkaadhem – Lady Willmurt (IRE)
**Trainer: Jonjo O'NEILL**      **Form Figures: 1**

Trained for his sole point by county Carlow handler Willie Murphy, and the Murphy farm also houses the sire of this horse. He is the younger sibling of two quality ex-pointers: A Hare Breath (full brother) and De Plotting Shed (half brother): akin to that pair, this gelding started his career with Murphy. His debut port of call was Bellurgan (**L**) (Good/Yielding) in April and in a compact seven runner field, he raced at the head of affairs and kept on from the second last to resist a challenge and score by a comfortable four lengths from Lovely Schtuff (subsequent winner). I ranked it a cosy win against inferiors rather than a spectacular effort. He is merely a middle sized bay gelding, and I must relate that I was shocked that he realised £275,000 at the Cheltenham April Sales (his siblings made figures below £100,000 when they sold). He looks a straightforward horse in that he settles nicely and has a fine racing attitude. However, at £200,000 + one may anticipate a future Grade 1 horse, I doubt if he is of that calibre: rather just a 115-130 two and a half miles and upwards middle tier handicapper, and not one that would be certain to land a bumper.

## GOOD MAN PAT (IRE) 4 b g Gold Well – Basically Supreme (IRE)
**Trainer: Alan KING**      **Form Figures: P1**

Ran twice in the space of a fortnight at the latter end of the spring: entrusted with favouritism for his debut at Lisronagh (**L**) (Yielding), he was ponderous at fences and on that sharp track it proved costly as he lost touch entering the final half mile and was pulled up. He picked himself off the canvas formwise as he scored on his second outing. At Necarne (**L**) (Yielding), he was smarter in the jumping aspect and positioned close to the pace for most of the journey, he asserted to lead away from the second last and won handily by twelve lengths in a sixteen runner field. He is a handy athletic individual, and those two performances may hint that he may have an inconsistency issue, though when in the mood he is capable of becoming a 115-120 track horse. Trained for this point success by Denis Murphy, the same handler also trained a half-brother called Classical Twist to win a four year old point in 2012 and it was sold on to Jonjo O'Neill for six figures and the horse never subsequently won one penny in prize-money. Alan King paid £70,000 for Good Man Pat and, barring accidents, he should have better luck with this fellow and he can be competitive in two and a half mile or above middling novice hurdles this winter.

### HEROESANDVILLAINS 4 b g Beneficial – Keys Pride (IRE)
**Trainer: Noel MEADE**           **Form Figures: 3U1**
Powerfully built bay gelding: packed in three point races in the space of a month indicating that he is a hardy durable character. Showed up close to the lead for much of his debut at Lingstown (R) (Soft) until just tapped for toe at the climax as he placed six lengths third. His second outing was short lived as he unseated rider over the second fence at Loughbrickland. The following weekend he set out his stall from the start of a maiden at Courtown (L) (Yielding/Soft) as he maintained a relentless gallop from the beginning, measuring his fences perfectly, he was too hot to handle for the opposition as he readily stayed in front to win by over two lengths, never looking in any trouble and leading home a one two for the Monbeg syndicate: with two subsequent winners in his midst that day, the form has been franked. Snapped up by Noel Meade for £140,000, this gelding could aspire to lifting a decent staying handicap chase later in his career: he may appreciate big galloping circuits and races run at a decent clip to maximise his stamina. He can win maiden/novice hurdle, his best days will be reserved for chasing.

### KUPATANA (IRE) 4 b f Westerner – Kildea Cailin (IRE)
**Trainer: Nicky HENDERSON**           **Form Figures: 1**
Although she has an extremely thin pedigree page with few winners to be found, this mare is an example that an individual in their own right can establish their own reputation. Scoring on her sole start at Monksgrange (L) (Yielding), she was an aggressive front runner and had all her rivals in trouble with half a mile to travel: continuing to jump competently, she never gave those fellow competitors a sniff, as she was driven clear to win by eight lengths, showing no signs of stopping, passing the winning post with wind still in her sails. She clocked a decent time in what was in reality a solo effort. She cost Nicky Henderson £120,000 at the Aintree sale in April. She may be of limited size, what is undeniable is that she has a real appetite for racing, a vital ingredient in racing mares over jumps. Ought to land a bumper and has bright prospects of gaining graded success as a hurdler. One of the smartest, if not the best, four year old mares of the spring pointing session.

### MADISON TO MONROE (IRE) 4 ro g Presenting – Caltra Princess (IRE)
**Trainer: Jessica HARRINGTON**           **Form Figures: 1**
A headline maker as Alan Potts fresh from his Gold Cup win in March stepped up to the plate and paid £300,000 for this gelding as he topped the Aintree Sales. He does have a rather unique dappled grey/roan colouring, quite distinctive, some might call it resembling a "show pony". He ran out of the Colin Bowe yard for his point, though I hear that Bowe and fellow point trainer Denis Murphy each owned shares in the horse. Consequently I have to question the actual merit of his sole run in the pointing world: he won the race at Monksgrange (L) (Yielding) making all, and to my eyes not too many in behind tried to test him (Denis Murphy saddling the third)...plus no subsequent franking of the form from those beaten that afternoon. He has an old fashioned lazy gait about him and I may be proven wrong, but my hunch is that he may become just a good 120-130 handicapper as opposed to a star graded jumper. Samcro won the corresponding race in 2016 and I don't think Madison To Monroe will match up to him. His dam has produced one winner, a low grade horse called Westend Prince: the dam herself

(Caltra Princess) ran seventeen times for Edward O'Grady, winning twice a ten furlong Flat handicap off 59, and a two and a half miles handicap hurdle off 86...bottom of the barrel stuff. In conclusion, I am more negative than positive on Madison's future and even winning a bumper will be no slam dunk.

### MAIRE BANRIGH 5 b m King's Theatre (IRE) – La Marianne
**Trainer: Dan SKELTON**          **Form Figures: 1**

Went into the record books as becoming the highest priced point-to-point mare to sell through the ring when she made a mind blowing £320,000 at the Cheltenham Festival sales in March: I was stunned by the magnitude of that price on the day of the sale, and even now in hindsight, I rate that transaction (from the purchaser's stance) as sheer madness, more money than sense springs to mind. This racy bay mare did make a winning debut at Lingstown (**R**) (Soft) in March. Trained by Richard Black (linked to Colin Bowe), she was primed for the day: Lingstown, which is a rather sharp track lends itself to front runners, and I often find when a prominent racer enjoys the circuit and wins easily, the performance can create the impression of world beater, when in fact key characteristics such as the ability to battle are not tested. The last three furlongs are in essence a freewheel down the hill to the line, and front runners on a roll are difficult to reel in. Barry O'Neill moved her to the front from the start and controlled an even pace, he relaxed the pace at the fourth last allowing the field to stack up behind (probably giving his mare a breather): he then kicked for home jumping the second last and to her credit she did open up smartly to win with more than the official five lengths up her sleeve. If you delve into the form, the fourth, Belmont Jewel, was twelve lengths behind, and she is now stationed with Michael Scudamore and finished last of six in a poor mares' maiden hurdle at Uttoxeter on her UK debut in May: so whilst Maire Banrigh posted a polished effort, including slick jumping, she in effect beat nothing. Her dam was merely an average jumps mare, winning twice and holding at peak a 108 hurdles rating: that dam La Marianne has produced Ballykan (140 rated chaser), however most of the pedigree is rather plain. To put the price of £320,000 into context, Fayonagh, one of the best young mares we have seen since Annie Power, was put through the same Tattersalls sales ring at Cheltenham in December and Gordon Elliott picked her up for £64,000. I suspect the fact that the sale of Maire Banrigh was conducted during the Cheltenham Festival of 2017, and new owner John Hales was extra keen to find another star may have led to a case of over exuberant bidding. Maire Banrigh will win mares' races for Dan Skelton, perhaps starting with a bumper, her point victory signalled that she was decent and potent fresh: she still has plenty to prove and a minimum of one win at Listed/graded mares level, in bumpers or over hurdles is demanded, to partially justify the expenditure on her.

### MASTER OF TARA (FR) 4 b g Kayf Tara – Ryme Bere (FR)
**Owner: Gordon ELLIOTT**          **Form Figures: 21**

Handled by Pat Doyle for his two point outings: inheriting bloodlines of a successful French jumping family on the damside. He ran an honest and close second to Sunset Showdown at Knockanard (**R**) (Yielding/Soft) in February, losing out in the final hundred yards. Three weeks later at Lemonfield (**L**) (Heavy), he indicated progression as taking the lead two from home, he readily drew clear for a cosy six lengths win. A powerful bay gelding with a prominent white blaze on his face, he composes himself well through a race and relaxes, and that may permit versatility when it comes to optimum trip, anywhere from two and a half to three miles. His stature suggests he may achieve more as a chaser than over hurdles, and with further development, he may be competitive in Grade 3 or higher over fences.

### MINELLAFORDOLLARS (IRE) 5 b g King's Theatre (IRE) – Another Dollar (IRE)
**Trainer: Gordon ELLIOTT**          **Form Figures: 11**

Trained by Denis Murphy, he came from seventh position at the third last to emerge as one of three fighting out the finish of a maiden at Lingstown (**R**) (Yielding/Soft) in December: he landed in front over the last and the eye catching aspect was that when Jamie Codd gave him a slap of the whip on touching down over that final fence, the response was excellent, as the horse found another gear to sprint to an eight lengths margin of victory. Owner John Nallen elected to switch him to Gordon Elliott to try and maintain or enhance the gelding's valuation. The latter was probably the outcome after he easily won a bumper at Navan (Heavy) in March. That success then convinced J.P. McManus to complete a private purchase from John Nallen. He now retains a 100% career record and should progress into a graded hurdler and chaser, though he might be below top class. His dam was an above average jumps mare and included in his family are horses like Monbeg Dude, Mala Beach and Bonny Kate. Another positive moving forward is that he seems to act on a variety of surfaces and I reckon two and a half to two miles six may become his optimum over hurdles.

### MINELLA TIMES (IRE) 4 b g Oscar (IRE) – Triptoshan (IRE)
**Trainer: Henry DE BROMHEAD**       **Form Figures: F**
A beautifully structured bay gelding: may have the ability to match his looks. Moved through from third, five out, to lead three out and had the race put to bed only to fall at the final fence on his one run at Belclare (**R**) (Yielding) in April: he was on his way to a 10 out of 10 first effort until trapped by the final fence. He relaxed and travelled as asked during the race and showed gears to inject pace in gaining control. On this evidence he could develop into a very classy horse: over many years, I have noted last fence "unfortunate" fallers tend to be horses worth following from pointing ranks....Gold Cup winners such as Mr Mulligan and War Of Attrition were also last fence fallers in points. John Nallen sold this four year old's older brother to Tom George in 2016, Cruiseaway, he too is talented but with issues. Nallen cashed in with a private sale of this four year old to J.P. McManus (six figures) and I gather that Henry de Bromhead is training him. Hopefully Minella Times will mature into a proper straight forward racehorse and, if he does, he would be one you would expect to see competing in decent races at future Cheltenham Festivals.

### MONBEG ZENA (IRE) 5 ch m Flemensfirth (USA) – Mandys Gold
**Trainer: Nicky HENDERSON**       **Form Figures: 1**
Full sister to the 135 rated Sizing Gold, a very solid physical unit and she left a fine impression by winning her sole start when pointing. Held up behind a fast pace at Baliinaboola (**L**) (Soft/Heavy), she improved her position during the final mile and was the only runner capable of reeling in the pacesetter Kygo. She drew alongside that rival at the last and drove clear on the run-in to win in a pleasing manner. The form of that mares' maiden has been well advertised since then, adding to the merit of the performance. Nicky Henderson paid £110,000 for her at Cheltenham in March: I gather she has always shown plenty when in the care of Donnacha Doyle/Monbeg, though keeping her sound was never easy. If she can be kept healthy then building into a 120 racemare is a possible: this chestnut five year old will appreciate two and a half miles and upwards and soft ground.

### MOONSHINE BAY (IRE) 4 b g Milan – Chantoue Royale (FR)
**Trainer: Jessica HARRINGTON**       **Form Figures: 41**
A lengthy gelding, he found his Monbeg rivals too good when placing a one paced fourth on his Courtown (**L**) (Yielding/Soft) debut in the race won by Heroesorvillains. He then outstayed some ordinary opponents when recording a win at Loughrea (**R**) (Good) in late April. In that triumph, he led at the second last and kept galloping whereas his rivals ran out of gas, resulting in an easy eight lengths winning margin. He has siblings who have won National Hunt races at distances ranging from two miles to two miles seven, so  tripwise he may have an element of versatility. He may lack gears, so chasing may offer him better opportunities than hurdling. A price of £120,000 was his transfer fee out of the Denis Murphy yard. For now, I think he is shy of graded class and may not be of Cheltenham Festival standard.

**MR WHIPPED (IRE) 4 br g Beneficial – Dyrick Daybreak (IRE)**
**Trainer: Nicky HENDERSON**　　　　　　　**Form Figures: 1**

A full-brother to another ex-pointer Ben the Boyo (now with Harry Fry). Denis Murphy brought him to Lingstown (**R**) (Soft) in March for his first start and partnered by Jamie Codd, he made an immediate impact. He consented to settle towards the rear, closed three out, nimble enough to manoeuvre himself into the best racing line rounding the hometurn, he quickened on the run to the last, gaining three lengths on Flawless Escape and held on to win by a length as that rival closed down on him in the dying stages. Both the runner up and third (subsequent winner Heroesandvillains) are talented, so this victory can be deemed solid form. As Lingstown is considered a speed biased track and adding in the gears he displayed, it is possible that Mr Whipped may enjoy racing at around the two and a half miles distance. Middle sized, his dam was a dual purpose operator and a multiple winner. He is now stationed with Nicky Henderson after a £160,000 purchase at the Cheltenham March sales. A good bet to land a bumper, and likely to build into a graded hurdler capable of contending at a future Cheltenham Festival.

**NOT MANY LEFT (IRE) 4 b g Oscar (IRE) – Lasado (IRE)**
**Trainer: Jessica HARRINGTON**　　　　　　　**Form Figures: 1**

Landed the geldings maiden at Largy (**R**) (Good/Yielding) in April on his only start (a race won in 2016 by Getabird): he was held up off a steady pace and improved his position to challenge for the lead at the second last: along with Burrows Edge they asserted. Holding the preferred inside racing line down approaching the final fence, he measured that fence accurately whereas his rival erred. Not Many Left climbed the tight bend with a lead of three lengths and held the renewed effort of Burrows Edge close to home. He looks a tough cookie and his game attitude will render positive results over time. He has plenty of positives in his pedigree, his dam is a half-sister to Grade 1 winner Harbour Pilot. Purchased by Jessica Harrington for £150,000 at the Punchestown auction. Stamina is his strong suit, and whilst he may be competitive in ordinary bumpers, I don't think he will be a star turn in that discipline. He will be a fair staying hurdler/chaser, capable of scaling Grade 3 ranks.

**ON THE BLIND SIDE (IRE) 5 b g Stowaway – Such A Set Up (IRE)**
**Trainer: Nicky HENDERSON**　　　　　　　**Form Figures: 1**

Paul Cashman purchased this chunky gelding for £20,000 when he was offered at auction as a foal. He allowed him to grow and produced him for his point debut as a five year old at Kilfeacle (**L**) (Soft) in January. He lined up alongside sixteen rivals and in a fast run race, he was anchored in midfield for two and a half miles: he made headway to become one of three in line running to the final fence and he dug deepest to rest the laurels in a tight finish. He beat five subsequent point winners, lending weight to the merit of the performance. He is the produce of an unraced dam, said dam is a half-sister of that tough stayer Knockara Beau. Nicky Henderson shelled out £205,000 to secure his services at Cheltenham sales in February. He will be a competitive staying novice hurdler this coming season, with prospects of bagging success at graded level. He looks primed for a two and a half miles staying novice hurdle at Newbury as a big galloping track will play to his strengths. He may be capable of booking himself a 2017 Cheltenham Festival date in either the Neptune or Albert Bartlett novice hurdles.

**PALMERS HILL (IRE) 4 b g Gold Well – Tosca Shine (IRE)**
**Trainer: Jonjo O'NEILL**　　　　　　　**Form Figures: 31**

A fair bench mark horse in that he raced twice in the early part of the four year old campaign: initially, he failed to match the ill-fated Flemenshill and Defi Bleu at Oldtown (**R**) (Yielding) when left trailing behind them from the second last, defeated some ten lengths that day finishing third. That was a two and a half miles maiden, and he appeared a more comfortable customer on his second run when moving up to the three mile trip. At Tyrella (**R**) (Yielding/Soft), he took advantage of a drop in class, as he toyed with his rivals, drawing away at his leisure from the second last to win by twenty lengths. He is the progeny of a Topanoora mare and stock from that line stay well and have a decent record in stamina events (such as Grand Nationals). Well put together as a physical specimen, he moved to McManus after a chunky £310,000 sales bid at Cheltenham auctions in March. He is another big money transfer who I have my doubts about his ability to make it at the top level (Grade 1s). I think his future path may be as a 120 rated hurdler and, perhaps his peak may be in staying chases in the 130-145 range, and one of the premier staying handicap chases may offer him the best opportunity of making headlines as a racehorse.

### PRAIRIENATIVE (IRE) 5 b g Robin Des Champs (FR) – Lost Prairie (IRE)
**Trainer: Willie MULLINS**                 **Form Figures: 1**

Won the first point of the 2016/17 season in the hands of Derek O'Connor at Toomebridge (**L**) (Yielding/Soft) on the 1st October. The track in County Antrim is a tight circuit with a very tricky home bend and it can often unnerve newcomers. Prairienative was allowed to find his feet and Derek O'Connor was at pains not to pressurise him on the home turn, preferring to ask for his effort once he was straightened up racing towards the final fence. Upsides jumping that fence, he asserted to win snugly by two lengths. A solid dark bay son of Robin Des Champs, he won that maiden for Wilson Dennison who had previously bought him as a two year old from the Costello family. That clan had raced with some success his sibling Final Gift. He became the first big money transfer of the campaign when Willie Mullins arranged a deal with Dennison on behalf of owner Graham Wylie. He did receive some five day bumper entries during the spring, but never fulfilled those engagements. I liked the way he settled on an awkward track (Yorkhill had trouble on this same circuit) and, if he recovers from whatever halted him appearing on the track proper last spring, then he has the engine to win a bumper and novice hurdles: extra progression is necessary for him to evolve into a graded animal.

### RAPID ESCAPE (IRE) 4 ch g Doyen (IRE) – Kenzie (IRE)
**Trainer: Gordon ELLIOTT**                 **Form Figures: 15**

Won the six runner maiden at Tinahely (**R**) (Yielding/Soft) in February at his ease: impressed as a horse who loved the jumping aspect of the task as he stole an advantage on his rivals at most obstacles with attacking leaps. He galloped clear from the second last to prevail by ten lengths. The Elliott team prepared him for that point for then owner Chris Donnelly and it was significant that, following a £240,000 transaction at Cheltenham March sales, he returned to the Elliott stable, with said trainer clearly encouraging Gigginstown to stump up the cash. He had been purchased at the 2016 Land Rover Sale at Goffs for £46,000, and that qualified him for the bumper linked to that sale at this spring's Punchestown Festival. Rapid Escape finished a close up fifth in that bumper, doing good work in the closing stages. The signs from that bumper added to the evidence from Tinahely are that this chestnut gelding appreciates soft ground and at least a distance of two and a half miles. He may win a modest bumper when he returns, that code will not be his favourite. He has bright prospects of winning a graded novice hurdle this season when he encounters his preferred conditions and long term, I think he will be a money spinner over fences, operating in graded company.

### RIO QUINTO (FR) 4 b g Loup Breton (IRE) – Seal of Cause (IRE)
**Trainer: Olly MURPHY**                 **Form Figures: 32**

Proved competitive in his two spins, placing third and second. Ventured north for the Monbeg team to contest the Broughshane (**L**) (Good) race in April. Whilst bang in the firing line jumping the second last, he could only muster one pace on the run-in and lost out by under two lengths (in third). He resurfaced four weeks later at Dromahane (**L**) (Good) and this time he led until passed by Reasonable Doubt with a mile to cover. From that moment he was the only horse to keep tabs with that eventual winner, always playing second fiddle up the finishing stretch, foiled by a length. He is a French bred with mostly Flat race bloodlines: he has a striking physical presence. Judged on his two point displays, he may be a little tripless or undercooked in terms of maturity. A £130,000 purchase at Cheltenham May sales, he will form the lynchpin of the

Midlands based yard of young Olly Murphy. Son of bloodstock agent, Aiden, Olly has served his apprenticeship in recent years as pupil assistant to Gordon Elliott and with his connections I am sure will fare pretty well in his rookie season as a trainer. Picking up a staying maiden/novice hurdle with Rio Quinto and hitting a rating of 115-120 would be a satisfactory first campaign under rules, as this bay gelding has the hallmarks of a horse likely to be a superior operator over fences.

## SENDING LOVE (IRE) 4 b g Scorpion (IRE) – Dato Vic (IRE)
**Trainer: Willie MULLINS**                **Form Figures: 1**

Purchased as a foal by Ulster based point handler Warren Ewing for £5,500, he already possessed a very nice pedigree page prior to appearing in a point. He is a half-brother to the talented/fragile point/bumper/hurdle winner Knocknanuss and is closely related to Dato Star (Champion bumper horse of 1995). A stout bay gelding with a white blaze on his face, two white rear socks and the owner of long old style ears, he hit the ground in style on his debut, landing the early season maiden at Kirkistown (**L**) (Yielding) by five lengths. Relaxed throughout the event, second five out, he was given the office to go and win his race on landing over the second last, and he readily asserted. He has a long stride pattern and covers ground easily. Guaranteed on the foot of the evidence of this performance to win one maybe two bumpers, I can most certainly envisage him becoming a graded class chaser, up to at least Grade 2 level. Were he to commence this coming winter firstly running in bumpers and then switching to hurdles, I would not be surprised to see him earn his right to have a shot at a Cheltenham Festival race. He did travel to that venue in February and, having gone under the hammer, he was knocked down to Mullins for £130,000, and I think he will prove value for money (as opposed to other £100k + purchases). Offspring of Scorpion have a bad reputation, as many handlers deem them hot headed and difficult to control...however, recent results recommend the good Scorpions such as Might Bite are high class and Sending Love may follow that trend.

## SENOR LOMBARDY (IRE) 4 b g Milan – Killoughey Babe (IRE)
**Trainer: Keith DALGLEISH**                **Form Figures: 1**

Faugheen won the 2012 edition of the four year old maiden at Ballysteen (**L**): as per norm this venue provided good/fast ground at the end of April and the 2017 four year race proved competitive attracting a field of fourteen. About six or seven were tightly boxed as they raced across the top of the track to the third last: as the tempo increased this bay gelding surged to the front, injected pace running downhill to the second last, and then maintaining his momentum he measured the final fence accurately to record a three lengths win. With the runner up Djarkevi scoring next time out, there is a view that this form is decent and trustworthy. Purchased by Colin Bowe for £34,000 at the 2016 Derby sale, this success was instrumental in yielding a chunky profit as the four year old made £125,000 when purchased at the Punchestown Goffs sale on the back of this triumph (a rare jumps acquisition for the Dalgleish yard). His dam is a half-sister to the 1999 Irish Grand National winner, Glebe Lad: in winning at Ballysteen, he was athletic and well balanced and a sound surface may bring the best out of him. He has a bright future and he may climax as a 130+ Saturday style chaser on the northern circuits.

## SLATE HOUSE (IRE) 5 b g Presenting – Bay Pearl (FR)
**Trainer: Colin TIZZARD**                **Form Figures: 5 - 1**

I profiled this powerful gelding in the 2016 four year olds section and noted him as a likely maiden winner this term: and so it proved: handled by Ian Ferguson for Wilson Dennison, he was ridden prominently and with maximum confidence at Tattersalls (**R**) (Soft) in November, where he hacked up by ten lengths to break his maiden tag on his second career start, he was in a different league to his seven opponents. There were two divisions of the four year maiden at this fixture: Cool Getaway won the other one, and it was noteworthy, that in a solo run Slate House clocked a faster time in his divide. A long striding customer who may appreciate the galloping circuits such as Newbury, he headed to Cheltenham Sales four months later for the March Festival auction: with Big Buck's amongst his relations and appealing form and physique, he made a chunky £260,000, giving Dennison a fine dividend on the £44,000 he had laid out when purchasing as a three year old store in 2015. He has the class to become a graded horse (130-140 chaser): my one concern is that as I pointed out in the essay on him in 2016, he was a beaten favourite on his other point run in Easter 2016 and it could be the case that, while he is always a pleasing homeworker, one may not be able to depend on him to translate such quality prep work to the track. That opening defeat may have been a blip or alternatively serve as a warning that there may be shades of inconsistency about him.

### SMALL FARM (IRE) 5 b g Westerner – Eastertide (IRE)
**Trainer: Willie MULLINS**                    **Form Figures: 1**

Full brother to 140-rated chaser Stilletto: robust bay gelding, he has raced once to date and that outing yielded a victory at Ballinaboola (**L**) (Soft/Heavy) in February. Sent straight to the front, he set a fast pace and had all bar Double Portrait in trouble travelling towards the finish: the latter mounted a late bid on the run in, but Small Farm resisted him to win by a neck, the pair drawing a furlong clear from the remainder. Double Portrait added substance to the form when he won his bumper at Cork. Front running suits Small Farm (and others in his family) and he may be as effective over two and two and a half miles on soft/heavy as three miles. I reckon juice in the ground will be a big advantage to him and, if he remains sound, then he could be a 130+ track horse in the making.

### SOME MAN (IRE) 4 b g Beat Hollow – Miss Denman (IRE)
**Trainer: Paul NICHOLLS**                    **Form Figures: 1**

Bred in the purple for the jumping game: his dam is a full-sister to 2008 Gold Cup winner Denman: this dam has already produced the 150 rated hurdler Polly Peachum. Some Man was a £36,000 purchase by the Monbeg team at the 2016 Land Rover Sale: that modest price given his pedigree may have been due to the limited size of this handy gelding. He debuted at Portrush (**L**) (Yielding) in March and faced only three rivals in a poorly supported maiden. Despite the poverty of runners, Some Man put a significant stamp on proceedings: he quickened to lead jumping the second last and settled the outcome in about ten strides, scoring by a leisurely five lengths. He indicated that key ability to inject pace which belongs to horses who possess those vital higher gears. Not surprisingly he was bought by Paul Nicholls for £165,000 at Aintree sales given his history with Denman. It was declared from the rostrum at that sale that this horse was a weaver (hyper-active in his box). In Some Man, Nicholls has rich raw material, which he may be able to cultivate into a proper graded hurdler/chaser and, whilst not a tank like Denman, this youngster may bag some high brow race during his track career. He looks poised to be potent from 2m 3f to 3 miles and may be versatile in terms of trip and ground.

### SPEAK EASY 4 b g Beneficial – For Bill (IRE)
**Trainer: Joseph O'BRIEN**                    **Form Figures: 1**

First progeny of top class jumps mare For Bill: that lady was champion pointing mare of 2009, and in fact won her first 7 races, 2 points, 3 bumpers and 2 hurdles: during a 19 race career, she won 11 times earning in excess of £160,000 in prize money, winning graded races in all codes of the jumping game....all her wins were on soft or heavy. Speak Easy encountered soft terrain for his sole pointing start at Kilworth (**R**) in March. In another small field (5 runners), he improved to lead four out and drew clear from the second last and held a six lengths advantage rounding the hometurn. He had to be kept up to his work by Richie Harding on the run-in as he either tired or idled, yet still won by six lengths. Whilst a success, the performance lacked star quality and as of now my inclination is to estimate him as a middle tier 115-125 track horse who may have his work cut out to match the achievements of his mother. Purchased by Joseph O Brien for £220,000 at the Cheltenham March sale, the Monbeg boys who had acquired him for £40,000 at the 2016 Derby Sale trousered a considerable profit by adding value inside the duration of nine months. A compact neat gelding possibly lacking scope, on the evidence of this only point run, he will not repeat the classy exploits of his mother and could struggle to become anything more than a middling handicapper.

## STOP THE WORLD (IRE) 4 b g Oscar (IRE) – Coolsilver (IRE)
**Trainer: Tom GEORGE**  **Form Figures: 2**
A sibling of Up For Review, a leggy bay gelding with plenty of white markings: ran once on Easter Sunday at Quakerstown (**L**) (Good/Yielding): he advanced from the rear to look a serious player on the run to the second last: when Brewin'Upastorm then quickened, he was left for dead, yet he kept on to finish an eight lengths second in a well contested fourteen runner race. If he had remained pointing, he would have been expected to win a maiden point at his leisure. Privately purchased from the Monbeg team, he should fill out into a powerful unit when he matures. I think he has the talent to make a useful hurdler, long term he may be destined to become an above average 135+ chaser.

## SUNSET SHOWDOWN (IRE) 4 b g Flemensfirth (USA) – Sunset Queen (IRE)
**Trainer: Rebecca CURTIS**  **Form Figures: 1**
Purchased by Gearoid Costello for £58,000 at the 2016 Derby Sale, he has the size and shape of a powerful old fashioned chaser. He turned up at Knockanard (**R**) (Yielding/Soft) in February in the charge of Denis Murphy (though Costello still apparently owned a significant share in the horse). He engaged in a decent three way scrap during the stiff uphill finish at the Cork track and managed to fend off Master Of Tara (an easy subsequent winner) in the final hundred yards to post a battling one and a half lengths win. Knockanard has a finishing climb which tests character, and some quality horses have been introduced to racing there, including Missed That and Keen Leader. This display showed that Sunset Showdown is a solid stayer and my instant impression that day was that down the line he will be a competitor in some of the brands of Grand Nationals. His older half-sister, Definite Ruby has bagged consecutive wins at the Punchestown Festivals of 2016 and 2017, and she enjoys chasing. This four year old will also be in his element as a chaser, I would not be anticipating too much from him in bumpers or hurdle races. J.P. McManus bought him in private transaction after this win and I heard from one source that as part of the deal the horse will be trained by Rebecca Curtis (Costello's partner).

## TEMPLEPARK 4 b g Phoenix Reach (IRE) – Kenny's Dream
**Trainer: Ben CASE**  **Form Figures: 31**
Sturdy UK bred gelding: ran for Wilson Dennison in the two four year old geldings maidens staged at Kirkistown (**L**) (Yielding) in the spring. On debut he was given an easy time by Derek O'Connor when it was obvious that Sending Love was in control of the maiden in February, as he was eased and nursed home in third, defeated seventeen lengths by a superior rival. The next time at Kirkistown in March (Yielding/Soft), he switched from the vanquished to become the conqueror, as he used that initial experience and simply steamrolled his eight opponents to win that event on the bridle beating Spin The Coin by eight lengths. He has two winning siblings and they have won on the all-weather at Dundalk and a fast ground point to point, so he may be as effective on a sound surface. Purchased for £75,000 at Aintree sales in April, if he had been the progeny of a more fashionable sire he may have commanded a higher price. Given that he will be housed in a low key yard, he may slip under the radar and pick up a small maiden/ novice hurdle at fair odds this winter. He can develop into a 115+ chaser and may be versatile in terms of preferred trip.

## THE DELLERCHECKOUT (IRE) 4 b g Getaway (GER) – Loreley (IRE)
**Trainer: Paul NICHOLLS**  **Form Figures: 1**
Coped best with the dreadful conditions at Lismore (**L**) (Heavy) as he finished alone to win a five starter race. He jumped best out of the tacky ground and, whilst he was pressurised by Difficult Decision heading to the second last, he was going best when that rival fell and from that moment he was left with a solo run to the line to claim the victory. Apart from neat jumping

and his capacity to handle horrible ground and stay three miles, little can be gleamed from the race as it lacked any substance. He ran in the point for the Monbeg team, I gather his rider on the day, Rob James owned a majority share in the horse. A sturdy bay gelding with room to muscle up, he comes from the family of Morley Street and Granville Again. Purchased at the 2016 Derby Sale for £40,000, the cashing in process must have been a pleasant experience for Rob James and his syndicate as owner John Hales bought the gelding for £260,000 at the Cheltenham March sales. On form alone, he did not warrant this sort of price, time will tell if the investment will pay off. A horse bound to be suited to the depths of winter conditions.

### TOSSAPENNY (IRE) 4 b g Presenting – Blueanna (IRE)
**Trainer: Evan WILLIAMS**                 **Form Figures: 1**

Denis Murphy picked him up for £31,000 at the 2016 Land Rover Sale: bred in house by Rathbarry Stud, his dam failed to bother the judge as a racemare. A middling sized bay gelding with a prominent white blaze on his face, he was always travelling well within himself on debut at Inch (**R**) (Good) in April. With Jamie Codd at the steering wheel, he jumped his way to the front as the third last (first of three fences up the finishing straight) and then sauntered clear for no pressure to win by six lengths from Net De Treve. It was a professional effort and suggested that this was a very straightforward uncomplicated horse. He should have no trouble reaching a minimum rating of 125 as a hurdler/chaser, and he floated that afternoon over the decent sod at that County Cork track. When then coming under the hammer at Cheltenham Sales eight days later, Williams prevailed with a winning bid of £170,000. This horse at this stage in his development appears to be above average. However, whether he can progress enough to become top class is open to question.

### WHITE MOON (GER) 5 gr g Sholokhov (IRE) – Westalin (GER)
**Trainer: Colin TIZZARD**                 **Form Figures: 5F1**

German bred almost white coloured grey gelding: stocky build. Looked far from fit when beaten a long way back in fifth on his January debut at Killeagh (**L**) (Yielding/Soft) in a race won by Minella Encore. He was better prepared for his second start at Cragmore (**L**) (Good/Yielding) in February: he was involved in a battle with Pallaskenry from three out (pair drawing clear): he was a length down and still trying when he took a very nasty final fence fall. He lay down winded for ten minutes and was lucky to survive the tumble. I was told he damaged muscles in his shoulder and was sore for five weeks. Somehow the Paul Cashman team worked the oracle and soothed the pain and managed to help him regain full fitness for a maiden at Dawstown (**R**) (Good) in May: this time his jockey Gerry Mangan took the bull by the horns and stretched the grey out into a clear lead: setting a strong tempo, he had his rivals under the cosh with a mile to travel and he kept up the pace to win unchallenged by fifteen lengths: with the second, Knockoura, winning a maiden on his next start, the form is commendable. White Moon is distinctive due to his colour and he could be an exciting grey, if he can be kept sound: staying races on flat galloping tracks may be his cup of tea.

# DECLAN PHELAN'S
# NATIONAL HUNT SERVICE 2017/18

The service for the 2017/18 season includes:

### (1) Full Irish Point to Point Dossier.

The 84 page indexed production contains 229 individual essays on track bound Irish pointers emerging from the 2016/17 pointing campaign.

It includes essays on 127 Four Year Olds and 102 Five Year Olds and upwards, all of whom raced in Irish points between October 2016 and June 2017. Prepared with punters in mind, these essays are designed to offer an introduction to each horse and arm you with a vital knowledge edge. My composition is the only such source covering the past pointing season in such depth.

### (2) Weekend Email Preview Service:

Covering 24 weekends from mid October to Aintree Grand National weekend in April. Posted via email by 8pm each Friday evening. The preview covers jumping action in the UK & Ireland and I focus on low key races because I deem them more punter friendly than the bookmaker promoted feature races. Extras include: a Boxing Day preview, a special Cheltenham Festival preview, and coverage of the Punchestown Festival in the spring. Plus some other bonus information.

If you would like to join the winter jumps service, contact via email **mrdeclanphelan@hotmail.com** for full details.

For Irish (only) clients, Declan's nightly views on the next day's action are available from 10pm on **1560 111 112**.

---

# www.mhpublications.co.uk
# Please see page 159
# for details of
# *Ahead on the Flat 2018*

# STABLE GOSSIP

**DAN SKELTON** continues to go from strength to strength with Paul Nicholls' former assistant sending out 118 winners last term. The stable look strong in the **novice hurdle** department this campaign and there is a belief that **CAUSE TOUJOURS** will develop into a high-class two miler. An easy winner at Warwick in a bumper on his Rules debut, the former Irish pointer travelled strongly in the Festival championship bumper at Cheltenham in March before fading inside the final furlong. A tall gelding by Khalkevi, he has reportedly done well during the summer and filled out. He is all speed and may prove best on a flat track.

The Neptune or even the Albert Bartlett Novice Hurdle is likely to be the ultimate target for ex-French trained **CAPTAIN FOREZ**. Still a maiden over timber, the Network gelding has been placed in all four of his races, including when three lengths runner-up to Finian's Oscar in the Grade 1 Mersey Novices' Hurdle at Aintree. Appreciating the step up to two and a half miles, the former Guillaume Macaire trained five year old had previously chased home Capitaine in the Grade 2 Kennel Gate Novices' Hurdle at Ascot before Christmas. Expect the John Hales owned gelding to win races this year but we won't see the best of him until he jumps fences in twelve months time.

**BEDROCK** was acquired out of William Haggas' yard for 70,000gns at the Newmarket Horses In Training Sale last October. Rated 83 and a dual winner on the Flat, he had three runs over hurdles last spring and was highly tried. Fifth in the Grade 2 Dovecote Novices' Hurdle at Kempton, the Fastnet Rock gelding was then only beaten six lengths by the unbeaten Triumph Hurdle winner Defi Du Seuil in Grade 1 company at Aintree. A twenty three lengths winner at Warwick (2m 3f) on the 1$^{st}$ May, he remains a novice for this season and has 'improved a lot' since his last run. The four year old is already rated 144 over hurdles.

The former Nicky Richards trained **BETAMECHE** has yet to run for Skelton but his new trainer harboured high hopes for the Kapgarde gelding last year before he suffered a 'leg.' A four and a half lengths winner of his sole bumper at Wetherby in April 2016, he beat Sam Spinner (rated 136 over hurdles) and Keeper Hill (138 rated Listed winner). His form is strong and the six year old is back in work and expected to make up for lost time this campaign.

**BREWIN'UPASTORM** was an expensive purchase (£250,000) at the Cheltenham April Sale having won his only Irish point-to-point by eight lengths for Timmy Hyde during the same month. Owned by Barbara Hester, the four year old did some very nice work soon after arriving and may contest a bumper before going hurdling. He is considered a smart prospect.

**BUCKBY BOY** is considered a nice prospect having finished fourth in his only bumper at Huntingdon last spring. A four year old by Shirocco, he wants decent ground and is capable of winning a bumper before going novice hurdling.

**NEW QUAY** is another four year old who came from the Irish pointing field. A gelding by Mahler, he raced twice for Sam Curling and, having finished third on his debut, he was a two lengths winner at Liscarroll (Yielding/Soft) in late March. Bought privately at the Aintree Sale for £90,000, he was highly recommended by crack amateur Derek O'Connor, who rode him in both his starts. He is described as 'a real nice horse' for bumpers and novice hurdles.

Rather like Al Ferof was transferred from Paul Nicholls to Skelton, owner John Hales has done likewise with another of his former Cheltenham Festival winners **AUX PTITS SOINS**. Rated 139 over fences and 146 over hurdles, he won over the larger obstacles at Kelso in December before disappointing at Doncaster and then reverting back to hurdles (runner-up in the Grade

2 Rendlesham Hurdle at Haydock). The seven year old is in fine form, by all accounts, and 'looks like a bull' at home. Expected to stay over the smaller obstacles for the time being, the West Yorkshire Hurdle at Wetherby (4th November) has been pencilled in for his reappearance. I remember Paul Nicholls telling me last season that, if he had another Grade 1 chaser in his yard, it was this grey.

The Grade 2 Elite Hurdle at Wincanton (11th November) is a possible target for ex-French gelding **KASAKH NOIR**. Absent since finishing sixth in the Fred Winter Juvenile Hurdle at Cheltenham in March 2016, he missed last season due to a leg injury. However, the Redback gelding remains a horse of some potential having only had four races over jumps. A dual winner at Newbury and Market Rasen, he is considered a well handicapped hurdler off 136 and can bag a good prize.

In other news from Lodge Hill Stables, the 152 rated chaser **THREE MUSKETEERS** has undergone surgery on his wind. A Grade 2 winning novice chaser, he has only had half a dozen races over fences and is still only seven.

\* \* \* \* \* \* \* \* \* \* \* \* \* \* \* \* \* \* \* \* \* \* \* \* \* \* \* \* \* \*

West Yorkshire based **SUE SMITH** is blessed with a good team of staying chasers and there is a belief within the yard that **I JUST KNOW** can win a big prize this winter. The seven year old was only rated 105 over hurdles but has been a different proposition since sent chasing. A ten lengths winner at Hexham last November (3m : Soft), the Robin Des Pres gelding has improved twenty seven pounds since following two more victories at Doncaster and Catterick off marks of 114 and 125. Third behind Label Des Obeaux in a competitive novices' handicap chase at Ayr on Scottish National day – a race the stable won in 2009 with their subsequent Grand National winner Auroras Encore – he is one to follow in those decent northern staying handicap chases over three miles plus. He has reportedly done very well during the summer and is in fine fettle.

The Smiths are believed to be looking forward to sending **JUST MINDED** over fences this term. A six year old by Kayf Tara who cost €40,000, he is a half-brother to Coral Cup winner Diamond King. A four lengths bumper winner at Carlisle on his reappearance last year, he won over hurdles at Market Rasen in March and was in the money on his other three starts over obstacles. Rated 122, he stays two and a half miles and is the sort to make a better chaser. By all accounts, he has thrived for his summer break at his owner Trevor Hemmings' stud.

One of the stable's brightest novice hurdle prospects for this season is the four year old **MIDNIGHT SHADOW**. Bought at the Doncaster May Sales last year for £28,000, he was a ten lengths winner of a junior bumper on his debut at Newcastle last December. Runner-up under a penalty behind the highly regarded Echo Express in a four runner event at Doncaster, he wasn't disgraced last time in the Goffs UK Spring Sales bumper at Newbury. Only twelve and a half lengths behind Harry Fry's Bullionaire in seventh, he shouldn't have any trouble winning northern novice hurdles.

\* \* \* \* \* \* \* \* \* \* \* \* \* \* \* \* \* \* \* \* \* \* \* \* \* \* \* \* \* \*

**NIGEL TWISTON-DAVIES** enjoyed an excellent season in 2016/2017 with 95 winners and total prize-money reaching £1,582,656. Flying Angel provided the yard with a Grade 1 winner at Aintree in April, while **BALLYANDY** captured the *Betfair Hurdle* at Newbury in February off a lenient looking mark of 135. A Grade 1 winner himself, the six year old subsequently finished sixth in the Skybet Supreme Novices' Hurdle at Cheltenham. Reported to have strengthened up during the summer, the Kayf Tara gelding has schooled well over fences and will go novice chasing over two and two and a half miles.

Another novice chaser to keep an eye on is the former Irish pointer **BALLYARTHUR**. Rated 129 over hurdles, he was a nine lengths winner at Leicester in January and finished runner-up on three other occasions last winter. He has had a breathing operation during the summer and his connections are enthusiastic about his prospects over fences. Watch out for him in a novices' handicap chase on his first run over the larger obstacles.

**BALLYMOY** was bought for £75,000 at the Doncaster Spring Sales in May having raced twice in Irish point-to-points for Wilson Dennison and Ian Ferguson. Fourth and third at Largy and Necarne respectively on decent ground during the spring, he will be suited by two and a half miles plus over hurdles and reportedly jumps well at home. Not the quickest, he is expected to pay his way in staying novice events.

**WHOLESTONE** was rated 145 over hurdles winning four of his six races last term. A dual Grade 2 winner at Cheltenham over two and a half and three miles, the Craigsteel gelding produced a terrific effort to finish third in the Albert Bartlett Hurdle at the Festival considering he returned home lame. Back to full fitness, the six year old is apparently being trained with the Stayers' Hurdle in mind. His form figures at Prestbury Park are 12113.

A couple of **unraced bumper performers** from the stable who have impressed at home to keep an eye on include the Paul and Clare Rooney owned **GOOD BOY BOBBY**. Purchased for €80,000 at the Tattersalls Derby Sale last year, the four year old is by Flemensfirth out of Princess Gaia and his homework has been very encouraging. The same comment applies to the Imperial Racing owned **IMPERIAL NEMESIS**. A well bred four year old by Stowaway, who was purchased for €26,000 at the Land Rover Sale in Ireland, he is a half-brother to Willie Mullins' Next Destination, who finished fourth in the Cheltenham Festival bumper last spring. He has improved over the summer and is going well on the Naunton gallops.

\* \* \* \* \* \* \* \* \* \* \* \* \* \* \* \* \* \* \* \* \* \* \* \* \* \* \* \* \* \* \* \*

Talking of Imperial Racing, they are also responsible for another potentially exciting unraced bumper horse in **IMPERIAL ELIXIR**. A four year old by Doyen who cost €22,000 last year, he is a half-brother to the aforementioned Philip Hobbs trained Steely Addition. He is trained by Twiston-Davies' former assistant and near neighbour **FERGAL O'BRIEN** (12 bumpers winner last season at a strike-rate of 24%). Reported to have 'gears to burn,' his homework has been of the highest order and is described as a 'serious horse' by his connections. A dirty scope prevented him from seeing a racecourse last spring but he may make his eagerly anticipated debut in a bumper at Cheltenham's first meeting (28th October). Ironically, the same black and white colours were carried to victory in the corresponding event in 2006 by subsequent Cheltenham Gold Cup winner Imperial Commander. Could lightning strike twice eleven years later?

\* \* \* \* \* \* \* \* \* \* \* \* \* \* \* \* \* \* \* \* \* \* \* \* \* \* \* \* \* \* \* \*

Finally, owner Paul Murphy has been responsible for useful horses over the years, including Aegean Dawn, Carole's Legacy and Skint amongst others. He has a promising four year old in training with his daughter **AMY MURPHY** in the form of the unbeaten **KALASHNIKOV**. I was working for *Racing UK* at Wetherby (Good/Soft) in late March and the Kalanisi gelding, who took the eye in the paddock beforehand, was well backed during the morning's trading before drifting out before the off on his debut in a thirteen runner bumper. Partnered by Jack Quinlan, he led approaching the final furlong before galloping a couple of lengths clear of the ex-pointer Minella Warrior. Strong at the finish, he is well bred being a full-brother to the same connections' five times winning mare Kalane. It is worth noting his sister is at her best on a sound surface and he may follow suit. He rates a smart prospect and one to follow in novice hurdles.

# UNRACED BUMPER HORSES

**AMEN CORNER 4 b g Yeats (IRE) – Feathard Lady (IRE)**
Owned by the **Masters Syndicate**, including **Graham Wylie**, the four year old is trained by **Willie Mullins** and will be making his debut in a bumper around November. Out of Colm Murphy's Christmas Hurdle winner Feathard Lady, the gelded son of Yeats is a full-brother to Grade 1 winning stablemate Augusta Kate.

**DEAL WITH IT 4 gr g Martaline – Topette (FR)**
This Martaline gelding is owned by **Gigginstown House Stud** and is now in training with **Henry De Bromhead**. Acquired at last year's Tattersalls Derby Sale for €135,000, he comes from a good family which includes the likes of Osana, Mon Perrain and Welsh National winner Notre Pere.

**ELECTRO LIDO (FR) 3 br g Voix Du Nord (FR) – Libido Rock (FR)**
Bought by **Willie Mullins** at the Tattersalls Derby Sale in June for €45,000, the three year old is a half-brother to triple Grade 1 winner Valseur Lido and is owned by **Sullivan Bloodstock Limited**.

**GENTLEMAN WALKER (FR) 4 gr g Walk In The Park (IRE) – Queen Isabella**
Another trained by **Willie Mullins**, he is by the same sire as stablemates Douvan and Min and belongs to **Mrs John Magnier**. Bought at the Tattersalls Derby Sale as a three year old for €160,000, his racecourse debut is likely to attract plenty of attention.

**JOLY MAKER (IRE) 3 b g Saddler Maker (IRE) – Mont Basile (FR)**
Only a three year old, he is probably one for the second half of the season. However, there was no shortage of interest in him at the Arqana Sale last November when bought by **J.P.McManus** for €130,000. He is a half-brother to a Listed hurdle winner at Auteuil.

# Don't forget to check out the Diary @ www.mhpublications.co.uk

Recent Extracts........

### 31st August 2017
"The good form of the Sir Michael Stoute stable continued at Kempton last night with **PIVOINE** getting off the mark for the season. A running on fourth at Bath last time behind the progressive **NATHAN**, the gelded son of **REDOUTE'S CHOICE** was fitted with a visor for the first time and Ted Durcan's mount certainly travelled much better in the eleven furlongs handicap. Quickening up approaching the final furlong, he was good value for his two and a half lengths success off a mark of 80. With his owners **BALLYMACOLL STUD** set to fold at the end of the year, he is likely to head to Newmarket in late October for the Horses In Training Sales. I suspect he will attract some interest being a well bred horse who stays well. Perhaps his long-term future will lie over obstacles, although so many horses at that particular sale are now sold to race abroad which is a great pity."

### 19th August 2017
"The Roger Varian trained **DEFOE** has enjoyed a tremendous three year old campaign winning all four of his races and setting up a possible tilt at the St Leger. Rated 88 when he won the London Gold Cup at Newbury in May, the son of **DALAKHANI** collected the Group 3 Geoffrey Freer Stakes at the same venue this afternoon. Ease underfoot is crucial to him and, granted such conditions at Town Moor next month, he warrants plenty of respect regardless of the opposition.

Although not quite at the same level, Alan King also has an improving three year old on his hands courtesy of **NATHAN**. Previously trained by Simon Crisford, he was a winner on his handicap debut at Bath last time and the Normandie Stud owned colt had no trouble following up at the Berkshire track in the opening ten furlongs event. Bred to improve over much further, I asked Alan about the prospect of sending him jumping this winter when we spoke earlier this month but he said his owner isn't keen, which is a pity because he would surely make a terrific juvenile hurdler."

### What The Clients Said:
*"Just want to say thanks for running the service again this year, I have ended up with a nice £756 profit from it so I'm obviously very happy with that so thanks a lot!"* **D.M.**

*"Superb information again Mark, I managed to get some 11/4, will certainly pay for Xmas. Different class."* **S.R.**

*"Thank you for an excellent tipping service throughout the three months. It has been a pleasure and profitable to be a member of your service. Your indepth knowledge and analysis of the race has been excellent. I honestly rate your service as one of the best and most profitable."* **D.K.**

# APPENDIX

As in previous years, I have attempted to highlight a number of horses, in various categories, who are expected to contest the major prizes during the 2017/2018 campaign.

**Two Mile Chasers:**

Nicky Henderson has won the Queen Mother Champion Chase on four occasions, including twice with the brilliant Sprinter Sacre. **ALTIOR** provided Seven Barrows with its sixth win in the Arkle Trophy in March when beating Cloudy Dream by six lengths and rounded off his unbeaten novice campaign with an eight lengths win from the reigning Champion chaser Special Tiara in the Celebration Chase at Sandown. His trainer said afterwards: **"At the moment the dream is very much alive. The irony is that you can find something so quickly after Sprinter (Sacre). There's still a long way to go but it's great to have something similar. We know where we've got to go next year and Altior is following in Sprinter's shoes. He'd get further if you wanted him to but I don't see any point if you don't need to. The Tingle Creek (9th December), Ascot and Cheltenham are the objectives."** Already a dual Festival winner and three from three at Prestbury Park, the seven year old is a short price favourite to add the Queen Mother Champion to his already impressive CV. The High Chaparral gelding has formed a fantastic partnership with Nico de Boinville (9 from 9).

Seven lengths separated Altior and **MIN** when the pair met in the Skybet Supreme Novices' Hurdle at Cheltenham in March 2016. Unfortunately, we were denied a rematch in the Arkle last spring when the latter was ruled out with a bruised cannonbone sustained in February. The ex-French gelding had been an impressive winner of both his starts over fences winning by ten lengths at Navan in November and then beating Ordinary World (third in the Arkle) by nine lengths in the *Racing Post* Chase at Leopardstown on St Stephen's Day. Back to full fitness, the Walk In The Park gelding is rated 160 over fences and will be a serious threat to Altior when the pair meet again. Currently top price 12/1 for the Champion Chase, expect him to be considerably shorter by next spring.

Stablemate **GREAT FIELD** is officially rated a pound higher over fences (161) having won all four of his races over the larger obstacles. Another ex-French gelding, he recorded wide margin wins at Gowran, Leopardstown and Thurles (Listed chase by 32 lengths) before beating the aforementioned Ordinary World by eleven lengths in the Grade 1 Ryanair Novice Chase at the Punchestown Festival (Good/Yielding). The Great Pretender gelding has won his races over fences by an aggregate of fifty eight and a half lengths. A free going, bold jumping front runner, he is inclined to make the odd mistake but is a thrilling horse to watch. Jody McGarvey rode him in all four starts last season and commented at Thurles in March: **"He's exciting. He jumped brilliantly apart from the second last. I went to take him back at that fence and he just hit it, but thankfully he kept going straight and went down to the last well. He's a real thrill to ride, he's got such an engine."** Pulled up in the County Hurdle at the Festival a couple of seasons ago, I would have reservations about him in a race such as the Queen Mother, especially if going head to head with Special Tiara from the outset. However, the J.P.McManus owned six year old will be hard to beat in small field conditions chase in his own back yard.

Paul Nicholls has won the QM Champion Chase a handful of times and he feels **POLITOLOGUE** may prove best over the minimum trip this season. A three times winner over fences and rated 154, the grey looked very good during the first half of the campaign winning in great style over two miles five at both Haydock and Ascot (Grade 2). Only fourth in the JLT Novices' Chase at the Festival, he dropped back to two miles at Aintree and was unlucky not to win the Grade 1 Maghull Novices' Chase when stumbling after the last and hitting the deck. **"How unlucky was Politologue? He absolutely winged the last and then just stumbled. He gallops and jumps** and two miles will probably be his job next year," said his trainer afterwards. Like Great Field, the Poliglote gelding is at his best attacking from the front and he would provide some spectacle over the Railway fences at Sandown in the Tingle Creek Chase.

**WAITING PATIENTLY** beat Politologue by a length and a quarter in a Grade 2 novice chase at Haydock in January (2m 4f : Soft) but hasn't been seen since. Unbeaten in three chases with his rating climbing from 123 to 150, Malcolm Jefferson's six year old has had a chip removed from a front joint but is back in work now. The Colin Parker Memorial Chase at Carlisle (5th November) is his intended comeback race and then a decision will be made regarding his optimum trip. His trainer is keen to pursue the two mile route, while his owner Richard Collins is eyeing the Betvictor Gold Cup at Cheltenham (18th November) before possibly stepping him up to three miles at some stage. Suited by soft ground, Jefferson mentioned the Flemensfirth gelding in the same breath as his former Festival bumper winner Dato Star when we spoke in late August, which is high praise indeed from a trainer who rarely talks his horses up.

### Two and a half Mile Chasers:
If it wasn't for the same owner's Gold Cup winner Sizing John, there is every possibility dual Grade 1 winner **FOX NORTON** would be heading to Kempton on Boxing Day for the King George even though the former Neil Mulholland owned gelding has yet to race beyond two and a half miles. Purchased by Alan and the late Ann Potts and transferred to Colin Tizzard last Autumn, he was beaten a head in the Champion Chase at Cheltenham having allowed the leaders, including Special Tiara, too much rope. Stepped up to two and a half miles in the Melling Chase at Aintree and ridden by Robbie Power (2 from 2) for the first time, he was an emphatic six lengths winner. **"This is a cracking boy, he really is. Fox Norton has everything at the moment. I think he'll make up into a King George horse - as long as Sizing John isn't there,"** commented Tizzard. The Lando gelding then rounded off a very productive spring by beating Un De Sceaux by a length and three quarters in the Grade 1 Champion Chase at the Punchestown Festival. He is another who is likely to head to Sandown for the Tingle Creek Chase (9th December), although he could start off in the Shloer Chase at Cheltenham (19th November), a race he won by nine lengths last season. His form figures at the home of National Hunt racing are 231112. I think his target at next year's Festival will either be the Ryanair Chase or Gold Cup rather than the Champion Chase.

One of the most impressive rounds of jumping from a novice I witnessed last winter came from the ex-French trained mare **BENIE DES DIEUX** on her chasing debut at Limerick (2m 3 : Soft/Heavy) over Christmas. Paul Townend's mount fenced brilliantly before sauntering to a thirty lengths success in the mares' beginners' chase. **"That was a fair performance. The plan wasn't to make it but she jumped the first couple so well that I let her roll along. She jumped like a stag and I never felt I was out of second gear,"** reported her rider afterwards. Unfortunately, the daughter of Great Pretender hasn't been seen since. Twice a winner over hurdles at Auteuil when trained in France, Willie Mullins' mare has only raced ten times during her career (won one of her three starts on the Flat). Reported to be back in work, she is an unknown quantity and lacks chasing experience but her jumping alone will ensure she wins more races. Time will tell at what level.

### Staying Chasers:
Jessica Harrington had a memorable 2016/2017 National Hunt season with 4 Grade 1 wins, 3 Cheltenham Festival winners, including the Gold Cup, 5 winners at the Punchestown Festival and an Irish National. **SIZING JOHN** joined her last Autumn from Henry De Bromhead and, having chased home Douvan on seven occasions throughout his career, including at Leopardstown over Christmas on his first run for his new yard, the Midnight Legend gelding stepped up in distance and hasn't looked back since. Following a two and a half lengths win in the Grade 2 Kinloch Brae Chase at Thurles in January (2m 4f), the seven year old tackled three miles for the

first time in the Irish Hennessy at Leopardstown. A three parts of a length scorer from Empire of Dirt, he then won the Cheltenham Gold Cup by nearly three lengths under Robbie Power. He then rounded off a superb season with a short head victory in the Punchestown Gold Cup. Unbeaten over three miles plus, he is set to chase the £1 million bonus, namely the *Betfair* Chase at Haydock (25th November), King George (26th December) and Cheltenham Gold Cup. If ever a horse was designed for those three races, it is him because the gelding has the perfect blend of speed and stamina.

**OUR DUKE** provides able back up in the staying division for Harrington following a novice campaign which saw the Oscar gelding win the Grade 1 Neville Hotels Novice Chase at Leopardstown (3m : Yielding) over Christmas and complete it with a fourteen lengths victory in the Irish National at Fairyhouse off a mark of 153. Racing prominently throughout, the seven year old galloped his rivals into submission. His delighted trainer said afterwards: **"Our Duke jumped beautifully and Robert rode him with such confidence. He was absolutely convinced that he was going to stay and rode him like that, and he actually loved the ground. I was a bit worried about the ground drying out but he absolutely loved it. He was very relaxed, and Robbie knows him so well. For a horse having his fourth chase ever in his life, it was a great performance. He looks like a Gold Cup horse for next year. We will keep him and Sizing John apart, and see what happens."** It certainly was the performance of a future Gold Cup contender. He, too, is unbeaten over three miles plus (11) and handles any surface. The Jnwine Champion Chase at Down Royal (4th November) has been mentioned as his first target and his record first time out is 11. With Robbie Power contracted to ride for Alan Potts, there could be a very good 'spare' up for grabs in next year's Gold Cup, if everything goes to plan for the pair between now and March. He strikes me as the biggest threat to his stablemate at this stage.

**THISTLECRACK** produced a brilliant display to win the King George at Kempton on Boxing Day on only his fourth run over fences. The former World Hurdle winner belied his lack of chasing experience as he handed out a three and a quarter lengths beating to stablemate and 2015 winner Cue Card. Unfortunately, the nine year old sustained a tendon injury shortly after chasing home the ill-fated Grand National winner Many Clouds in the Cotswold Chase at Cheltenham in January. Colin Tizzard hopes to have his five times Grade 1 winner back for Boxing Day but there is always a question mark once a horse has suffered with tendon problems. Regardless of what happens in the future, the Kayf Tara gelding has been a magnificent horse for his connections earning £644,653 in prize-money with his form figures over three miles plus reading 121111111112.

Another chasing star who will hopefully return from a spell on the sidelines is the dual Festival winner and eight times Grade 1 winner **DOUVAN**. The Walk In The Park gelding had won all thirteen of his races for Willie Mullins, prior to the Queen Mother Champion Chase and was sent off 2/9 favourite, as a result. However, a mistake at the third fence appeared to knock him out of his stride and Ruby Walsh's mount was never travelling thereafter. Having finished a well held seventh, it was later revealed the gelding had suffered a stress fracture to his pelvis. Despite the fact he has yet to race beyond two miles one, there is a possibility he will be stepping up in distance this winter which brings the King George into the equation. Therefore don't be surprised if he accompanies Faugheen to West London on Boxing Day. Touted as the best horse Mullins has ever trained, he has already proved on seven occasions he can cope with Sizing Europe over two miles. It will be interesting to see if it is the same old story over an extra eight furlongs.

The leading British staying novice chaser last term was the Nicky Henderson trained **MIGHT BITE**. A half-brother to the stable's Grade 1 winner Beat That, he was nearly twenty lengths in front when hitting the floor after the final fence in the Kauto Star Novices' Chase at Kempton over Christmas. The Scorpion gelding's confidence didn't appear to be dented though as he won by thirty lengths at Doncaster in February before producing one of the most remarkable performances of the season in the RSA Chase at Cheltenham. Nico De Boinville's mount was in control jumping the penultimate fence but then made a mistake at the last fence before veering badly right on the run-in. Despite being headed by his stablemate Whisper, he regained the advantage in the shadows of the post to win by a nose. It was much more straightforward at Aintree as he beat the same rival by a couple of lengths. **"Might Bite's jumping was great again. No funny antics today which was a relief because I was worried about going around that stable bend twice. Having done what he did at Cheltenham, you just had to think about it but he was very good there and Nico was at pains not to give him a smack. That was the only change. I said whatever is happening between the last two, don't hit him. That's him done for the year. I'd think the King George is the obvious place to be thinking about,"** remarked Henderson at Aintree. The *Betfair* Chase at Haydock (25th November) may enter calculations en route to the King George. His form figures at Kempton are 1F and, while there is no doubt the eight year old has his quirks, he is a very talented chaser with a big engine.

The Eddie Harty trained **CONEY ISLAND** looks capable of winning a big staying chase this winter. A two and a quarter lengths winner of the Grade 1 Drinmore Novices' Chase at Fairyhouse in December, his trainer commented: **"It was only his second run over fences and it was a case of running in another beginners' chase or giving him his chance in a Grade 1. We obviously made the right choice. He's gone and won like a proper horse and that's what I hope he is. He stays well but he also has plenty of toe."** The six year old was only beaten half a length by the aforementioned Our Duke in Grade 1 company over three miles at Leopardstown later the same month. From the family of Wichita Lineman, the Flemensfirth gelding was being aimed at the RSA Chase at Cheltenham until a foot problem ruled him out. Rated 157, he has only raced three times over fences and his record over three miles is 122. The J.P.McManus owned gelding could emerge as a live outsider for the Gold Cup. He is available at 40/1 in places for steeplechasing's Blue Riband.

Following the retirement of Sandra Hughes from the training ranks earlier this year, it was announced her stable star **ACAPELLA BOURGEOIS** will join **Willie Mullins**. A dual Grade 2 winning hurdler, the Network gelding won two of his seven races over fences last season. Both wins were gained at Navan, including a devastating performance in the Grade 2 Ten Up Novice Chase over three miles (Soft/Heavy). Roger Loughran's mount soon established a healthy advantage and never looked like being reeled in eventually winning by thirty two lengths from subsequent Grade 1 winner Road To Respect. **"The ground is the key to him; he just goes on really testing ground and his jumping was superb,"** stated Hughes. Disappointing on livelier ground at Cheltenham and Punchestown, his record on soft or heavy surfaces is 312111. Interestingly, Ruby Walsh is unbeaten on the seven year old having ridden him to victory in the Grade 2 Michael Purcell Novice Hurdle at Thurles in February 2016. He is officially rated 149 over fences and could win a big staying handicap chase in testing conditions in Ireland this winter.

Finally in this section re staying chasers, I feel the following six horses are worth watching out for in races such as the **Ladbrokes Gold Cup (formerly the Hennessy Gold Cup)** at Newbury **(2nd December), Welsh National (27th December)** or **Grand National**.

**BELAMI DES PICTONS** (Officially rated 148) is trained by Venetia Williams who won the Hennessy Gold Cup with Teeton Mill (1998) and Welsh National twice (Jocks Cross (2000) & Emperor's Choice (2014)). This lightly raced six year old has won three of his four races over fences by an aggregate of nearly fifty six lengths. Unbeaten over three miles, he was a wide margin winner at Warwick and Leicester off marks of 138 and 148. His form figures on soft or heavy ground are 3111411. Bought for €120,000, the Khalkevi gelding has won five of his six races since joining his current yard.

**BELLSHILL** (148) won two of his four starts over fences and was ten lengths third behind Might Bite in the RSA Chase. Despite one or two jumping issues last term, the seven year old invariably comes good in the spring and could emerge as a Grand National contender one day, possibly even this season. I am a big fan of horses who have performed well on the Mildmay course at Aintree as they often translate it to the National course. The King's Theatre gelding's form figures on the Mildmay course are 22 and his record at Grade 1 level is 0113021F3.

**MALL DINI** (141) finished a frustrating fifth in the Kim Muir Chase at the Cheltenham Festival in the spring. The Milan gelding had won the Pertemps Final twelve months earlier before his attentions were turned to chasing. Still a novice over fences, Pat Kelly's charge was campaigned largely over shorter trips last winter before returning to three miles in March. Beaten three lengths by Domesday Book, he came from a long way back under Katie Walsh. Davy Russell (31433133323) gets the best out of the seven year old and, while he handles testing ground, he is arguably better on a quicker terrain. He strikes me as a National type, possibly the Irish or Scottish versions at the moment.

**NOBLE ENDEAVOR** (154) was given a brilliant ride by Davy Russell to win the Paddy Power Chase at Leopardstown last Christmas. Leading at the last, Gordon Elliott's charge powered clear on the run-in to win by three and a half lengths off a rating of 143. Third at Cheltenham behind Un Temps Pour Tout, the eight year old was beaten nearly twenty lengths in sixth in the Irish National last time. Suited by decent ground, the Flemensfirth gelding has only raced ten times over fences and looks Grand National material, especially with Russell (324136) on his back.

**ROCK THE KASBAH** (142) may attempt to provide Philip Hobbs with his second win in the Welsh National following Dream Alliance's success in 2009. The Diana and Grahame Whateley owned gelding boasts some excellent form at Chepstow (2211) and is unbeaten at the track over fences. A two lengths winner in October (2m 3f), he scored by a length over nearly three miles at the same venue in February. A running on sixth in the Bet365 Gold Cup at Sandown last time, he was only two and a quarter lengths behind Henllan Harri and the handicapper has kindly left his mark alone.

**SINGLEFARMPAYMENT** (146) is ideal for the Hennessy according to his former trainer Tom Lacey. If forced to choose, I would suggest he is tailormade for the English National – a strong traveller who jumps well and possesses a touch of class. Transferred to Tom George last term, the seven year old only won one of his five races over fences but came within a short head of winning the Ultima Handicap Chase (3m 1f : Good/Soft) at the Cheltenham Festival. Headed on the line by Un Temps Pour Tout, who was winning the race for the second time, he had jumped and moved through the race like the best horse in the race only to be denied late on. To add insult to injury, the gelding was raised a further four pounds. Effective on heavy and good ground, he remains unexposed over fences.

## Two Mile Hurdlers:

**BUVEUR D'AIR** provided J.P.McManus and Nicky Henderson with their sixth win in the Champion Hurdle at Cheltenham in March. The Crillon gelding started the season by winning over fences at Haydock and Warwick in the space of fifteen days. However, his connections had a change of heart and the six year old reverted back to the smaller obstacles. Following a ready win in the Contenders Hurdle at Sandown in February, he beat stablemate My Tent Or Yours by four and a half lengths in March under Noel Fehily before making it five out of five during 2016/2017 with a five lengths win from the same rival in the Aintree Hurdle. A half-brother to Punchestowns, Barry Geraghty (2 from 2) did the steering on Merseyside. Rated 169, he has won 6 of his 7 races over hurdles and will continue to be a major force in the top two mile events.

As discussed, the same owner's Triumph Hurdle winner **DEFI DU SEUIL** will remain over timber this season with a view to hopefully developing into a Champion Hurdle contender. Rated 157, he has won all seven of his races over obstacles, including that mighty impressive performance in March when beating Mega Fortune by a hard held five lengths. Philip Hobbs remarked: **"Defi Du Seuil was always going very well and it's a big relief. He's such a fantastic horse."** The Voix Du Nord gelding completed the Cheltenham/Aintree double when defeating Divin Bere by a length and a half. His reappearance is expected to come in a four year old hurdle at Cheltenham (28th October).

Willie Mullins has won the Champion Hurdle four times in the last seven years, including with 7 times Grade 1 winner **FAUGHEEN** in 2015. The Germany gelding has only raced on four occasions since and the last time we saw him on a racecourse was at Leopardstown in the Irish Champion Hurdle at the start of last year when producing arguably his best ever performance trouncing stablemate Arctic Fire by fifteen lengths. A stress fracture ruled him out of last season's Champion Hurdle but the nine year old is believed to be back in work and will attempt to win the Christmas Hurdle at Kempton on Boxing Day for a third time following his victories in 2014 and 2015.

Intriguingly, Ireland's champion trainer could be represented next March by dual Festival winner **YORKHILL** even though the former Irish pointer was jumping fences last term. The Presenting gelding has produced two stunning displays at Cheltenham, including when beating Top Notch by a length in the JLT Novices' Chase in March. However, he lost his unbeaten record over the larger obstacles on his final start in the Ryanair Gold Cup at Fairyhouse's Easter Festival. Jumping to his left throughout, he made a mistake at the last and handed the Grade 1 event to Road To Respect. His record racing left-handed under Rules is 1111 compared to 1111412 going right-handed. I contacted the seven year old's owner Graham Wylie in August and he commented: **"He's an enigma. He has the ability to win any of the championship races at the Festival but we think he is a better hurdler than a chaser, but he does love to go left handed rather than right handed. My guess is to see what race he starts off on this season and that will tell you which way Willie wants him to go this season."** Whichever route he takes, Yorkhill is a top-class horse on his day.

Nicky Henderson has a clutch of two mile hurdlers who are unlikely to be competing in Grade 1s but could win a big handicap or two. **CHARLI PARCS** looked a star in the making on his British debut at Kempton over Christmas when beating Master Blueyes by eight lengths. **"He has plenty of speed and today when Noel pulled him out he jumped a hurdle and was gone - that wasn't the plan. He is a good jumper of hurdles, very quick and is a proper juvenile hurdler,"** stated Henderson. However, the wheels rather fell off thereafter falling two out against the same rival in the Grade 2 Adonis Hurdle over the same course and distance in February. The former Arnaud Chaille-Chaille trained gelding still took his chance in the Triumph Hurdle but could only finish sixth. Purchased for €250,000, the Anabaa Blue gelding remains lightly raced and can prove better than his current mark of 145. He could be one for the Ladbroke Hurdle at Ascot (23rd December), a race his stable have won four times since 2002 (Chauvinist (2002), Jack The Giant (2007), Sentry Duty (2008) and Brain Power (2016)).

As discussed, another ex-French gelding **CHARMING ZEN** has joined the Seven Barrows team during the summer. A ten lengths winner on his hurdles debut at Les Sables-d'Olonne in October when trained by Patrice Quinton, he was bought by Anthony Bromley on behalf of Jared Sullivan at the Arqana Sale the following month for €210,000. On his first start for Dan Skelton, he beat the 134 rated Apasionado by five lengths in a two miles novices' hurdle at Doncaster in February. Bromley, who was representing the winning connections, said afterwards: **"Charming Zen showed a good attitude considering it was only his second run. He will probably go up in distance now. He has some good entries, but I doubt he will go** to Cheltenham, maybe Aintree, but really he is a horse for next year and will be a chaser eventually." Entered in the Supreme and Neptune Novices' Hurdle at Cheltenham last spring, he has yet to be allocated a mark but is an interesting horse nevertheless.

Nicky Henderson has yet to win the Greatwood Hurdle at Cheltenham (19th November) but he has come close with the likes of Aigle D'Or (2008), Cash And Go (2012) and Vaniteux (2014) all finishing second. Given the fact that four year olds have won three of the last six renewals, he may decide to aim his Festival runner-up **DIVIN BERE** at the two mile contest off his mark of 148. The ex-French gelding has only raced three times for his current connections winning on his first start in the UK in January. A neck scorer from subsequent Grade 2 winner Master Blueyes conceding four pounds in the Chatteris Fen Juvenile Hurdle at Huntingdon in January, the Della Francesca gelding was beaten by the same margin in the Fred Winter Juvenile Hurdle at Cheltenham off a rating of 139. Stepped up in class, he produced a career best effort when a length and a half runner-up behind Defi Du Seuil in the Grade 1 four year old hurdle at Aintree. Only raised three pounds since, he can win a lucrative handicap before returning to Graded contests.

If the hugely talented **JENKINS** can get his jumping together then there would be few better handicapped hurdlers in training. Rated 137, he was a high-class bumper horse winning by nine lengths at Newbury on his debut before finishing second at Punchestown. Sent jumping last Autumn, the Azamour gelding overcame some sloppy leaps to beat Bags Groove (rated 133), Captain Forez (148) and Grade 1 winner Pingshou (150) by upwards of five lengths at Newbury's Hennessy meeting. Henderson commented: "**Jenkins is a lot more laid back than he was last year and his schooling has been good, Barry (Geraghty) said he could improve in all sorts of departments and I was delighted - he was very good over the last two. I thought it was an excellent performance. He's very smart and will have learned tonnes today. We'll wander along quietly and I'd be mindful about running him on very soft ground.**" Sent off 1/2 favourite for another novice hurdle at Kempton on Boxing Day, he was very disappointing trailing in a well beaten fourth behind Elgin. Not seen again until mid April, he was workmanlike in victory at Ffos Las (2m : Good) from A Bold Move. David Bass, who also rode him on his racecourse debut, said afterwards: "**The positive was that Jenkins jumped really well and he finished his race well. He's still a baby and we are learning about him. When he won his bumper I thought he was one of the best horses I'd ever ridden in a bumper. We are on the right path with him.**" Reported to have had some work done on his wind since, Jenkins still has time on his side and could still win a good prize over hurdles. Unbeaten in two visits to Newbury, he looks tailormade for the *Betfair* Hurdle at the Berkshire track in February. Nicky Henderson has already won the valuable two miles event on five occasions.

Granted two or two and a half miles on a flat track and decent ground, **VERDANA BLUE** is a very useful mare. A bumper winner at Killarney when trained in Ireland by Edmond Kent, she was bought for £65,000 at the Cheltenham November Sale. A half-sister to Alan King's dual hurdle winner Wilde Blue Yonder, she has raced five times over hurdles and, following an inauspicious start at Exeter, she won her next two races at Hereford (2m : Good/Soft) and Taunton (2m 3f : Good). The daughter of Getaway then belied her odds of 25/1 by finishing a highly creditable fourth in the Grade 2 Dawn Run Mares' Novices' Hurdle at the Cheltenham Festival. Only beaten three and a quarter lengths, she held every chance at the final flight. Third over an extra half a mile at the same track in a Listed hurdle in April, she didn't appear to relish the final climb up the hill at Prestbury Park hence a flatter track may suit her better. Rated 136, Verdana Blue gets on well with Jerry McGrath and is one to watch out for when conditons are in her favour.

**Two and a half Mile Hurdlers +:**

**NICHOLS CANYON** claimed his eighth Grade 1 victory when winning the Stayers' Hurdle at Cheltenham in March and remains unexposed over three miles (312). A three parts of a length winner, he failed by a head to follow up in the equivalent event at the Punchestown Festival behind his old rival **UNOWHATIMEANHARRY**. Harry Fry's nine year old won four of his five races last term with his sole defeat coming in the Stayers' Hurdle in March. His record at Prestbury Park is 11112 and he will continue to be hard to beat in races such as the Cleeve Hurdle at the track in January. According to their respective connections, the pair will once again contest the big staying events with Cheltenham their ultimate target in March.

Amongst last season's novices, it would be no surprise to see **THE WORLDS END** emerge as a threat to the 'old guard.' A faller in his only Irish point when trained by Sean Doyle, the Stowaway gelding won 4 of his 6 races over timber last year earning an official rating of 149. While useful over shorter distances, Tom George's gelding improved markedly when stepping up to staying trips winning a Grade 2 at Haydock in February by nine lengths. He was still going well when crashing out at the penultimate flight in the Albert Bartlett Novices' Hurdle at Cheltenham. Thankfully, none the worse, Adrian Heskin's mount gained compensation with a half length win in the Grade 1 Sefton Novices' Hurdle at Aintree's Grand National meeting. **"That was a tough performance after what happened at Cheltenham. The Worlds End was travelling very, very easily there - probably easier than he was today - but he had a hard fall. I'm usually the first to go over fences very quickly, but I'd say this one still has improvement in him over hurdles. He's going to strengthen up and he might stick to hurdles for now,"** explained his trainer. A horse with a high cruising speed, he is effective on soft and good ground, he handles flat and stiff tracks and his form figures over 2m 7f plus are 1F1.

**APPLE'S JADE** is a top-class filly and her connections may elect to pursue the mares' hurdle route once again, especially after her Grade 1 victories at Cheltenham and Punchestown in the spring. A length and a half scorer in the David Nicholson Mares' Hurdle from Vroum Vroum Mag and Limini at the former, Gordon Elliott's charge then beat another Willie Mullins trained runner Airlie Beach by fourteen lengths in the Mares' Champion Hurdle at the latter. Yet to race beyond two and a half miles, the daughter of Saddler Maker looks a strong stayer and there is every reason to believe she will stay three miles if necessary. Her record at Grade 1 level is 2112111 and her form figures over 2m 4f are 1211. Gordon Elliott has indicated the five year old will reappear over two miles in the WKD Hurdle (runner-up last year) at Down Royal (3rd November) once again before stepping up in trip. Decent ground brings out the best in her.

Despite only being a four year old, Triumph Hurdle third **BAPAUME** could develop into a smart stayer this winter. Willie Mullins' ex-French gelding was a Grade 2 winner at Leopardstown over Christmas before finding Defi Du Seuil too pacey at the Festival in March. Only beaten five lengths, the Turtle Bowl gelding won the Grade 1 four year old hurdle at the Punchestown Festival by a length and a quarter before finishing half a length second in the champion four year old hurdle at Auteuil (2m 3f) in June. The gelding lacks the gears to be a Champion Hurdle horse but could be a Stayers' Hurdle contender one day.

Willie Mullins has any number of mares who are likely to be targeted at the David Nicholson Mares' Hurdle at Cheltenham next March. These include Grade 1 winners **AIRLIE BEACH, AUGUSTA KATE, VROUM VROUM MAG**, plus **LET'S DANCE, LIMINI** and **MERIE DEVIE** (although according to Graham Wylie she may go novice chasing).

# INDEX

## SELECTED HORSE = BOLD          Talking Trainers = Italics

# Value Racing Club

## "Winning Together"

Our aim at Value Racing Club is to introduce new people into the world of horse racing and provide a cost effective and simple way of becoming a racehorse owner. There are never any hidden extras such as vet bills or travel costs. Once the initial purchase has been paid, no further monies are required during the entire racing season.

### What we offer and benefits:

- An opportunity to become involved in racehorse ownership.
- What we pay for a horse is what you pay, no added fees of any kind.
- A one-off cost covers the entire racing season.
- Stable visits arranged to watch your horse work on the gallops.
- Free owners badge every time your horse runs.
- Each syndicate keeps 100% of all prize money won.
- 72% overall strike rate of our runners finishing in the first three places.
- Horses in training with David Pipe, Dr Richard Newland, Chris Wall & David Dennis.
- Racing UK pundit Mark Howard is our Club Ambassador.
- We are members of the ROA "Racehorse Owners Association" & RSA "Racehorse Syndicates Association".

**Big race wins include the £70,000 Imperial Cup, £30,000 Betfred Summer Hurdle, £20,000 Six Nations Chase.**

**Over £200,000 of prize money won for owners in the last 3 years.**

**Website:** www.valueracingclub.co.uk **email:** contact@valueracingclub.co.uk **Twitter:** @valueracingclub

### Call James for more information: 07939800769

# EMAIL ONLY SERVICE

Similar to the last couple of years, I am running an **EMAIL ONLY SERVICE** from October to December exclusively. To give new clients an idea of what is on offer, I have included some examples from last year's service.

### What The Clients Said:

*"Just wanted to say a "BIG thank you for the two fantastic "tips" on Friday and Saturday - Throthethatch (got 6/4) and yesterday's one - Ravenhill Road (got 2/1) an amazing profit of £400 over the past two days. Fantastic tipping - well done and well worth the wait for success. Keep up the great work!!"* **A.G.**

*"I would just like to thank you for the 2 winners sent out on the October email, not a moments worry with either of the selections. Top class information."* **C.Y.**

*"Fantastic start to the three month service Mark, very many thanks, much enjoyed the romp of Ravenhill, never seemed in any danger even though he seemed a little green. Why has it taken me over 30 years to find such a professional fella?"* **G.H.**

*"Absolutely buzzing after today's winner Ravenhill Road! Got some 11/4 last night. I see it was smashed in all day and went off evens fav!"* **P.F.**

*"Thanks Mark, spot on as always. Not often one can get 3/1 about an evens shot with never a moment's worry. That's this season's emails paid for once again after just 2 selections."* **S.L.**

*"Amazing tipping 2/2 Unbelievable performance from Ravenhill Road today winning by 14L thus following yesterday's comfortable victory for Throthethatch has rewarded email service followers alike. Your attention to detail and patience is second to none."* **N.R.**

*"Absolutely top class stuff with 2 from 2 and both winning easily. You must be delighted with such a great start. Your service is excellent, clear and trustworthy which means an enormous amount to ordinary race fans."* **J.C.**

*"I managed to get 3/1 last night and obviously he won at evens very easily. Having been a client for a while now I am not really surprised at such brilliant info. Superb and well done."* **M.F.**

*"Mark, what can I say, you are definitely the man with your finger on the pulse that was a really easy winner top man Mark once again thanks."* **T.S.**

*"Thank you again for more fantastic information Mark. You ground work and interpretation of the form and information is second to none."* **R.J.**

*"BOOOOOOOOOM simple majestic never a moments worry 5/2 price massive this horse was a different league, thank you magic Mark Howard your info is a different league sir."* **C.R.**

*"One again Mark, fantastic info, backed at 3-1 last night!! Won at a canter again!! What a start for the email service!"* **R.C.**

*"Your inside information could not have been more right - he destroyed that field. Thank you Mark for the second time in just over 24 hours!"* **E.L.**

*"The first monthly selection was well worth waiting for. Thanks again for the most wonderful and well constructed information. Still the only true professional I trust with my cash to provide me with not only top tips but as always the best racing read of the year with One Jump Ahead."* **K.E.**

*"Yet again subscription paid for with first bet, the best information about anyone who's serious about betting has to consider your email service sir, my favourite 3 months of the year thanks again Mark number 1."* **C.R.**

*"A belated THANK YOU for the excellent tips/information on Friday/Saturday. Top class stuff. A brilliant start to the e-mail service."* **S.G.**

*"Well done mark information again spot on I do enjoy the email service and read the book everyday. I am really impressed with your hard work and professionalism."* **T.S.**

*"Good evening Mark just got home from shouting the Henderson horse home in the last thanks very much brilliant information."* **C.W.**

*"Good work Mark first time with you, I am very impressed with service not only the winners but the explanations that go with them."* **D.P.**

*"Just to say brilliant winner again today. Like all your services and updates first class, best information."* **T.Y.**

*"Another good winner today, first time in for the 3 months, you've now got a customer for many years to come. Raising a glass of red this very moment to your good self."* **P.P.**

*"Thanks for the great information today. I've been buying your books for over 10 years and they are great value and the best around. As well as your updates and the Email service. The information is second to none."* **C.W.**

*"Thanks for the email re American Tom, looked impressive and one to keep on the right side of. Look forward to the next update, keep up the fantastic work."* **S.P.**

*"Top research, contacts and information once again you put us in the right direction. Your hard work and enthusiasm for the game gives you the rewards you deserve. Thanks again for the great service."* **R.J.**

*"Yet again sir you deliver 5/2 price was an early Christmas gift, keep up the good work Mark the service is second to none."* **C.R.**

*"Many thanks for your detailed information provided throughout the year, it is without doubt the best value for money information that can be had (win or lose). What I like about you Mark is you really care for the client and you feel it when a selection you have put up does not run true. You know you can't tip winners all the time, but your strike rate is better than the rest and is without doubt the best value that money can buy.....Very Well Done!"* **S.D.**

# OCTOBER 2016 – 2 WINNERS FROM 4 RUNNERS

| | | | |
|---|---|---|---|
| Friday 14th | THROTHETHATCH (Advised @ 7/4) | 1st | 11/8 |
| Saturday 15th | RAVENHILL ROAD (Advised @ 3/1) | 1st | Evens |

**Friday 14th**

*"The former Lucinda Russell trained **THROTHETHATCH** has his first run for Dan Skelton in the opening handicap hurdle at Fakenham tomorrow (2.05). The seven year old runs off a lenient looking mark of 111, and is reportedly in fine form at home having completed his preparation with a good work out on Tuesday morning. Rated five pounds lower over timber compared to fences, the seven year old was a three times winner last term and goes well fresh (217 days). A five lengths winner from Morning Royalty at Haydock in December, receiving eight pounds, Jimmy Moffatt's runner-up has won twice since and is now rated 135 over fences. Absence since finishing second at Ayr in March, the ex-Irish pointer was transferred to Skelton during the summer. Dan told me when we spoke in August that the gelding has undergone a wind operation and more improvement should be forthcoming (wears a tongue tie for the first time). The stable sent out Return Flight to win at Southwell earlier this month on his first run for the yard and there is plenty of stable confidence behind Throthethatch in tomorrow's eleven runner two and a half mile handicap hurdle."*

**SELECTION: THROTHETHATCH (7/4 William Hill) 2.05 Fakenham  WON @ 11/8**

**Saturday 15th**

*"The bumper at Market Rasen tomorrow has divided and, whilst working at Carlisle on Thursday, I spoke to Brian Ellison. The Malton trainer is represented in both divisions and he passed on some very positive news regarding former Irish pointer **RAVENHILL ROAD**, who contests the second division at **5.05**. A five year old gelding by Exit To Nowhere, he was a fifteen lengths winner of his only point at Broughshane in early May (Good) for Stuart Crawford. Subsequently bought for £100,000 at the Doncaster May Sales on behalf of Phil Martin, expert Declan Phelan wrote in his Irish point dossier: **"£100,000 is the price this chestnut commanded at the Doncaster May Sales: eleven days earlier he had made a winning debut at Broughshane (g/f). In that race, against very exposed poor opposition, he was always swinging on the bridle and once asked to lead at the second last, in a matter of a hundred yards he opened up a big margin on the field, winning eased down by fifteen lengths. Rating horses who trounce poor opponents is pure guesswork. On this evidence he should win a good ground bumper and will win maiden/novice hurdles on the northern circuit. Brian Ellison has an excellent record with Irish pointers, so it is conceivable that this five year old could easily become one of the top ten novice hurdlers based in the north this season."** Brian told me yesterday that he considers Ravenhill Road to be in a different league to his runner in the first division, Instant Replay. He described the gelding as a class act, who has been working brilliantly with 140 rated horses at home. He will be very disappointed if he doesn't go close. The ground at the Lincolnshire venue is currently described as good to soft and more rain is forecast overnight. An easy surface would be an unknown but his dam (Zaffarella) won on soft twice and heavy for Lucinda Russell in 2009 and 2010. The fact he is a five year old is a plus too, because his main dangers, namely Mister Whitaker, Test Pilot and Temple Man are only four. Brian has trained two winners this month suggesting his team are in decent form and seven pounds conditional Kaine Wood, who is on board, rode a bumper winner at Southwell earlier this month (he has also ridden 8 winners on the Flat). I suggest backing Ravenhill Road each-way at 3/1."*

**SELECTION: RAVENHILL ROAD (3/1 Bet365, BetVictor, Coral, Paddy Power, Skybet William Hill) 5.05 Market Rasen  WON by 14 lengths @ Evens**

# NOVEMBER 2016 – 2 WINNERS FROM 4 RUNNERS

| Wednesday 9th | MESSIRE DES OBEAUX | 1st | 6/4 |
| Friday 18th | CLAIMANTAKINFORGAN (Advised @ 11/4) | 1st | 11/4 |

*"The Email Service could do with a winner so I am hoping one of my chief contributors Anthony Bromley has pointed us in the right direction. As many subscribers will be aware, Anthony is racing manager for leading owner Simon Munir and he is confident* **MESSIRE DES OBEAUX** *will win the two and a half miles handicap hurdle at Bangor tomorrow (3.00). Below are Alan King's comments regarding the four year old on page 97 of One Jump Ahead:* **"A potentially high-class horse who has size and scope. Still a novice over hurdles, he arrived from France quite late last year and ran two good races for us. We threw him in at the deep end by contesting the Victor Ludorum and Fred Winter Hurdles at Haydock and Cheltenham respectively. Third on the first occasion, he then finished seventh at the Festival. Dropped four pounds since, he has been bought by Simon Munir and Isaac Souede during the summer. He will continue over two miles and there are plenty of options for him. I love him."** *Given such comments, a mark of 128 looks lenient to say the least and, bearing in mind Messire Des Obeaux is a full brother to Paul Nicholls' Cheltenham Festival runner-up Bouvreuil, he ought to improve for the step up to two and a half miles for the first time. The ground at the Welsh track is currently described as good (watered) but there is significant rainfall forecast this evening and overnight. Anthony texted me to say he won't run if the ground is too quick but he is expecting it to be on the soft side by racetime."*

**SELECTION: MESSIRE DES OBEAUX (6/4 Skybet, 11/8 Bet365, Ladbrokes, William Hill) 3.00 Bangor. WON by 10 lengths @ 6/4**

*"Talking of the Top 40 Prospects, there are no less than 4 runners at Haydock Park tomorrow and I can report a lot of stable confidence behind* **CLAIMANTAKINFORGAN** *in the concluding bumper at 3.45. Three different sources have described the former Irish pointers as a smart prospect and he is fully expected to get his Rules career off to the best possible start. Irish point expert Declan Phelan wrote in One Jump Ahead:* **"This gelding suffered an abrupt end to his Inch debut...slipping up on the flat inside the first two hundred yards: happily, he atoned in no uncertain manner on Easter Monday: contesting what is traditionally one of the best northern area four year old maidens at Loughanmore, he took apart a field of fancied opponents. Leading from three out, he steadily upped the ante and dropped his dangers one by one to pull clear from the final fence for an authoritative five lengths success on the yielding to soft terrain. He hinted in this display that he is equipped with many of the qualities a top jumper requires: clean jumping, powerful gallop, resolute attitude, and running to the line with vigour. Joining Nicky Henderson via a £110,000 sales ring transaction, it is more than conceivable that he may figure in Graded staying novice hurdles this winter, winning at Grade 1 level is attainable."***

**SELECTION: CLAIMANTAKINFORGAN (11/4 Bet365, 5/2 Betfred, BetVictor, Paddy Power, Skybet, Totesport) 3.45 Haydock. WON @ 11/4**

# DECEMBER 2016 – 1 WINNERS FROM 4 RUNNERS

Sunday 11th     AMERICAN TOM (Advised @ 5/2)     1st    Evens

*"Leading owner Rich Ricci texted me last Saturday evening suggesting I keep an eye out for his novice chaser **AMERICAN TOM**. The ex-French gelding is declared to run in the two mile beginners' chase at Punchestown on Sunday (2.35). Rich said: "They tell me this lad is a proper machine." If that is the case, he looks well worth backing tomorrow. Absent for 386 days, he won over hurdles at Gowran last season before injury intervened. Entered in Grade 1 events at Leopardstown over Christmas over two and three miles, he is already prominent in the ante-post lists for the Cheltenham Festival novice races. I think it is significant Ruby Walsh heads to Punchestown rather than to partner Douvan at Cork."*

**SELECTION: AMERICAN TOM (5/2 Paddy Power, William Hill 9/4 Bet365, Skybet) 2.35 Punchestown**

The service will run for 3 months (ie. October, November & December) with the option of buying each month at £30 or £75 for all 3 (save £15).

## OCTOBER 2016............................................................. £30.00
## NOVEMBER 2016 ......................................................... £30.00
## DECEMBER 2016 .......................................................... £30.00

## OR ALL 3 MONTHS .................................................... £75.00

Total Cheque / Postal Order value £.............. made payable to MARK HOWARD PUBLICATIONS Ltd. Post your order to: MARK HOWARD PUBLICATIONS. 69 FAIRGARTH DRIVE, KIRKBY LONSDALE, CARNFORTH, LANCASHIRE. LA6 2FB.

NAME: ...............................................................................................................................

ADDRESS: ........................................................................................................................

..........................................................................................................................................

.................................................................................. POST CODE: ..................................

Email Address: ................................................................................................................

# *ONE JUMP AHEAD UPDATES*

I shall be producing **5 One Jump Ahead *Updates*** throughout the 2017/18 National Hunt season. Each *Update* comprises information about the horses in **One Jump Ahead**, **an update from top Bloodstock Agent Anthony Bromley**, **Bumper News**, **Ante-Post Advice** (recommendations for the major races), **Big-Race Previews** and **News from Ireland** from one of the most informed Irish experts Declan Phelan. **Please note, the *Updates* are ONLY AVAILABLE VIA EMAIL (Not Post).**

It is £6 per *Update* (except £10 for the Cheltenham Festival version) or £34 for ALL 5 via **EMAIL**.

**Summary of the 2016/2017 *Updates*:**

### What The Clients Said:

*"Very well done in the Update - just back from overnight stay in Cotswolds planned before yesterday's very helpful double North Hill Harvey and Behind Time, which certainly more than paid the expenses."* **S.W.**

*"Just a few words to thank you for a very profitable Cheltenham, the Update was excellent, a credit to yourself, once again many thanks for superb information at an unbelievable price."* **C.Y.**

*"Just to congratulate you on following up from Tarquin Du Seuil win, Buywise third, with North Hill Harvey's win and Behind Time's win as well. Keep up the good work, you never fail to produce with your Updates."* **S.W.**

*"Just like to say absolutely brilliant info in your email your professional and knowledge is second to none I had my best punting weekend ever and I have been backing horses for nearly 40 years. Well done mate and keep up the fantastic work."* **D.W.**

*"Thank you Mark for the info on Behind Time. Absolutely spot on. Could be the new Unowhatimeanharry! Green as grass and won how he liked. Superb!"* **G.W.**

*"Absolutely brilliant once again, four of the best, great results at one of the of the most difficult meetings to find winners anywhere, getting 4 is something else, well in front again, many thanks."* **J.S.**

*"That Update has been different gravy pal, you're a brilliant judge -  won me a fortune this weekend ."* **J.R.**

*"Just had to mail and thank you for the excellent tipping of today Taquin was excellent. Very well done and onwards and upwards for the rest of the season."* **A.H.**

*"As Names to Note said the step up in trip and the soft ground did the trick for Delusionsofgrandeur at Catterick today. Plus, at 12/1 a nice little midweek boost to the account."* **S.P.**

*"The info regarding Sweet as a Nut was excellent and I can't think of anywhere else where I would have read such a spot on few paragraphs analysing a hunter chase at Limerick! The info re Charli Parcs was also very good plus Bacardys. These three plus Defi de Seuil made a nice four timer today. The information you provide in these updates plus the 'bonus' information you provide on your racing diary is truly priceless!"* **J.S.**

*"Just a quick line to say that I'm enjoying the Update. Special thanks today to Declan Phelan for Bacardys and Sweet As A Nut. The paragraphs on Page 15/16 couldn't have been more accurate. Managed to get some 6's last night, although I think there was some 7's around with Paddy Power."* **M.**

*"I have purchased your book for the last 14 or 15 years and have over the last few years also purchased the Cheltenham Update. I am not a big gambler by any means, usually having a maximum stake of £10, but buying the Cheltenham update has always been a very profitable. Last year I made a profit of over £600 for the 4 days. The Update yesterday provided me with a return of £561 on an outlay of £ 127, which has paid for my week of gambling and hopefully with more winners should again prove profitable. It is not only your own information for each race that makes for great reading, it is the little snippets of information you pass on, from Gordon Elliott (Proved to be very profitable last year and already this year, with Labaik and Apple's Jade), and also Denis O'Regan (Tully East). I also had a bet on Tiger Roll, a horse highlighted in your book a couple of years ago. Congratulations again on another excellent publication. Your knowledge and contacts are priceless."* **M.H.**

*"Back from another good Cheltenham thanks to your thorough Update. Friday was a great day, the last race Gardefort 33/1 was so near but to mention only 3 horses in the first 4 was outstanding."* **J.B.**

*"Thanks very much for high lighting Brio Conte for today, he won with plenty in hand. Thanks also for Sizing John in Gold Cup."* **J.S.**

*"Great info in the Update as per usual. Fantastic regarding Brio Conti for the Saturday. As always keep up the great work."* **S.P.**

*"Many thanks yet again for the Chelt update. Plenty of value around. As well as Sizing John, surely the best tip in it though was Gordon Elliott's note on Labaik - 'if he jumps off he's worth a £5 e.w.' Certainly was at 50/1 in the morning!"* **W.P.**

## The PADDY POWER MEETING 2016

**4 WINNERS: DEFI DU SEUIL (5/4), TAQUIN DU SEUIL (Advised @ 10/1 – WON @ 8/1), NORTH HILL HARVEY (Advised @ 12/1 – WON @ 6/1), BEHIND TIME (9/2)**

Quote: *"**TAQUIN DU SEUIL** won the JLT Novice Chase at the Festival in 2014 (beat subsequent Ryanair Chase winner Uxizandre) and, while his career hasn't progressed in the manner expected, he is still dangerously handicapped off 156. A winner at Warwick last season, he finished sixth in the Ryanair Chase but didn't look at his best. However, there was plenty to like about his reappearance run over hurdles at Chepstow. A running on sixth behind Ballyoptic in the Silver Trophy at Chepstow, his course form reads 612196. Any ease in the ground would be in his favour."* **Advised @ 10/1 WON the BetVictor Gold Cup @ 8/1**

Quote: *"**NORTH HILL HARVEY** was a late withdrawal from the Elite Hurdle at Wincanton last weekend and could run here instead. Dan Skelton's former pointer won on the New Course at Cheltenham last December and, while only ninth in the Supreme NH on this track, he would have been closer had he not made a mistake at the penultimate flight. Fourth at Aintree last time, he goes well fresh and handles testing ground. Harry Skelton rides him in favour of stablemate Ch'tibello."* **Advised @ 12/1 WON the Greatwood Hurdle @ 6/1**

Quote: *"**BEHIND TIME** is featured on page 50 of One Jump Ahead as a handicapper to follow. The five year old showed very little in his first two races at Newbury and Taunton but* the Stowaway gelding was a different proposition at Exeter last time. Beaten a short neck by Captain Chaos (rated 139) receiving only seven pounds, he makes his handicap debut off a rating of 115. The step up in trip is expected to suit and this event is invariably won by a very well handicapped youngster. Indeed, Harry Fry won the race last year with subsequent Grade 1 and Festival winner Unowhatimeanharry off 123. Behind Time has only raced on soft and heavy ground." **WON @ 9/2**

Plus: **CRACK TIEPY (4/9), CRACKING SMART (13/8), DELUSIONOFGRANDEUR (3 wins including @ 17/2), MASTER OF IRONY (2/1 & 13/8), NOT NEVER (6/4), PERCY STREET (6/4).**

Quote: *"Danny Cook is known to be excited by the prospect of partnering* **DELUSIONOFGRANDEUR** *over fences this season. A former winning Irish pointer, he developed into a useful novice hurdler for* **Sue Smith** *last season winning twice at Hexham and Catterick (beat subsequent Grade 2 winner Jonniesofa) over trips ranging from two and a half to three miles one. Rated 139 over timber, he stays well and appreciates plenty of cut in the ground. The six year old gelded son of Mahler will reportedly be ready to run in a beginners' chase in the next couple of weeks."* **WON 3 times, including at Catterick (13/12/16) by six lengths @ 17/2**

Quote: *"Another dual purpose trainer,* **John Quinn**, *has enjoyed plenty of success from the horses he has acquired at this sale over the years, including Cockney Sparrow (35,000gns), Forced Family Fun (30,000gns), Pearl Castle (28,000gns) and Rutherglen (40,000gns). The Malton handler paid* **46,000gns** *for* **MASTER OF IRONY**. *A three times winner for Qatar Racing and Ralph Beckett on the Flat, he scored decisively over ten furlongs at Windsor during the spring. Rated 87, he is just the sort his new trainer excels with and the half-brother to Captain Cat can develop into a decent northern novice hurdler."* **WON TWICE @ 2/1 & 13/8**

*OWNERS ENCLOSURE:* **GRAHAME WHATELEY**
Quote: **SNEAKY FEELING**: *"Another very nice youngster who has yet to run for us. He finished fourth in one of the strongest four year old point-to-points run in Ireland last season. We will start him off in either a bumper or novice hurdle at a lowly level and let him find his feet. He is a lovely horse for the future."* **WON @ 25/1 at Newbury (14/12/16)**

## CHRISTMAS SPECIAL 2016

KING GEORGE: **THISTLECRACK (Advised @ 11/8 WON at 11/10)**

Quote: *"**THISTLECRACK** was a top-class staying hurdler winning the World Hurdle last spring and earning an official mark over timber of 174. Switched to fences this Autumn, Colin Tizzard's eight year old has won all three of his starts with the minimum of fuss. Easy wins have been gained at Chepstow, Cheltenham and Newbury. A four times winner racing right-handed, he has won 9 of his 10 races over three miles and he has already gained four Grade 1 wins during his career. He obviously lacks chasing experience but it is worth recalling Coneygree won the Cheltenham Gold Cup on only his fourth run over fences. There is no doubting his ability."* **Advised @ 11/8 WON the King George at 11/10**

The **IRISH ANGLE** by Declan PHELAN: WINNERS: **BACARDYS (4/6, 12/1 & 10/1), CARTER MCKAY (1/2 & 8/13), NEXT DESTINATION (8/15), SWEET AS A NUT (3/1 & 4/6), WHITE ARM (9/2)**

Quote: *"Down at **Limerick** on **December 27th** they stage a maiden hunters' chase (**2.45**): the market will be dominated by three main players: Dimple, Quarry Rua and Sweet As A Nut. My*

preference is for the latter: the grey Dimple was exposed on eight unsuccessful outings in the UK: movcd to Andy Slattery, he spruced up his ideas and completed a hat trick of point wins at Lingstown last Sunday: on paper those wins make pleasant reading, sadly there is little substance to them. Quarry Rua is also a 3-times point winner: he won two last winter and then ran ok in a couple of bumpers in Cork. He won hard held on his return to pointing at Ballindenisk at the start of this month. **SWEET AS A NUT** won a maiden point at Ballyvodock in January: he hardly broke sweat on his seasonal reappearance at Castletown in October.... he beat a subsequent 3 time points winner by fifteen lengths. Next up at Rathcannon, he was poised to win and challenging at the second last he was tightened for room and, although officially down as having run out, it was more a case of pushed out...undoubtedly the moral winner of that race. In his last outing, Sweet As A Nut took a hike in class as he faced off against proven hunter chase and track stock in the best Open lightweight of the autumn session. In that race at Dromahane in November, he was bang in the picture until just nudged out of the verdict close to the line. In finishing three lengths off Sydney Paget, he ran an absolute cracker....the winner is a leading Open horse and certainly runs to a mark above 120 in most points: Buckers Bridge a decent track horse placed a dozen lengths behind Sweet As A Nut in this race, and he next time up won an Open in a canter. Since that third place at Dromahane the owner/trainer of Sweet As A Nut, Trixie Barry, has turned down some tempting offers. Said owner has a dream to run the horse in the Cheltenham Foxhunters. To get a ticket for that race in March this son of Vinnie Roe must win in Limerick. The terrain at Limerick is bound to be holding and testing and of the three horses in focus, Sweet As A Nut is the most versatile regarding underfoot conditions: he does travel like a horse with some class through a race: he has toe and this 2m 6f trip will play to his strengths and I expect him to land the prize for his Fermoy connections."
**WON by 15 lengths at Limerick @ 3/1**

**THE HORSE I AM MOST LOOKING FORWARD TO SEEING OVER CHRISTMAS: RICH RICCI: MONTALBANO (WON @ 8/11)**

**THE HORSE I AM MOST LOOKING FORWARD TO SEEING OVER CHRISTMAS: ANTHONY BROMLEY: MESSIRE DES OBEAUX (WON the Challow Hurdle at Newbury @ 100/30)**

*TALKING TRAINERS*: **GORDON ELLIOTT: WINNERS: APPLE'S JADE (7/2), A TOI PHIL (7/2 & 6/5), BARRA (5/4), DINARIA DES OBEAUX (10/11), MEGA FORTUNE (9/2), MICK JAZZ (7/1), NOBLE ENDEAVOR (6/1), OUTLANDER (11/1), POLI ROI (2/7), SAMCRO (8/13), SUTTON PLACE (4/1 & 4/6), THE STORYTELLER (Evens & 5/2), TOMBSTONE (9/4).**

Quote: **NOBLE ENDEAVOR**: *"He is in good form at home and is also an intended runner in the Paddy Power Chase on Tuesday (27th). A horse with a lot of ability, he needs things to go right but we were pleased with his run in the Troytown Chase at Navan last time finishing fourth. He looks well and appears to have improved since his last run."* **WON the Paddy Power Chase at Leopardstown (27/12/16) @ 6/1**

Plus: **CAP SOLEIL (11/8 & 9/2), CHARLI PARCS (5/4), ESPOIR DE TEILLEE (10/1), SUPERB STORY (11/8), WONDERFUL CHARM (4/6 & 1/2)**

Quote: *"Cheltenham stages a **Listed bumper for four year olds over a mile and six furlongs (3.40)**. At the time of writing, there is an element of guesswork regarding the line up but I suggest readers bear the following in mind, if featuring amongst the entries. Fergal O'Brien has had 9 bumpers winners from only 29 runners (31%) this season and the unbeaten **CAP SOLEIL** looked a quality filly when winning by two and a half lengths on her debut in a junior bumper at Newbury earlier this month. Sent off evens favourite, the Kapgarde filly didn't come off the bridle under Paddy Brennan. Provided the race doesn't come too soon (only 18 days ago), she looks set to play a leading part."* **CAP SOLEIL won @ 11/8**

Quote: *"The legendary owner is also responsible for the Nicky Henderson trained juvenile hurdler CHARLI PARCS. McManus paid €250,000 at the Arqana Sale last month for the former Arnaud Chaille-Chaille trained three year old. Successful on his debut over hurdles at Enghien in early November, he beat Poker Play by a length and the runner-up has won since. Indeed, the runner-up was subsequently bought by David Pipe for £280,000 at the Cheltenham December Sale. Charli Parcs could make his British debut at Kempton on Tuesday and a big run is anticipated from the son of Anabaa Blue."* **WON by eight lengths on his British debut at Kempton (5/4)**

Quote: *"Irish point expert Declan Phelan spoke positively regarding ESPOIR DE TEILLEE on page 155 of OJA. A faller at the last on his only start 'between the flags,' he was subsequently bought by Roger Brookhouse for £220,000. In training with rising star Neil Mulholland, the West Country based handler commented recently: "He's a beautiful horse who covers the ground effortlessly and I really do think he has some potential. He'll start off in a bumper around Christmas and I'd like to think he could run in one of the championship bumpers at some point."* **WON at Ffos Las (9/4/16) @ 10/1**

Quote: *"J.P.McManus invariably targets one of his novices at the Betfair Hurdle at Newbury (11th February) and it will be interesting to see if he has the valuable two mile event in mind for MOVEWITHTHETIMES. His famous green and gold silks have been carried to victory aboard Get Me Out of Here (2010) and My Tent Or Yours (2013) in recent years, plus Darlan was still going well when falling two out in 2012. Paul Nicholls' gelding has been allocated a generous looking mark of 136 having won two of his three races over timber this season. The son of Presenting lacks experience but he hasn't been hard pressed to win at Fontwell and Wincanton and didn't enjoy the smoothest of passages when fifth in the Grade 2 Sharp NH at Cheltenham in November. Hampered turning for home, he was beaten less than four lengths by Moon Racer. I am reliably informed the champion trainer has backed Movewiththetimes at 33/1 for Skybet Supreme NH at Cheltenham. Therefore, if he heads down the handicap route, take the hint."* **2nd in the *Betfair* Hurdle at Newbury (11/2/17) @ 6/1**

Quote: *"County Hurdle winner SUPERB STORY hasn't been seen since pulling up in the Galway Hurdle at the end of July. Dan Skelton's five year old raced wide throughout in Ireland and was never able to get into a good position. Officially rated 145 and seven pounds higher than when providing his trainer with his first Cheltenham Festival winner, the Duke of Marmalade gelding is due to reappear in a £40,000 handicap hurdle at Musselburgh (2.50) on New Year's Day. Decent ground is ideal for him and the lengthy absence won't be an issue because he is very good fresh, plus he is a course and distance winner (when trained by Charlie Mann). His homework in recent weeks has been excellent."* **WON @ 11/8**

## FEBRUARY 2017

**WINNERS: BRIO CONTI (8/1), BUVEUR D'AIR (1/4, 5/1, 4/9)**

Quote: *"BALLYANDY is trained by Nigel Twiston-Davies, who sent out Splash of Ginge to win this as a novice three years ago. A top-class bumper performer (won 4 out of 6), the Kayf Tara gelding won the Cheltenham Festival bumper last March. Things haven't quite gone to plan over hurdles though this season and the six year old remains a maiden over obstacles. Placed behind Moon Racer at Perth and Cheltenham, he was then stepped up to two and a half miles at Sandown last time. Beaten half a length by subsequent Grade 1 winner Messire Des Obeaux in the Winter NH at the Esher track, he was outstayed after the last. Unbeaten at Newbury and effective on any ground, he will be suited by a strongly run two miles – although it is possible he will be ridden from the front, which has been an advantage in this race during the last few years. On his bumper form and to a lesser degree his hurdles efforts, the handicapper hasn't overburdened him off a mark of 135. Novices have won 5 of the last 7 renewals."* **WON the Betfair Hurdle at Newbury @ 3/1**

Quote: **BRIO CONTI**: *"A grey gelding by Dom Alco, he won a bumper at Stratford last spring before falling at the first on his hurdles bow at Kelso in October. He then finished an excellent half length second behind subsequent Grade 2 River Don NH winner Constantine Bay over the fixed brush hurdles at Haydock's Betfair Chase meeting. Ten lengths clear of the third that day, he almost certainly found the drop in trip at Cheltenham next time against him. The six year old wasn't disgraced though and still held every chance between the final two flights in a novice event won by Pingshou. Given a break, Brio Conti returned in a two mile three and a half furlongs maiden hurdle at Doncaster at the end of last month and produced a really taking effort. Although a shade keen early on, he was always going strongly for Sean Bowen and, having been produced at the second last, he ran on well to beat Wenyerreadyfreddie by nine lengths. One of his owners, namely John Hales, was interviewed afterwards and he left viewers of ATR in no doubt that the gelding is held in high esteem."* **WON at Kempton (18/3/17) @ 8/1**

Quote: **BUVEUR D'AIR**: *"I think the race which will really suit him is the **Aintree Hurdle** – he is a half-brother to Punchestowns and therefore the step up to two and a half miles ought to suit."* **WON the Champion Hurdle (5/1) & Aintree Hurdle (4/9)**

## The CHELTENHAM FESTIVAL 2017

**5 WINNERS: ALTIOR (1/4), YORKHILL (6/4), LET'S DANCE (Advised @ 6/4), DEFI DU SEUIL (5/2), SIZING JOHN (Advised @ 10/1)**

**Plus: SINGLEFARMPAYMENT (E/W – 2nd @ Advised 8/1), GOLD PRESENT (E/W – 2nd @ 14/1), BELLSHILL (E/W – 3rd @ Advised 12/1), MONALEE (E/W – 2nd @ Advised 9/1), GARDEFORT (EW – 2nd @ Advised 33/1)**

Quote: *"**DEFI DU SEUIL** has been the star juvenile hurdler on either side of the Irish Sea this winter. A bumper winner in France for Emmanuel Clayeux, he is unbeaten in five races over hurdles for Philip Hobbs and is rated 155. The stable have won this with Made In Japan (2004) and Detroit City (2006) and the fact the Voix Du Nord gelding is already a three times winner at Prestbury Park is a major plus. A nine lengths winner of the Finesse Hurdle at the Trials meeting in late January, he had previously won the Grade 1 Finale Hurdle at Chepstow by thirteen lengths. His jumping that day was indifferent (Barry Geraghty feels he will jump better on a sounder surface) and his best form has been on soft ground. Richard Johnson (2 from 2) is expected to deputise for the sidelined Barry Geraghty. A winner on good and soft ground, he has outstanding claims."* **WON the Triumph Hurdle @ 5/2**

Quote: *"**SIZING JOHN** was placed in both the Supreme NH (2015) and Arkle (2016) and may follow in the hoofprints of previous Gold Cup winners War of Attrition and Kicking King who both ran well in those novice events before capturing steeplechasing's Blue Riband. The Midnight Legend gelding has chased home Douvan on no less than seven occasions during his career including at Leopardstown over Christmas. That was his first run for Jessica Harrington having been moved from Henry De Bromhead. Since then, he has benefited from avoiding Willie Mullins' superstar and also stepping up in distance. A two and a quarter lengths winner of the Kinloch Brae Chase at Thurles (Don Cossack won the same race prior to the Gold Cup) from Sub Lieutenant, he then produced an even better performance next time. Tackling three miles for the first time, he ran on well to beat Empire of Dirt in the Irish Hennessy at Leopardstown. Another who is very much unexposed over three miles, he isn't guaranteed to stay another two and a half furlongs but stamina looks his strong suit nowadays."* **WON the Cheltenham Gold Cup @ 7/1**

Quote: *"Jessica Harrington won this with Space Trucker in 1999 and she is set to be represented by **ROCK MY WORLD**. Third in the race last year off 146, the gelding is only a pound higher this time having run below par on his last three starts. Off the track since October (146 days), he prefers decent ground and has had a wind operation since his last appearance. Expect Robbie Power (2112512372) to be back on board for the first time since last April."* **WON the Grand Annual Chase @ 10/1**

Quote: *"It is seventeen years since Samakaan won the race for Venetia Williams and **GARDEFORT** was running well in last year's race until making a mistake at the fourth last and never recovered. A five times winner over fences, he scored by a length and a quarter at Wincanton last time and has only been raised three pounds since. Daryl Jacob (1 from 1) partnered him at the Somerset track and recommended this race immediately afterwards. Suited by ease in the ground, the forecast rain would play to his strengths. He is an interesting outsider."* **Advised @ 33/1 – 2nd in the Grand Annual Chase**

## MY BEST CHANCE AT THE CHELTENHAM FESTIVAL: GRAHAM WYLIE: YORKHILL (WON @ 6/4)

## THE HORSE I AM MOST LOOKING FORWARD TO RIDING AT THE CHELTENHAM FESTIVAL: DENIS O'REGAN: TULLY EAST (WON @ 8/1)

*TALKING TRAINERS*: **GORDON ELLIOTT: WINNERS: APPLE'S JADE (7/2), LABAIK (25/1)**

Quote: **APPLE'S JADE**: *"We are looking forward to running her because she has come on a lot since Punchestown. Better ground will suit her and she is in very good form at home. Bryan (Cooper) is very keen on her chances."* **WON @ 7/2**

Quote: **LABAIK**: *"He is a horse with a lot of ability. If he jumps off, he is worth a £5 each-way."* **WON the Supreme NH @ 25/1**

## PAUL NICHOLLS
Quote: "Keep an eye out, too, for **BRIO CONTI** at Kempton on Saturday (18th March): *"I would have really fancied him in the Martin Pipe Conditional Jockeys' Hurdle on Friday but he won't get in. He will therefore run in the consolation race the following day at Kempton. I think he will have a massive chance in that."* **WON at Kempton (18/3/17) @ 8/1**

## The IRISH ANGLE by Declan PHELAN
Quote: *"My bet in this race is **APPLE'S JADE**. A leading juvenile in 2016, finishing runner up in the Triumph prior to coasting to victories at Aintree and Punchestown Festivals. Upon moving to Gordon Elliott, she has maintained that high standard over hurdles (not always the case with five year olds in their second term hurdling). Far from cherry ripe when defeated at Down Royal, she did not enjoy the run of the race in the Fighting Fifth, yet nearly rescued the cause with an impressive late surge, foiled in the end by a nose. For me, the key piece of form on offer is the Hatton's Grace at Fairyhouse: a proper 2m 4f Grade 1: that afternoon I sided with Vroum Vroum Mag: inside the final two furlongs Apple's and VV engaged in an epic battle with Apple's poking her head in front at the loppypop stick. My initial, albeit at the time, biased opinion, was that VVM should have won if Ruby had got involved earlier. Upon reviewing the race many times, I changed my mind and felt that Apple's took the measure of VVM, and if the race had gone on for another furlong or two, she would not have been passed. That afternoon, on the weight for age scale Apple's received four pounds, that allowance is now gone, though the aspect of extra physical maturity should compensate. Apple's then enjoyed a near three month break and returned at Punchestown: the ground was heavier than ideal, Limini pounced on her approaching the last and beat her two lengths. Bryan Cooper merely tapped Apple's Jade*

a couple of times with no intensity. After the race she looked to me like a mare that was on a cob-web blowing exercise, and I believe she will strip significantly fitter for the run. As another three times Grade 1 winner, including a Grade 1 at 2m 4f, plus holding an official rating of 151, in this race you will see the real Apple's Jade in bloom. She will sit close to the pace and when it comes to the crunch that doggedness and no surrender characteristic she demonstrated at Fairyhouse will be in evidence and help her win this prize." **WON @ 7/2**

Quote: "**YORKHILL** will be the classic exchange/divided opinion horse of the Festival. There is no denying that he has a massive engine under his bonnet and is one of the top five jumps horses in training; the divisive debate abounds whether the horse can keep his focus and jump cleanly and record a facile win in this race, or will he bring out some bad habits and post a performance littered with minor mistakes. His 2016 Neptune victory was one of the moments of that Festival, especially watching Ruby Walsh taking a pull heading to the last and almost laughing at Yanworth. Forewarned is forearmed and Ruby Walsh knows what to expect with Yorkhill; he has educated him in his two spins over fences: his only track defeat was at Punchestown last April, and he may by then have gone to the well once too often that springtime. This winter he has had a rather easy time and he is currently as fresh as a daisy compared to others in the line-up who have had a rough winter. I would agree with the view that he would be a serious contender for the Champion Hurdle had he been diverted in that direction. What is unusual about this horse is that his family are three milers, including the likes of The Listener and others therein. The speed he shows is almost a freak of nature. I think he wins bar a bad mistake and at 2/1 he is a fair price against less talented rivals." **WON @ 6/4**

Quote: "Like most observers I had doubts about **SIZING JOHN** on the count of stamina before he won the Irish Gold Cup: in hindsight the fact that he had been generally campaigned at the two mile range for much of his career masked the truth that on pedigree three mile trips were a viable alternative: he is the young horse with the most speed in the race, and as of now he is 1 out of 1 in 3 mile Grade 1 chases, and this late vocation to staying chasing could easily take this race by storm." **WON the Cheltenham Gold Cup @ 7/1**

## The AINTREE GRAND MEETING 2017

**5 WINNERS: DEFI DU SEUIL (4/11), BUVEUR D'AIR (4/9), RATHER BE (Advised @ 16/1 – WON @ 10/1), THE WORLD'S END (3/1), YANWORTH (9/4)**

Quote: "Nicky Henderson has won this twice in the last four years (Minella Forfitness (2013) & Theinval (2015)) and, at the time of writing, has seven entries. The one who stands out is the novice **RATHER BE**, who looks ahead of the handicapper off a mark of 136. Bought for €78,000 and a half-brother to stablemate and smart hurdler Sign of A Victory, he was beaten less than ten lengths in the Cheltenham Festival bumper last season. A winner over jumps at Hereford (Good) and Huntingdon (Good/Soft) in October and December respectively, the six year old failed by a head to concede nine pounds to Alan King's Coeur De Lion (seventh in the Triumph Hurdle) at Sandown (Heavy). Last time, he was badly hampered and unseated his rider at the second flight in the Martin Pipe Conditional Jockeys' Handicap Hurdle at Cheltenham. Unexposed over the distance (1U), he is well regarded and handles any ground. He ought to be very competitive off his rating." **Advised @ 16/1 WON @ 10/1**

Quote: "**THE WORLD'S END** fell in his only Irish point but has won a bumper and three times over hurdles since joining Tom George. Rated 149, the Stowaway gelding has improved since tackling longer trips. A nine lengths winner of a Grade 2 at Haydock (2m 7f) in February, he was still travelling strongly when falling at the penultimate flight in the Albert Bartlett NH at

*Cheltenham. Unexposed over three miles, he handles any ground and, assuming his fall hasn't left its mark, he is another very much for the shortlist."* **WON the Grade 1 Sefton Novices' Hurdle @ 3/1**

Quote: *"YANWORTH is rated 163 having won 7 of his 9 races. Despite winning his first three starts this term, Alan King's seven year old didn't convince in the Ascot, Christmas or Kingwell Hurdles. A hard fought winner on each occasion, he was a big disappointment in the Champion Hurdle only finishing seventh behind Buveur D'Air. The Norse Dancer gelding looked a stayer when leading close home in his three wins this term and he looks well worth a try over this distance (another who is running beyond 2m 5f for the first time). He finished strongly in the Neptune Investments NH last season and the World Hurdle was mooted as the likely plan until his owner J.P.McManus bought Unowhatimeanharry. The head of Barbury Castle has won this twice with Spendid (2002) and Blazing Bailey (2008)."* **WON the Liverpool Hurdle @ 9/4**

Quote: **LALOR:** *"A five year old by It's Gino, he finished runner-up on his first two outings at Wincanton before running out a thirteen lengths winner at the same track last month. Always going well under Daryl Jacob, he sauntered clear. His trainer Richard Woollacott stated afterwards:* **"I think Lalor is quite nice because he's a big, weak, unfurnished horse. He might run with a penalty, but wouldn't run on anything quicker than good to soft."** *It was rumoured afterwards that champion trainer Paul Nicholls made a six figure bid for the five year old which was rejected. All three of his races have been on soft or heavy ground."* **WON the Grade 2 bumper @ 33/1**

Quote: *"DOUBLE W'S was an easy winner of his first two races over fences at Carlisle and Wetherby before possibly finding the ground too slow at Newbury's Hennessy meeting. Runner-up behind Upsilon Bleu at Doncaster, he didn't appear to get home in the 2m 4f novices' handicap chase at Cheltenham last month. Eventually beaten over twenty lengths, he held every chance jumping the second last. A strongly run two miles on drying ground brings out the best in Malcolm Jefferson's seven year old. He is only four pounds higher than his last win."* **WON the Red Rum Chase @ 8/1**

# ONE JUMP AHEAD UPDATES 2017/2018
# ORDER FORM (EMAIL ONLY)

## AVAILABLE AT £6.00 EACH (£10 Cheltenham) OR £34 FOR ALL 5

- **CHELTENHAM PADDY POWER MEETING 2017**
  **(Will be emailed on Thursday 16th November 2017)**

- **CHRISTMAS SPECIAL 2017**
  **(Will be emailed on Thursday 21st December 2017)**

- **FEBRUARY 2018**

- **MARCH 2018 - CHELTENHAM FESTIVAL PREVIEW**
  **(Will be emailed on the Sunday before the Festival)**

- **APRIL 2018 – AINTREE PREVIEW**
  **(Will be emailed on the Tuesday before the Meeting)**

Total Cheque / Postal Order value £.............. made payable to MARK HOWARD PUBLICATIONS Ltd. Post your order to: MARK HOWARD PUBLICATIONS. 69 FAIRGARTH DRIVE, KIRKBY LONSDALE, CARNFORTH, LANCASHIRE. LA6 2FB.

NAME:  ........................................................................................................................................

ADDRESS: ..................................................................................................................................

....................................................................................................................................................

..................................................................................... POST CODE: ...................................

Email Address: ............................................................................................................................

If you have not received your *UPDATE* via email 24 hours before the meeting starts, please contact us immediately.

Available to order via www.mhpublications.co.uk

# AHEAD ON THE FLAT 2018

The 18th edition of *Ahead On The Flat* will be published in early April for the 2018 Flat season. It will be formulated along the same lines as previous years with a ***Top 40 Prospects*** (the 2017 edition included **CRACKSMAN, CRYSTAL OCEAN, MOJITO, POET'S WORD** & **ULYSSES**), ***Maidens, Handicappers*** and ***What's The Craic In Ireland?*** In addition, there will be the usual stable interviews with some of the top trainers in Great Britain (this year's included **Ralph Beckett, Roger Charlton, Keith Dalgleish, James Fanshawe, William Haggas, Mark Johnston, David O'Meara, Hugo Palmer, David Simcock** and **Roger Varian**). *Ahead On The Flat* will contain 152 pages and the price is £9.99.

I shall also be producing **three** *Ahead On The Flat Updates* **(EMAIL ONLY)**. There will be a **Royal Ascot Preview** (6 winners in 2017 including **ATTY PERSSE (Advised @ 8/1)** & **THE TIN MAN (Advised @ 8/1))**, plus 6 2nds & 6 3rds, a **York Ebor Preview** (6 Winners in 2017 including **MARSHA (Advised @ 10/1), THREADING (Advised @ 5/1)** & **ULYSSES (4/1))**, and an **Autumn** *Update*. The Royal Ascot version is £10 with the other two £6 or £19 for the ALL THREE.

---

## ORDER FORM

- **AHEAD ON THE FLAT 2018 (Book ONLY)**     £9.99

**AHEAD ON THE FLAT UPDATES 2018 (can be ordered individually at £6.00 EACH (£8 ROYAL ASCOT) or ALL 3 updates for £17.00):**

- **ROYAL ASCOT PREVIEW 2018**     £10.00
- **YORK EBOR MEETING PREVIEW 2018**     £6.00
- **AUTUMN PREVIEW 2018**     £6.00
- **ALL 3 UPDATES (EMAIL ONLY)**     £19.00
- **AHEAD ON THE FLAT + 3 UPDATES**     £27.99

Total Cheque / Postal Order value £............. Made payable to **MARK HOWARD PUBLICATIONS Ltd. Please send to: MARK HOWARD PUBLICATIONS Ltd. 69 FAIRGARTH DRIVE, KIRKBY LONSDALE, CARNFORTH, LANCASHIRE. LA6 2FB.**

NAME: ...........................................................................................................................

ADDRESS: ....................................................................................................................

........................................................................................................................................

........................................................................ POST CODE: ...........................

Email Address: ............................................................................................................

# Value Racing Club

## "Winning Together"

Our aim at Value Racing Club is to introduce new people into the world of horse racing and provide a cost effective and simple way of becoming a racehorse owner. There are never any hidden extras such as vet bills or travel costs. Once the initial purchase has been paid, no further monies are required during the entire racing season.

### What we offer and benefits:

- An opportunity to become involved in racehorse ownership.
- What we pay for a horse is what you pay, no added fees of any kind.
- A one-off cost covers the entire racing season.
- Stable visits arranged to watch your horse work on the gallops.
- Free owners badge every time your horse runs.
- Each syndicate keeps 100% of all prize money won.
- 72% overall strike rate of our runners finishing in the first three places.
- Horses in training with David Pipe, Dr Richard Newland, Chris Wall & David Dennis.
- Racing UK pundit Mark Howard is our Club Ambassador.
- We are members of the ROA "Racehorse Owners Association" & RSA "Racehorse Syndicates Association".

**Big race wins include the £70,000 Imperial Cup, £30,000 Betfred Summer Hurdle, £20,000 Six Nations Chase.**

**Over £200,000 of prize money won for owners in the last 3 years.**

**Website: www.valueracingclub.co.uk email: contact@valueracingclub.co.uk Twitter: @valueracingclub**

## Call James for more information: 07939800769